Working with Children and Young People

New International Studies in Applied Ethics

VOLUME 5

EDITED BY

Professor R. John Elford and Professor Simon Robinson,
Leeds Metropolitan University

PETER LANG

Oxford · Bern · Berlin · Bruxelles · Frankfurt am Main · New York · Wien

Working with Children and Young People

Ethical Debates and Practices
Across Disciplines and Continents

Anne Campbell and Pat Broadhead (eds)

PETER LANG

Oxford · Bern · Berlin · Bruxelles · Frankfurt am Main · New York · Wien

Bibliographic information published by Die Deutsche Nationalbibliothek.
Die Deutsche Nationalbibliothek lists this publication in the Deutsche
Nationalbibliografie; detailed bibliographic data is available on the Internet at
http://dnb.d-nb.de.

A catalogue record for this book is available from the British Library.

Library of Congress Cataloging-in-Publication Data:
Working with children and young people : ethical debates and practices
across disciplines and continents / Anne Campbell and Pat Broadhead
(eds).
    p. cm
  Includes bibliographical references and index.
  ISBN 978-3-0343-0121-3 (alk. paper)
  1. Teachers--Professional ethics. 2. Teaching--Moral and ethical
aspects. I. Campbell, Anne Jemima, 1947- editor of compilation. II.
Broadhead, Pat, 1951- editor of compilation. III. Brock, Avril. Are we
doing it by the book?
  LB1779.W627 2010
  371.102--dc22
                        2010046068

ISSN 1663-0033
ISBN 978-3-0343-0121-3

© Peter Lang AG, International Academic Publishers, Bern 2011
Hochfeldstrasse 32, CH-3012 Bern, Switzerland
info@peterlang.com, www.peterlang.com, www.peterlang.net

Printed in Germany

*This book is dedicated to Pam Nason,
a contributing author who died in the autumn of 2010.
Her work will be remembered for its
democratic approaches and scholarship.*

Contents

Foreword   xi

ANNE CAMPBELL AND PAT BROADHEAD

1   Introduction   1

PART I   Striving to be ethical: Professionals' perspectives   13

AVRIL BROCK, CAROLYNN RANKIN AND LOUISE BOYLE SWINIARSKI

2   Are we doing it by the book? Professional ethics for teachers
and librarians in the early years   15

ANNE CAMPBELL AND DOUG MARTIN

3   Every Child Matters: New ethical challenges arising in schools   37

ANGELA ANNING

4   Research with vulnerable people:
The importance of sensitivity   59

PAM NASON AND ANNE HUNT

5   Pedagogy as an ethical encounter:
How does it look in our professional practice?   79

BRUCE JOHNSON

6   Maintaining professional ethics during a 'moral panic'
over sex education: A case study   103

BRIDGET COOPER

7   Valuing the human in the design and use of technology in
    education: An ethical approach to the digital age of learning   123

PART 2   Striving to be ethical: Engaging with children and
         young people   141

SUSAN GROUNDWATER-SMITH

8   The dilemmas we face: Designing a curriculum for
    vulnerable children in short-term care   143

DOROTHY BOTTRELL

9   Shifting perspectives, representations and dilemmas in work
    with young people   159

EMMA RAMSDEN AND PHIL JONES

10 Children as active agents in gaining and giving assent:
    Involving children as co-researchers   179

LIZ WEBSTER AND PAT BROADHEAD

11 Their life, their choice: Ethical challenges for supporting
    children and young people in the self-management of
    Type 1 diabetes   197

KAYE JOHNSON

12 Promoting ethical understandings in child co-researchers   215

JO ARMISTEAD

13 Reflecting on ethical considerations around young children's
    engagement when researching children's perspectives   237

BRIDGET COOPER

14 Developing an ethic of care with children and young people:
Opportunities and challenges   259

PAT BROADHEAD AND ANNE CAMPBELL

15 New ethical horizons: Lessons learned for changing practices   283

Notes on contributors   293

Index   299

Foreword by the General Editors

This book explores ethical issues relating to the inter-agency and interdisciplinary care and education of children. The volume identifies a wide range of key issues, explores the related aspects and suggests ways of ensuring that appropriate and ethical responses are made across a range of contexts and circumstances. It is a timely publication, given the proliferation of integrated working and practice in recent years. The contributors draw particular attention to the ways in which codes of practice in different professions match and mismatch. It is imperative that all concerned with the welfare of children understand these issues and learn how to respond to them in creative ways. Promoting the best interests of children and young people must be paramount.

The contributions to this collection are markedly international. They are exemplary in focusing on the ethical issues that are encountered both in practice and in research. Extensive and well-illustrated case-studies are used throughout. Running throughout the book is an emphasis on the ethics of care and the immediacy and quality of educational relationships and communities. The overlap and interplay between learning, development and therapy is deftly handled, forming the theoretical basis for inter-professional ethical practice.

This book will be essential to all who are concerned with the education, care and welfare of children and young people.

R. John Elford
Simon Robinson

ANNE CAMPBELL AND PAT BROADHEAD

1 Introduction

Working with Children and Young People: Ethical Debates and Practices Across Disciplines and Continents brings together thinking and practice in the United Kingdom, Australia, the United States of America and Canada. It covers the perspectives of professional practitioners in education, social care and health settings, library contexts and youth work. It also covers the views of children and young people who are involved with the education and care professions, in early years settings, residential provision, health contexts and youth work. In presenting these perspectives the publication aims to enhance understandings of the ethics of professional practice through the lenses of practitioners, children and young people.

In the last twenty years or so there has been much development internationally in the area of multi-professional, multi-agency work. Paralleling this has been the integration of services to provide support, education and social and health care for children and young people. There have also been many instances of children's services being headlined in the media as tragic cases are reported and at times used to fuel political debates. These are fields of practice which are fraught with ethical dilemmas and this book would hope to address, in an integrated way, the issues and challenges facing the various professions around the globe as they strive to meet the diverse needs of children and young people.

This book is interdisciplinary. One of its main foci is on the professionals who work 'around' the child: workers such as education, health and social care professionals, youth workers, play workers and play therapists. The book is primarily about professional ethics and practice, through research ethics that arise from examples in the book. Children's and young people's voices and experiences of understanding ethical behaviour are the second area of focus. It is an academic book about principles, practice and policy and draws, where appropriate, on examples from actual practice to illuminate key points.

Chapters address the following: the values and principles underpinning professional and inter-professional practice; the promotion of ethical understanding in children and young people; how ethical practices are confronted and shared across disciplines; the framing and re-framing of ethical values as part of ongoing professional development and learning; the development and potential shifting of personal and professional positions over time.

We would hope to provide a theoretical underpinning for an examination of professional ethics through the following: dilemmas experienced by professionals in the practice fields, examples of practices and strategies promoting multi-agency work and new engagements with power relationships as new ethical stances are taken. Stories of social, health and education workers, as they strive to provide integrated or joined up services for children and families, are provided to illustrate and illuminate cases of practice in the varying fields.

An exploration of the different arrangements in different international contexts, policies, practices and research provides a global perspective to the collection and underlines its importance. However, as authors we have been aware that we are dealing with complex and challenging ideas and have tried to avoid drawing simplistic solutions to complex problems. Reducing ethical behaviour and principles to codes suffers the same fate as quality assurance procedures and processes, ticking boxes rather than thinking about dilemmas and complex situations that require ethical problem-solving and deep thinking. Creating a reflective and discursive ethical culture and stance within an organisation, we would argue, would result in a more comprehensive approach to shaping professionalism and more ethical approaches to policy and practice.

Part 1: Striving to be ethical: Professionals' perspectives

The book is divided into two parts: the first, *Striving to be ethical: Professionals' perspectives*, contains seven chapters and focuses on the voice of the professionals in interdisciplinary settings, libraries, schools, early years settings and health contexts.

Avril Brock, Carolynn Rankin and Louise Boyle Swiniarski in Chapter 2 discuss ethical issues in two professional spheres: early years educators and early years librarians in the United Kingdom (UK) and the United States of America (USA). They explore how ethics is at the centre of practice and identify the resultant need for increased professional knowledge. Their discussion covers ethics in professionalism, ethical codes for professionals and ethical dilemmas through the personal voices of practitioners. Previous research by Brock (2006), which identified ten tenets of ethical practice, permeates the chapter and indicates the complexity of conceptualising ethics. A key, important question for professionals is raised and discussed, that of whether increased regulation and accountability to clients and policy makers has resulted in less autonomy? New challenges, they argue, need further professional integrity.

Comparison between the UK and USA with regards to ethical codes for working with young children identifies differences and stimulates discussion about how ethical codes need to be responsive to change and amendment as practice develops and policies change. As argued earlier, an ethical culture and stance, as well as documented codes could have more comprehensive influences in organisations. Four ethical dilemmas constructed by the authors illustrate some of the challenges facing practitioners across the two nations. One theme evident in these dilemmas is that of the selection of materials and presentation of knowledge and how this can lead to censorship and omission in provision. Another theme is how important the environment is and how hidden messages in curriculum can shape young children's experiences.

The authors conclude, in tune with the aims of this book, that new insights and opportunities can be gained through sharing practice and thinking in multidisciplinary and international contexts.

In Chapter 3, Anne Campbell and Doug Martin examine some of the ethical implications for schools and for school staff in the light of substantial policy changes in England. They discuss the considerable ethical challenges arising from the Every Child Matters legislation (DfES 2003) which includes one of the biggest challenges to recent workforce reform, that of creating and sustaining effective multi-professional or integrated teams of professionals who are concerned with the care and education of children and young people. In their discussion of the policy background and the integration of children's services they describe the plethora of government initiatives and identify prescriptive practices which provide fundamental ethical challenges to those working both within schools and in the broader community because of complex interpretation and application.

From informal interviews with staff, a pupil and a parent, the experience of one primary school is detailed in short, but insightful, vignettes. Each of the stories presented report positive points and illustrations of multi-agency working in supporting children and families in need but the authors recognise that some parents or professionals may be less committed for a variety of different, complex reasons. Good effective leadership is identified as essential where an overview of cases is maintained and knowledge of professionals working on cases as well as the vital, good family relationships which encourage communication and empathy are developed. Understanding the social and cultural context of the school is found to be important in taking an ethical stance to the challenges that arise. One of the major tensions discussed is that of who needs to know what? There is a need to maintain appropriate professional dialogues and to foster the ability to identify and filter confidential information to the relevant person.

The authors warn of the dangers of intrusive practice for children and families at risk and caution professionals and their organisations to be mindful of the need for ethical decision-making and to avoid the use of value-laden language. One of the biggest challenges is if and when to intervene. These complex situations provide many opportunities for professional learning in the development of multi-agency approaches.

Angela Anning, in her chapter about research in interdisciplinary settings, starts by contesting the notion of 'vulnerability' and the messy and shifting realities of unique settings. She calls on qualitative researchers to be rigorous in their methodologies and to be aware of the power relationships that exist in multidisciplinary settings. In discussing ethics in research practice she examines definitions of vulnerability and how it is a relative concept dependent on cultural norms, socio-economic conditions and expectations in communities. She also highlights the fact that 'vulnerable' populations are disproportionately represented in research due to political concerns about costs and benefits and solving 'problems'.

Illustrations of dilemmas in researching vulnerable subjects are presented and discussed to provide examples of how informed consent, ensuring confidentiality, gaining trust and protecting participants require ethical research practices. She concludes by reminding us of the instability of the construct of vulnerability and of the risk of stereotyping people and the danger of perpetuating dominant hegemonies in the research and development work that we do.

Chapter 5 leads on from Anning's work and focuses on the role of language in professional practice and the negotiation of power, position, privilege and politics within a childcare community in New Brunswick, Canada. Pam Nason and Anne Hunt outline the political context of their work in developing an official curriculum framework for early learning and childcare and professional learning and discuss the global nature of policies encouraged by 'policy borrowing' across the world. They describe the risks they took in putting forward a proposal within the constraints of a government funded initiative: restricted academic freedom; reproduction of a colonising discourse and regulation of practice. They make explicit their commitment to pedagogy as an ethical encounter which foregrounds responsibility and relationship to the Other (Dalberg and Moss 2005).

Through providing 'open spaces for dialogue and critique' twelve value statements were articulated which provided starting points for a curriculum framework. They subjected their draft framework to processes of critique amongst practitioners and academics which resulted in contradictory discussions. Messy, multi-layered and context-specific as professional practice is, they proposed that such discussions can contribute to ongoing conversations about professional ethics. The chapter documents their journey through the complex arena of the diversely populated terrain of the early learning and childcare sector. From the position of open debate they began to imagine new possibilities for acting in solidarity with the first nation population of Mi'kmaq, Maliseet and Passamoquody peoples. They finish by reflecting on the process of 'turning the inside out' that they have undertaken and hope that they have 'unmasked their agendas' and contributed to the ongoing critical dialogue in ethics in co-constructing a curriculum framework.

Changing continents in Chapter 6, Bruce Johnson from South Australia invokes 'virtue ethics' as a long tradition to illustrate the more fundamental and implicit agreements among groups of professions. The chapter offers an analysis of the 'trials and tribulations' of a group of health and education professionals who re-asserted their ethical commitment to secular principles. A detailed account of a major clash of values between a group of sexuality educators and administrators and their opponents, an alliance of Pentecostal, evangelical Christian groups, pro-family and anti-abortion lobbyists and conservative politicians (known as the traditionalists) forms the core of this chapter.

Johnson depicts and analyses the 'moral panic' through the lens of a researcher and provides a clear, calm account based on interview data and documentary evidence. He identifies the role of the media and politicians as key in the exaggeration and distortion of events and encouraging the use of emotive language. The sexuality educators experienced a steep learning curve in *realpolitik* to enable them to restate their philosophical and ethical principles in order to move forward with their programme. Johnson quotes Stevens et al. (2009) when he hopes that the 'use of critical reason, factual evidence and scientific methods of inquiry' will prevail over 'faith and mysticism in seeking solutions to human problems and answers to important human questions'.

In Chapter 7 Bridget Cooper addresses the particular ethical challenges in the design and use of technology in education. She argues that as technology is improved there is a need to consider the moral and affective issues in learning with technology. Cooper stresses the importance of links between the affective domain and learning and advocates a multisensory, mutually respectful approach to avoid learner alienation and to recognise that human relationships are at the heart of the learning process.

Cooper warns of the dangers of using technology unethically: exclusion related to gender or culture resulting in inequity; alienation and the reduction of human contact. She does, however, assert that good technology can affirm and enhance humanity. Useful examples from research and development projects are used to illustrate how empathic, Information Communications Technology (ICT), integrated classrooms can be created and sustained.

She concludes by stating that wider application of holistic, ethical and interactive approaches in using technology could enable rapid intervention in global problems and respond to the sharing of rapidly evolving knowledge. This, she asserts, would raise the quality of individual and collective lives.

Part 2: Striving to be ethical: Engaging with children and young people

The focus in the second part of the book shifts from practitioners and their learning to children and young people and their engagement in ethical issues as they experience them. Inevitably, there is an overlap and most chapters also focus on adult learning. Key themes emerge of listening to children and young people and of taking their ideas and concerns seriously. Part 2 concludes with a chapter addressing the development of an ethic of care for professionals in the broader field that we consider in the book and serves to bring together in an holistic way important issues of permeation and communication.

Susan Groundwater-Smith, in writing about curriculum design for vulnerable young people in Chapter 8 argues that to discuss rights is to discuss dilemmas. Those dilemmas in schooling she argues rest upon the moral questions surrounding rights. Her chapter documents through a case study a curriculum designed to have meaning and relevance for children in short-term residential care. Groundwater-Smith sets the context sensitively, recognising the delicacy of work with young people at risk. Her role in the project was as critical friend composing think-pieces to be shared with teachers to help shape and improve the curriculum.

Two fundamental touchstones for the curriculum are articulated by Groundwater-Smith; accelerated literacy whereby a teaching and learning scaffold that develops skills through reading and writing and shared texts which are engaging and age-appropriate and enable fast progress; and the nurturing of emotional literacy and resilience whereby student wellbeing is of high importance. She also reminds us that making decisions about curriculum and materials is first and foremost an ethical concern. The maxims of: no harm; voice; equity; benefit; integrity; liberty and care voiced by Ahmed and Machold (2004) serve to support the weighing up of curriculum dilemmas and conclude the chapter.

Ethical dilemmas in youth work and work with individual work pro-grammes are raised by Dorothy Bottrell in Chapter 9. The scenarios used to discuss issues are fictional though representative of Bottrell's doctoral work in Sydney, Australia. Ethical dilemmas presented and analysed cover important issues such as the tensions between emancipatory aims and social control functions in youth work; and managing young people for connec-tion or correction. Bottrell deals with issues of ensuring safety; marginali-sation; complicity; suspension and truancy from school; participation in illicit activities and anti-social behaviour in ways that provide insights into the experiences of youth in the current climate. She espouses a commit-ment to shifting perspectives that re-inscribe and target 'problem youth' and invokes the fundamental principle of listening to young people which she claims is an ethical process necessitating response and advocacy.

Bottrell stresses the importance of dialogical ethics and commitment to 'the common good' in the community development role of youth work and social justice. She argues that engaging in the dialogical process in com-munity development aspects of youth work shifts emphasis from changing young people to changing the dominant narratives towards more emanci-patory perspectives for young people.

In Chapter 10 Emma Ramsden and Phil Jones tread a delicate pathway of current approaches to child consent and assent with regard to partici-pation in research activity during dramatherapy. Instances of children as researchers and co-researchers are on the increase as participatory styles of research emerge and challenges are raised as to how children are informed and involved in research. The research described in the chapter is Ramsden's doctoral study of children's voices in dramatherapy sessions. Children are positioned as co-researchers and not subjects and encouraged to make choices from a place of parity, safety and trust.

Vignettes are constructed to show children's responses in the gaining assent process enabled by 'Reggie' an anthropomorphic research frog. Throughout the chapter there is a real sense of children's voices being listened to and a lively, childish feel created by the pseudonyms chosen by children, such as Lady Gaga, Rocksus and Lava. Key issues of power dynamics and regular negotiation of active participation are raised and discussed. Ramsden and Jones want children to be recognised as worthy of respect and to acknowledge them as active meaning makers, decision makers and social agents. In so doing they claim that children will be empowered and the quality of research data will be enhanced.

Continuing the theme of choice for children and young people, Liz Webster and Pat Broadhead in Chapter 11 focus on the 'Getting Sorted' programme for young people with Type 1 diabetes. The chapter describes how the programme of self-help workshops has aided further development in young people's self-management of their condition. The ethical challenges encountered by Webster and her team focused on trying not to be too defensive about the increasingly critical comments from young people about their parents' responses to their condition and their clinical experiences. Similar to Ramsden and Jones in the previous chapter, the programme sought to involve the young people in participatory research as co-researchers. Drawing on the work of Kellett et al. (2004), the team shifted their thinking, language and understanding to work *with* rather than *on* young people.

These workshops revealed how young people want to keep autonomy, self-care and self-esteem at the heart of the treatment and how there needs to be a shift in power from a wholly medical model to one which listens to the voices of young people. The challenges of convincing medical professionals of the need to build good relationships still need tackling in the future and will require sensitive and ethical approaches to create better conditions for young people's self-management in an informed and effective way.

Further developing the theme of children and young people as researchers, Kaye Johnson in Chapter 12 describes the ethical dilemmas posed by conducting research in her own primary school in South Australia. The dilemmas she identifies in her role as head teacher and researcher relate to her as an insider with privileged knowledge alongside her role as principal in a position of power and of remaining in the setting after the conclusion of the research. She addresses issues of consent and confidentiality and emphasises listening to and asking children about participating in research.

There are several useful tools for those wishing to undertake research with children such as a table about roles and examples of research questions and a pamphlet about informed consent. Johnson concludes her chapter with a set of dispositions that she advises should be shared by teachers and school leaders who engage with children as co-researchers. These seem to be in tune with all of the authors' principles in this book and centre on recognition of diversity, having confidence in children's competence, willingness to listen and commitment to democratic processes in the pursuit of ethical research.

In Chapter 13 Jo Armistead resonates with issues raised by Ramsden and Jones in Chapter 10 and Kaye Johnson in Chapter 12, by exploring the role and involvement of children in research with particular reference to participatory approaches to gaining consent and assent. With regards to the policy background, Armistead contests from a postmodern perspective the development of national, centrally imposed, quality frameworks in England which view quality as a socially constructed phenomenon, with multiple stakeholders defining quality early years provision at local levels. The doctoral study, which was the basis of this research, aimed to develop a deeper understanding of what children as stakeholders valued within their own early years provisions, and to highlight the continued absence of recognition of children's views in government policy in the early years. The research gave voice to young children's perspectives on quality in provision.

In tune with the previous chapters identified above, issues of power, participative methods which recognise children as experts in their own lives and children's rights are raised and discussed. Armistead devised an innovative nursery play tool to stimulate conversation and dialogue with children with a measure of success which could help other researchers in their quest for young children's voice.

It seems fitting to focus on developing an ethic of care at this point in the book. In Chapter 14 Bridget Cooper asserts that the quality of empathy is at the heart of developing an ethic of care and claims that empathy needs to permeate all levels of an organisation and its communication channels. She writes about the global context in the aftermath of a world banking crisis and argues that inequality breeds resentment and lack of trust. Cooper draws on her doctoral work to illustrate the role of empathy and emotions in creating good relationships in education.

Similarly to Brock et al. in Chapter 2, Cooper recognises the powerful messages implicit in the 'hidden curriculum' of schools which can shape and influence young people's thinking and behaviour. She advocates modelling an ethic of care and highlights the importance of ethical leadership while calling on individuals to commit to a joint venture to envisage and support everyone's potential.

The concluding chapter in this book aims to tease out some layered complexities in ethical issues in work and research with children and young people and for adults working with children, young people and families, many of whom live on a day-to-day basis with personal difficulties, in relation to two areas of focus:

- The challenges for ethical practices of care and education as integrated teams emerge and develop
- The challenges for adopting ethical research practices with children and young people

This final chapter address the above two areas through three themes which we believe underpin professional learning. These themes are:

- Recognising and confronting challenges to ethical practice
- Deepening one's personal commitment to ethical practices
- Supporting life-changes through ethical practices

Editors and authors identify the need for a substantial step-change in perspectives and practice for both professionals and researchers. From these might come the policy changes also needed to progress from the rhetoric of *hearing* the child's, the young person's and the marginalised adult's voices – often a relatively superficial exercise – to enabling their voices to actively shape policy development and to subsequently and positively influence the quality of experiences within and beyond their own lives. We reiterate this point in the final chapter because it is a central tenet in this book.

We hope this book might make a difference and improve both the thinking about ethical practice and the practice itself.

References

Ahmed, P., and Machold, S. (2004). 'The Quality and Ethics Connection: Towards Virtuous Organisations', *Total Quality Management*, 15 (4), 527–45.

Brock, A. (2006). 'Dimensions of early years professionalism – attitudes versus competences?' Reflection paper on *Training Advancement and Co-operation in the Teaching of Young Children (TACTYC)* <http://www.tactyc.org.uk> accessed 21 October 2009.

Dahlberg, G. and Moss, P. (2005). *Ethics and politics in early childhood education*. New York, NY: Routledge.

Department for Education and Skills (DfES) (2003). *Every Child Matters – the Green Paper*. London: DfES.

Kellett, M., Forrest, R., Dent, N. and Ward, S. (2004). 'Just teach us the skills, we'll do the rest: Empowering ten year olds as active researchers'. *Children and Society*, published online 5th February 2009, DOI: 10. 1062/Chi.807. <http://onlinelibrary.wiley.com/doi/10.1111/chso.2004.18.issue-5/issuetoc> accessed 25 February 2010.

Stevens, F., Tabash, E., Hill, T., Sikes, M. and Flynn, T. (2009). 'What is Secular Humanism?' Council for Secular Humanism. <http://www.secularhumanism.org/index> accessed 21 October 2009.

PART I

Striving to be ethical: Professionals' perspectives

AVRIL BROCK, CAROLYNN RANKIN AND
LOUISE BOYLE SWINIARSKI

2   Are we doing it by the book? Professional ethics for teachers and librarians in the early years

Ethics is a key dimension of professionalism (Brock 2006) and should be at the foundation of practice for those who work with young children and their families. This chapter explores ethical issues affecting the two professions of early years educators and early years librarians in the UK and the USA. The discussion draws on research undertaken through eliciting the voices of professionals from both trans-disciplinary and transatlantic perspectives. The chapter explores how these two professions have ethics at the centre of practice, focusing on the pre-eminence of the needs, wants and interests of their 'clients' – children and families. It also focuses on the ethical environment that encompasses a commitment to work in collaboration, and share expertise with, other professional colleagues. As new thinking is offered through exploring the thinking and practice of professionals working across boundaries, so the ethical demands intensify and increased professional knowledge is required (Brock and Swiniarski 2008). The chapter demonstrates new insights and opportunities gained through the sharing of interdisciplinary and international perspectives within the field of educators and librarians in the early years. The discussion will include:

- Ethics in professionalism
- Codes of ethics for professionals working with young children
- Personal voice and ethical dilemmas

Ethics in professionalism

How do contemporary professionals define and sustain their ethical values and beliefs in the early twenty-first century? Professionals have an ethical responsibility (often supported by a code of conduct) to act in clients' best needs, interests and rights. They should possess characteristics of dedication and commitment with clear standards of behaviour and a strong service ethic (Helsby 1996; Osgood 2006). Professionals should be morally accountable in their ethical relationships which should be established in an ethos of trust and confidentiality (Winch 2004). In the ever-changing demands of contemporary society, technology and globalisation, the different professions have to be responsive to client and public need and not hide behind complexities or assumptions regarding their roles (Garet et al. 2001). Each profession needs to face new challenges with integrity, balancing the needs of its members with those of the society for which it works. In discussing responsibility at work, Gardner reminds us that:

> Professionals are groups of individuals who are afforded a certain degree of autonomy and status for tackling important individual or societal problems involving complex judgements under uncertainty, and for doing so in a thoughtful and disinterested manner. (2007: 10)

A professional's ethical practice is dependent on professional knowledge acquired through education, qualification and experience, which will have generated specific skills, values and beliefs. Brock's (2006) seven dimensions of professionalism – knowledge, education and training, skills, autonomy, values, ethics, and reward – is drawn from an investigation of literature across the disciplines of philosophy, sociology and education and empirical research in the field of early childhood education and care (ECEC). Brock (2006) believes these seven common traits of professionalism are interconnected and have equal importance, as a 'well-rounded' professional requires all of the seven dimensions. Her research indicates the complexity of conceptualising 'ethics' – a key dimension that incorporates the following ten tenets of ethical practice:

- Adherence to a professional code of conduct and/or self regulating code of ethics
- Consideration of standards or norms, which may include measures of what is quality
- Beliefs, values and principles – applicable and acceptable to workers and clients – consistent with inclusiveness rather than exclusiveness
- Ethical relationships between practitioner and client, centred on pre-eminence of an individual's needs, interests, rights and opinions
- Responsibility to the well-being of individuals or society at large respecting confidentiality
- Moral integrity with elements of vocation, altruism or 'good work' underpinning values
- Promotion of well-being, truth, democracy, fairness and equality for both clients and society
- Trustworthiness in professional knowledge and practical wisdom developed through experience and continuing professional development
- Commitment to working in collaboration with colleagues and sharing of expertise
- Collective and collaborative action regarding ethical practice through articulating professional voice and engaging in advocacy

A discussion of many of these ten tenets of ethical practice identified by Brock (2006) will permeate the chapter, along with the work of many professionals within an ethical code that reflects these tenets. We raise two questions: has increased regulation and accountability to clients and policy-makers resulted in less autonomy to uphold their ethical principles? Have the individual professional's ethical values, difficult to maintain in a climate that requires evidence of quality and demands target-setting to prove effectiveness, become more divorced from the practice demanded by society and government policy? Goodson (2003: 32) states that a new 'professionalism needs to reinstate moral and ethical vocation as the guiding principle'. As Clarke (2006: 703) argues, the evaluation of policy initiatives

and judgments of the value of state investment focuses mainly on quanti-
tatively measurable outcomes, rather than the qualitative data from users.
Does this make the professional's aspirations for truly ethical practice
harder to achieve? In Goodfellow's (2004) opinion there needs to be a
better balance between the ethics of care in professions and society's values.
Indeed a professional's ethical practice should 'foreground active personal
responsibility' when making decisions and forming ethical relationships
(Dahlberg and Moss 2005: 12). A commitment to a clear, shared emotional
and intellectual understanding of the complexity of values and ethics is
therefore important for any contemporary professional.

Codes of ethics for professionals working with young children

So what is the role of the early years professional when we focus on educators and librarians? What ethical principles need to be considered by these
individuals when aspiring to work as reflective practitioners? They have
a responsibility to do the best for their client groups of children, families
and communities, in ways that are built upon strong and secure values,
beliefs and knowledge. Professionals who work with young children have
proclaimed that their vocation, values, ethics and personal fulfilment are key
to their commitment and professionalism (Moyles 2001). Other researchers
(Nias 1989; Osgood 2004) also find that passionate and caring emotions
are fundamental and crucial to providing good quality provision for young
children. The interactive and reciprocal relationships formed between the
children, parents, families and other adults are key. A code of ethics for
these professionals would provide all parties with clear guidelines of what
is expected from everyone involved in working with young children. Preer
(2008) reminds us of the challenge of being able to separate personal belief
from professional responsibility, and the next section will explore codes of
ethics for educators and librarians in the UK and the USA.

Codes of ethics for professionalism in the English education system

Search on the internet for 'codes of ethics' and you will easily find sites for the British Psychological Society, the British Association of Social Workers, Counselling and Psychotherapy, museums, librarians and innumerable sports organisations. Then try a search for codes of ethics for education and you will be able to access those for the USA, Canada, New Zealand, Australia, Phillipines and Malta. However, you will have very limited results for ethical codes for education professionals in England, whether it is for early years, primary, secondary, further or higher education. This seems rather unusual in a contemporary society for such a large body of professionals – surely, as Brock's (2006) dimensions reveal, ethics is a key facet for any self-respecting professional. Codes of ethics are difficult to locate when you access the websites and documentation for the General Teaching Council (GTC), the Children's Workforce Development Council (CWDC), the newly developed Early Years Professional Status (EYPS) and the teacher Training and Development Agency (TDA). An informal survey with twenty lecturers and educationalists teaching, researching and writing in the field of childhood and early years found that they could not recall there ever having been a national code of ethics for the ECEC profession.

The TDA website informs us that teachers' professional duties are framed by legislation, statutory and non-statutory guidance, including the 'Education Act (2002), the Children Act (2004), the Children's Workforce Strategy (2005) and Every Child Matters'. It advises that teachers have rights and responsibilities for their professional practice, which are formulated by local authorities, schools and other organisations. The TDA standards for teachers focus on the three areas of Attributes, Knowledge and Understanding, and Skills – but at no point is 'ethics' mentioned. The attention for the teaching profession seems to be very focused on achieving standards and competence – a rather narrow view of professionalism (Brock 2006).

On the CWDC (2009) website a search of 'ethics' does address listening to the 'clients' through participation that 'means ensuring the structures, resources and processes are in place' to act on information from children, young people and their families. But still no code of ethics is in place for the ECEC! When writing the standards for the National Professional Qualification for Children's Centre Leadership in 2005, the CWDC consulted ECEC professionals. At one meeting in Leeds there was a strong recommendation to include a section on ethics; however, this was not incorporated into the standards.

The GTC developed a Code of Conduct for teachers in 2001, which included ethical principles that advocate public service and accountability to the community, values consistent with education and teaching, high standards from well-informed views and evidence-led advice. One of the GTC's funded research projects (Cordingley et al. 2003) evaluates the impact of continuing professional development for teachers, and within this document the importance of ethics is emphasised. However, Laight's (2009) research questions how many educators actually access and acknowledge the GTC as a significant influence on their professional work. Whilst there is a definite account of ethical principles for this professional body, it still does not reach a wide audience or establish a national code of ethics accessible to all educators. This is also the case for the National Union of Teachers' (NUT) code of ethics, located within its professional code of conduct.

In Rodd's (2004) view, ECEC professionals should own a code of ethics that has moral obligations and responsibilities to children and families based on trust, values, respect and empowerment. She reflects how the USA, Canada, Australia and New Zealand developed their codes of ethics in the 1990s to ensure that children's rights were identified and enhanced. It may be valuable for early years educators to seek advice from these international ECEC professionals, as well as from other professional bodies in the UK. Early years educators in the USA, as well as librarians in the UK and USA have professional codes of ethics; the next sections explore these codes of ethics to seek this advice.

Codes of ethics for professionalism in early years in the United States of America

Each profession's ethical positions are often defined in a Professional Code of Ethical Conduct. Codes of Ethics are a set of principles or rules of behaviour within a profession that have been recognized universally or considered to be beneficial for positive outcomes (Breitborde and Swiniarski 2006). Many educators post in their schools or centres the code they have accepted as a moral compass for all to know and adhere to. In the United States, professional organizations and teachers' unions have promulgated their principles in generic codes for educators of the early years through college/university teaching. As the largest educators' organization in the country, The National Education Association (NEA) adopted its code in 1975 by its Representative Assembly. Its 'Code of Ethics for the Education Profession' focuses on two basic principles: Principle I, Commitment to the Student, and Principle II, Commitment to the Profession. Its preamble frames the philosophical foundation of the code:

> The educator recognizes the magnitude of the responsibility inherent in the teaching process. The desire for the respect and confidence of one's colleagues, of students, of parents and of the members of the community provides the incentive to attain and maintain the highest possible degree of ethical conduct. The Code of Ethics of the Education Profession indicates the aspiration of all educators and provides standards by which to judge conduct. (NEA 1975)

Some schools use the NEA Code as a template for their individual codes, in which they define standards to judge actions or behaviours. In these individual codes, students are often permitted input. Providing students' voices in the consecration of moral expectations lends a personal ownership and commitment. All agree on what behaviour is acceptable and encouraged and what is not (Breitborde and Swiniarski 2006).

Codes are designed as guides for teachers and administrators who work with children, families and communities. While the NEA code is the umbrella code for the education profession in the United States, there are other associations and organizations that provide Codes of Professional Conduct for specific fields within the profession. Not all educators necessarily belong to NEA, while others feel a need to chart moral expectations for a more focussed group. Such is the case for Early Childhood Education professionals in the United States. The National Association for the Education of Young Children (NAEYC), the most extensive early years care organization nationwide, revised its Code of Ethical Conduct in 2005 for professionals who work with or are associated with the education and care of young children from birth to age eight. Along with teachers, the code includes such professionals as administrators, educators of early childhood providers and teachers, governmental regulatory officials or any specialists who directly or indirectly impact young children in primary schools, hospitals, community programmes, as well as childcare centres (NAEYC 2005).

The NAEYC Code has been endorsed or adapted by other associations such as the Association of Childhood Education International and the National Association for Family Child Care, an organization that addresses care given in a home setting to children not related to family operators. The Association of Childhood Education International (ACEI), headquartered in Olney, Maryland, USA, has a global mission for the education of children from birth through early adolescence. Its genesis is in the former International Kindergarten Union of the late nineteenth century. The organization changed its name to be more inclusive of professionals working with children from infancy through the middle school years. In 2000 the organization began the task of writing a Code of Professional Ethics for its membership. After years of research, an Ethics Committee was convened which in 2005 proposed an endorsement of the NAEYC code to the ACEI Executive Board. With the Board's recommendation, the association promptly approved the action at its annual international conference of Spring 2005. Freeman and Swick (2007) expand on this protocol to recommend:

> That all organizations involved in the care and education consider the possibility of endorsing each other's position statements ... This collaboration might be ... an ongoing sharing of resources that could enhance the public's perception of teachers' professionalism

In their writings, Freeman and Swick note the practicality of having a code when faced with moral dilemmas in teaching. They illustrate how reliance on the code offers support in sensitive ethical situations that can arise especially in dealing with families. Freeman and Swick outline practical steps teachers can use to implement the NAEYC Code:

1. Identify the issues and stakeholders
2. Brainstorm for resolution
3. Refer to the code to determine defensible courses of action
4. Apply the code in context of your best judgment

(Adapted from Freeman and Swick 2007: 165)

In addition to the adaptation of the NAEYC Code, the Association for Childhood Education has a specific code for its executive board, headquarters staff, and volunteers working for the association to sign in agreement with the 'Mission of ACEI':

> The Mission of ACEI is to promote and support in the global community the optimal education and development of children, from birth though early adolescence, and to influence the professional growth of educators and the efforts of others who are committed to the needs of children in a changing society. (ACEI 2007)

This code also includes clauses that provide expectations for legal compliance, responsible stewardship, openness and disclosure, personal and professional conduct, conflicts of interest, as well as an inclusiveness and diversity policy.

In writing their Code of Ethical Conduct, the NAEYC identified *core values* that have been held as long time commitments in the fields of early childhood education and care universally. These values are the underpinnings of the Code's *standards of ethical behaviour*, namely:

- Appreciation of the uniqueness of childhood in the human life cycle
- Knowledge of child development and the learning process
- Support for the bond of children and family

- Recognition of family, culture, community and society to understand each child
- Respect for the dignity, worth and uniqueness of all children, families and colleagues
- Respect for diversity of all
- Recognition that children reach full potential in relationship with trust and respect

(Adapted from NAEYC 2007)

The Association of Childhood Education feels these standards are equally relevant to its mission and constituencies.

Implications for early years educators in England in a global age

The Association of Childhood Education's endorsement of the NAEYC code provides an optional route for English early years educators to consider. Since ACEI is an international organization with British members, there is an opportunity to work within the organization for adapting standards that fit with the social/cultural needs of Britain. The NAEYC standards have a universal base for early childhood education as they are founded on a set of internationally accepted and acclaimed values. Research and study into the development of the NAEYC code might be the first step to acceptance or serve as a model for a British code. In America, the NAEYC has been effective in enforcing the code in early childhood programmes, since it is the national accrediting organization for early education schooling as well as early childhood education teacher training programmes in colleges and universities for all states.

The implications of a mandate for a Code of Professional Ethics for early years educators in the UK are critical in this age of global education. Sharing resources and ideas on each side of the Atlantic would heighten awareness of the moral dimension of the profession, derive global codes of expected behaviours for the early years and improve the professionalism of the field. International partnerships with interdisciplinary memberships should explore the possibilities of authoring such a code or building on the foundations of established work.

As well as exploring ethical codes of practice internationally, it would also be beneficial to reflect on codes from other professional bodies in the UK. Brock and Rankin's (2008; 2009) interdisciplinary partnership brings together the fields of ECEC and librarianship. They have demonstrated the rich potential of how partnerships between these two professions can draw families into the world of literacy and all it can offer – promoting the generic message that reading with young children is important. This section has discussed codes of ethics for early years educators, the next section now turns to the ethical codes for the profession of librarianship.

Codes of ethics and codes of conduct for librarians – The USA and UK perspectives

Gorman (2000) proposes eight values that that offer foundational support to librarianship: stewardship, service, intellectual freedom, rationalism, literacy and learning, equity of access, privacy and democracy. One of the hallmarks of a profession is the framework of values that underpin the work of practitioners, and the International Federation of Library Associations has compiled a collection of professional guidelines for librarians and other library employees adopted by national library or librarian associations or implemented by government agencies. McMenemy et al. (2007) point out that despite being a profession that is centuries old, the literature on ethical issues in librarianship is sparse before the 1970s. The American Library Association was the first to begin to develop a code in 1938; last amended in 2008 it is broadly based and attempts to cover the whole profession – including professional development and ethical management:

> As members of the American Library Association, we recognize the importance of codifying and making known to the profession and to the general public the ethical principles that guide the work of librarians, other professionals providing information services, library trustees and library staffs. (ALA 2008)

In the UK, the Library Association did not adopt an ethical code until 1985, over 100 years after it was formed as a professional body. The Library Association was reconstituted as the Chartered Institute of Library and Information Professionals (CILIP) in 2002 and, by the terms of its Royal Charter, CILIP has a responsibility to 'the public good'. CILIP has developed a set of twelve Ethical Principles and a Code of Professional Practice for Library and Information Professionals. The code sets out the expectations in five sections covering personal responsibilities, responsibilities to information and its users, responsibilities to colleagues and the information community, responsibilities to society and responsibilities as employees. The introduction to the CILIP code reminds us that library and information professionals are frequently the essential link between information users and the information or piece of literature which they require. They therefore occupy a privileged position which carries corresponding responsibilities. The purpose of the Principles and Code is to provide a framework that helps library and information professionals who are members of CILIP to manage the responsibilities and sensitivities which figure prominently in their work. As mentioned earlier, a consideration of ethical issues is an essential quality of the 'reflective' practitioner.

McNenemy et al. (2007) point out that ethical codes are useful documents for two specific reasons. Firstly, they offer members of the professional association a model of behaviour that is expected of them, establishing the parameters of acceptable behaviour. Secondly they communicate a set of values to the wider world, including employers and other stakeholders. However, although ethical codes are in place for librarians in both the USA and the UK, it is perhaps debatable as to how useful and relevant they are in terms of supporting and guiding the every day work of practitioners when facing ethical dilemmas. Hauptman (2002: 135) writes that:

Codes, rules, regulations and even laws do not create or foster an ethical environment; a true commitment on the part of the organization and its individual members is mandatory if we are to operate fairly, and offer all patrons and clients the service that they deserve while avoiding social harm.

Preer (2008) argues that the starting point of professional conduct is adherence to the core ethical values of librarianship; providing service and access, avoiding philosophical and financial conflicts of interest, and protecting patron confidentiality. She comments that just as practice changes, ethical standards evolve to encompass new understandings of our roles. The complexity of these issues will now be explored within the interdisciplinary and international domains of early years educators and librarians.

Personal voice and ethical dilemmas

Eliciting the voices of professionals can fill in gaps in the perceptions of theorists and proffer implications for policy-makers through providing insights into ethical beliefs and practices. A professional voice for those working in the field is required to be a part of any ongoing debate about what is important for young children and their families. In the next section we introduce four ethical dilemmas to illustrate and exemplify issues faced by practitioners in early years education and library settings. These reflect the ten tenets of ethical behaviour identified by Brock (2006).

Ethical dilemma 1: Rights and responsibilities – Where is the guidance?

A small group of educators (academics and practitioners) when discussing Ethics in the ECEC in England raised a number of contentious issues. There was a view that ethics is usually about protecting the rights of individuals, but also that individuals have responsibilities. This is Tanya's perspective:

I don't know of any national code of ethics for early years education. When I came across Reggio in 2000 and their list of rights and responsibilities, I felt I needed something more formal in our setting, so we put it in our hallway for everyone to see. Ethics is about protecting everyone's rights: children, parents, staff. We're growing up in a strong rights culture, but people aren't always aware of their responsibilities. For me, the biggest thing about ethics is to do with film and photography. We've been involved in PICL (Parents Involved in their Children's Learning) and that's when I started looking for statements on ethics from Pen Green. They believe that all participants have equal voices to decide what was OK, however I'm concerned about longitudinal effects. For example, some years ago our school was filmed to show different settings and professional roles in the early years. Several years later I saw a banner at an outdoor play environment promotion that showed a photo of my daughter up a tree. It had originally been taken only for the video which had a specific distribution, yet here it was used for a completely different purpose of which I had no knowledge. A clearer ethical statement about everything we are involved in is required. There should be a national code – I'm surprised we don't have one. I can see that different authorities may want their own local level code that acknowledges specific communities, but I would like to see an overarching code of ethics, rights and responsibilities to get the balance right.

In Brock's (2006) research with early years educators, ethics was a key dimension of their professionalism. The research participants had a high level of commitment to being professionals and to helping young children, their families and the community with whom they worked. They had a broad and encompassing view of parents, carers and children and showed that the forming of strong, supportive relationships was an important part of the professional role. That they were committed to collaborative and collective behaviour was clear and they gave much qualitative evidence of how they met young children's needs. Their values were centred on a professional, albeit tacit, self-regulating code of ethics, pre-eminence of clients' interests and well-being and a commitment to working inclusively and collaboratively. This was the case for the educators consulted during the research. We raise the question, therefore: would a national code of ethics based on such principles be beneficial for *every* professional working with young children?

Ethical dilemma 2: The hidden curriculum defines the moral code

Lisa Pannell is gathering her kindergarten class together for a reading from its Global Bookshelf Corner. She has selected as today's choice, 'For Every Child'. This picture book by Castle (2000) is published in association with UNICEF to introduce young children to the UN Convention on the Rights of the Child. Fourteen principles from the convention are delivered in the book's text and illustrated by fourteen artists from all corners of the globe. The children are clustered around their teacher to see the text and hear the reading on comfortable personal mats that designate their self spaces for story time. They know the rules for listening to the story, asking questions, and respecting the comments from their peers. Ms Pannell opens the book and reads through to its end. The children then are asked to respond, interpret what they heard, and illustrate each principle together in small groups. A class book is completed with each group's efforts as a culminating activity to be shared with other classes and displayed in the Global Bookshelf collection.

Lisa Pannell selected *'For Every Child'* to draw attention to the UN Convention on the Rights of the Child (CRC). Although Madeleine Albright, as the US Ambassador to the United Nations, signed the convention in the early 1990s, the United States' Congress has yet to ratify the convention. As a result, CRC gets little attention in the United States and is often excluded from the American schools' overt curriculum, which is the curriculum each state mandates for standards, outcomes and behaviours. The CRC is an example of a topic ignored in school and thus a part of the *null* curriculum. The choice to include or exclude it is a value of the hidden curriculum.

The hidden curriculum is subtle and includes all of the knowledge, values, attitudes, norms or beliefs that children acquire in school but which is not stated in formal objectives or policies (Breitborde and Swiniarski 2006). Ms Pannell's case in point is a deliberate attempt by a teacher to transform a piece of the *null* curriculum into class discourse by heightening awareness of information that is relevant to her children yet often avoided. While she does not state her intention, she is teaching the hidden curriculum in her behaviour, her actions and her choice to read about the CRC. Other covert values are evident in her teaching by the way she has arranged her class with the use of group activities for a consensus of interpretation of the CRC principles. She uses strategies that help her children know that each child has a personal place in the classroom and equal opportunities to voice personal thought, but also that all share the responsibility to listen to each other. Collaboration in her class is encouraged over competition and children's work is honoured.

The hidden curriculum can ask and answer moral questions in positive or negative terms. The climate of a childcare centre, a kindergarten class, or an entire school can be defined in responses to questions like the following:

- Who owns the classroom, the curriculum, the materials?
- Who makes the decisions?
- Who can interact with whom, when and why?
- Who is worth listening to?
- Who has good ideas?
- What part do I play in the classroom?
- What part do I play the world?

(Swiniarski and Breitborde 2009)

The questions raised by the USA classroom environment present ethical decisions for the early years educator. In the next example we consider the environment of a Children's Centre in the UK, and the ethical issues relating to the challenges of partnership working between professionals.

Ethical dilemma 3: A dilemma for the early years librarian –
Confidentiality versus referral

The decisions a professional makes and the work of a professional affects large numbers of people, our patrons, our stakeholders, our societies. Buchanan and Henderson remind us that this clearly differentiates professionals from lay persons. (2009: 95). Partnership working can present challenges and ethical dilemmas for professionals, particularly in cross-sector partnerships where participants can often have different strategic priorities and political drivers. In the UK, agency partnerships in Children's Centres are helping parents to support their children's early language and literacy, as well as communicating important messages about emotional and social development and health issues (Rankin, Brock et al. 2007).

Consider the potential ethical dilemma facing Alex, an early years librarian in the busy inner city Rainbow Children's Centre. Joe, aged three, regularly comes with his grandmother to the story time in the Rainbow Children's Centre and they often stay for a while to play with other children after the sessions. Joe wasn't making much of an attempt to speak and was often quite aggressive with other children. His Grandmother was worried about Joe's speech and language development and his behaviour and she eventually felt confident enough to mention her concerns to Alex while chatting after a story time. Alex is facing an ethical dilemma as there are issues of respecting privacy and confidentiality, and data protection legislation. However, the local partnership organisations in this particular Children's Centre have a record keeping and information sharing agreement. Alex, as the early years librarian in the Rainbow Children's Centre is empowered to use this process and he makes a referral to the family support team. Joe and his family now have speech therapy support. Alfino and Pierce (2001) remind us that in addition to its practical or financial value, information also has a social or moral nature. Using professional judgement in the choice of action, Alex is aware of his role as a referral agent. The next ethical dilemma discusses professional obligations in relation to censorship and intellectual freedom.

Ethical dilemma 4: Choosing the books: The ethics of information
supply and intellectual freedom, USA

A key aspect of professional practice in librarianship is collection development, the selection of material to support a particular user community. In the ECEC context it is important to have knowledge about children and their families' culture, heritage, language and interests so as to ensure that a breadth of valuable resources is provided (Rankin and Brock, 2009: 81). Hauptman (2002) raises the issue that in collection development many of the choices that selectors make have strong ethical implications. Ethical selection policies require that we choose appropriate materials while attempting to ignore social and personal prejudices that may cause us to censor unacceptable materials. In ethical dilemma two we have already made reference to the UN Convention of the Rights of the Child, and in a discussion about intellectual freedom, Buchanan and Henderson (2009) note that the USA has the notorious stigma of being one of only two nations (with Somalia) not to ratify the UN Convention on the Rights of the Child. They remind us that libraries have long adopted the position that children and young adults have the right to free expression. The American Association of School Librarians has suggested that 'school library media professionals assume a leadership role in promoting the principles of intellectual freedom within the school by providing resources and services that create and sustain an atmosphere of free inquiry', yet there are concerns about the 'widespread devaluation and elimination of school librarians' (2009: 26).

In an example of book selection and intellectual freedom, McNenemy et al. (2007) cite the controversy over intelligent design and creationism versus evolution, a challenging issue for librarians in the USA. This has raised serious ethical dilemmas regarding censorship and the banning of books that are deemed unsuitable or inappropriate. In another example, Buchanan and Henderson (2009) discuss intellectual freedom in a case study of Tommy, a child in kindergarten who is not able to borrow a copy of the children's picture book *And Tango Makes Three* by Richardson and Parnell (2007) because it is in the adult section. This case study raises the ethical dilemma about intellectual freedom and a library's policy to shelve alternative lifestyle books in the adult section. Does the librarian have an obligation to keep all controversial books out of the children's section?

Conclusion

This chapter has demonstrated the new insights and opportunities that can be gained through the sharing of professional ethics, by considering multi-disciplinary and international perspectives within the fields of early years educators and librarians. A respect for each other's professional domain and a willingness to explore, and question, beyond one's own code of practice empowers the reflective practitioner. However, more work needs to be done. The notion of using a personal moral compass as an ethical guide is addressed in professions such as health and social care, yet there is limited evidence of research and theory within education and librarianship. The early years education community in the UK does not have a codified statement of ethical practice: should this apparent gap be addressed by the profession? Librarianship is well served by codes of practice. Preer (2008) offers a reminder that many of the most important professional values have been tested and debated in the course of formulating and adopting codes of ethics for the library profession. However recent publications on ethics in librarianship appear to include very little on issues in early years provision. In this chapter we seem to have raised questions more than we have provided answers. The complexity of providing positive conditions for all children and their families in twenty-first-century environments continues to offer ethical challenges. Doing it by the book using existing codes would seem to be just the starting point; there are many more chapters to be written.

References

Abbott, L., and Nutbrown, C. (2001) (eds). *Experiencing Reggio Emilia: Implications for Preschool Provision.* Buckingham: Open University Press.

Association of Childhood Education International (ACEI) (2007). 'Code of Ethics for ACEI'. Olney, MD: Association for Childhood Education International. <http://www.acei.org/codeofethics> accessed 6 June 2009.

American Library Association (ALA) (2008). 'Code of Ethics of the American Library Association' <http://www.ala.org/ala/aboutala/offices/oif/statementspols/codeofethics/codeethics.cfm> accessed 3 July 2009.

Alfino, M., and Pierce, L. (2001). 'The Social Nature of Information', *Library Trends*, 49 (3), 471–85.

Breitborde, M. and Swiniarski, L. (2006). *Teaching on Principle and Promise: The Foundations of Education*. Boston, MA: Houghton Mifflin.

Brock, A. (2006). 'Dimensions of Early Years Professionalism – Attitudes Versus Competences?' Reflection paper on *Training Advancement and Co-operation in the Teaching of Young Children (TACTYC)* <http://www.tactyc.org.uk> accessed 21 October 2006.

—— and Rankin, C. (2008). *Communication, Language and Literacy from Birth to Five*. London: Sage.

—— and Swiniarski, L. (2008). 'An International Teaching Partnership's Ideas to Transform Early Education Practices for Global Understanding and Cultural Sensitivity', *Education*, 3–13 (33), 281–92.

Buchanan, E. and Henderson, K. (2009). *Case Studies in Library and Information Science Ethics*. Jefferson, NC: McFarland.

Castle, C. (2000). *For Every Child: The Rights of the Child in Words and Pictures*. New York, NY: Phyllis Fogelman Books.

CILIP. 'Code of Professional Practice for Library and Information Professionals' <http://www.cilip.org.uk/NR/rdonlyres/CC88B3D0-9F93-4FF0-B448-7BFF5EBCE61C/0/CodeofProfessionalPracticeforLibraryandInformation Professionalspdf> accessed 3 July 2009.

Children's Workforce Development Council (CWDC) <http://www.cwdcouncil.org.uk> accessed 1 June 2009.

Clarke, K. (2006). 'Childhood, Parenting and Early Intervention: A Critical Examination of the Sure Start National Programme', *Critical Social Policy*, 26, 699–721.

Cordingley, P., Bell, M., Rundell, B., and Evans, D. (2003). *The Impact of Collaborative CPD on Classroom Teaching and Learning*. London: EPPI-Centre, Social Science Research Unit, Institute of Education, University of London.

Dahlberg, G. and Moss, P. (2005). *Ethics and Politics in Early Childhood Education*. Abingdon: Routledge Falmer.

Freeman, N. and Swick, K. (2007). 'The Ethical Dimensions of Working with Parents: Using the Code Of Ethics When Faced with a Difficult Decision', *Childhood Education*, 83 (3) 163–9.

Gardner, H. (ed.) (2007). *Responsibility at Work: How Leading Professionals Act (or Don't Act) Responsibly*. San Francisco, CA: Jossey Bass.

Garet, M., Porter, A., Desimone, L., Birman, B. and Yoo, K. (2001). 'What Makes Professional Development Effective? Results from a National Sample of Teachers', *American Educational Research Journal*, 38, 915–45.

General Teaching Council for England (GTC) <http://www.gtce.org.uk> accessed 1 June 2009.

Goodfellow, J. (2004). 'Documenting Professional Practice through the Use of a Professional Portfolio', *Early Years: An International Journal of Research and Development*, 23, 63–74.

Goodson, I. (2003). *Professional Knowledge, Professional Lives: Studies in Education and Change.* London: Open University Press.

Gorman, M. (2000). *Our Enduring Values: Librarianship in the 21st Century.* Chicago: American Library Association.

Hauptman, Robert (2002). *Ethics and Librarianship.* Jefferson, NC: McFarland.

Helsby, G. (1996). 'Professionalism in English Secondary Schools', *Journal of Education for Teaching*, 22, 135–48.

Laight, J. (2009). 'Critical Discourse Analysis of Journals for Teachers: A Comparative Study of the General Teaching Council and National Union of Teachers' Magazines'. Unpublished research, Leeds Metropolitan University.

McMenemy, D., Poulter, A. and Burton, P.F. (2007). *A Handbook of Ethical Practice: A Practical Guide to Dealing with Ethical Issues in Information and Library Work.* Oxford: Chandos Publishing.

Moyles, J. (2001). 'Passion, Paradox and Professionalism in Early Years Education', *Early Years: Journal of International Research and Development*, 21, 81–95.

National Association for the Education of Young Children (NAEYC) (2005). 'NAEYC Code of Ethical Conduct and Statement of Commitment' <http://www.naeyc. org/about/positions/PSethof.asp> accessed 6 June 2009.

National Education Association (NEA) Representative Assembly (1975). 'Code of Ethics of the Education Profession, National Education Association' <http:// www.knea.org/profession/codeofethics.html> accessed 6 June 2009.

National Union of Teachers (NUT) website <http://www.nut.org.uk> accessed 1 June 2009.

Nias, J. (1989). *Primary Teachers Talking: A Study of Teaching as Work.* London: Routledge.

Osgood, J. (2004). 'Time to Get Down to Business? The Responses of Early Years Practitioners to Entrepreneurial Approaches to Professionalism', *Journal of Early Childhood Research*, 2, 5–24.

——(2006). 'Deconstructing Professionalism in Early Childhood Education: Resisting the Regulatory Gaze', *Contemporary Issues in Early Childhood Journal*, 7, 5–14.

Preer, J. (2008). *Library Ethics.* Westport, CT: Libraries Unlimited.

Rankin, C. and Brock, A. (2009). *Delivering the Best Start: A Guide to Early Years Libraries*. London: Facet Publishing.

——, Wootton, C. and Halpin, E. (2007). 'The Role of the Early Year's Librarian in Developing an Information Community: A Case Study of Effective Partnerships and Early Years Literacy within a Sure Start Project in Wakefield'. Conference Proceedings of the Canadian Association for Information Science <http://www.cais-acsi.ca/proceedings/2007/rankin_2007.pdf> accessed 3 July 2009.

Richardson, J. and Parnell, P. (2007). *And Tango Makes Three*. London: Simon & Schuster.

Rodd, J. (2004). *Leadership in Early Childhood*. Maidenhead: Open University Press/ McGraw-Hill Education.

Swiniarski, L. and Breitborde, M. (2009). 'Global Education: Beginning with Ourselves, Changing the World'. Unpublished keynote paper for the Queen's Conference on Education, Queen's University, Kingston, Ontario, Canada.

Training and Development Agency for Schools (TDA) <http://www.tda.gov.uk> accessed 1 June 2009.

Winch, C. (2004). 'What Do Teachers Need to Know About Teaching? A Critical Examination of the Occupational Knowledge of Teachers', *Journal of Educational Studies*, 52, 180–96.

3   Every Child Matters:
New ethical challenges arising in schools

This chapter looks at the ethical implications for schools and for school staff in becoming multi-professional and integrated. It details the substantial legislation that is forcing policy changes arising from the Every Child Matters agenda in England (DfES 2003). One of the biggest challenges arising from recent workforce reform is that of creating and sustaining effective multi-professional or integrated teams and the unification of professionals and practices of those who are concerned with children and young people. These professionals are now expected to plan, work, think and problem-solve in much closer collaboration than previously and this is forcing substantial changes on schools.

These newly emerging, integrated roles should benefit from opportunities for working together to develop formal policies and procedures that guide their multi-professional team work (Anning et al. 2006) and help build new kinds of professional identity recognised as necessary for integrated working. The building of services 'around' the child and the family (Sloper 2004) presents new ethical challenges with regard to confidentiality, the protection of children, and in relation to children's and parents' rights.

Abbott (2005) notes that education as a broad agency, was finding it challenging to work in multi-disciplinary ways, in relation to children and families in difficulties. In the last ten years an increasing number of other professionals have moved in to work in schools in support of the curriculum, such as Higher Learning and Teaching Assistants (HLTAs), Family Support Workers and Learning Mentors. The Every Child Matters policy strongly endorses the ethic of professional team-working by portraying educational settings as appropriate contexts for inter-professional collaboration, but little has been written about how schools experience the challenges in developing ethical practice through these new forms of integrated and multi-agency working.

This chapter considers the day-to-day ethical issues for staff, pupils and parents in one primary school. These are explored through interviews with staff supporting children in challenging social and educational circumstances. Interviews with a parent and her child also provide insights into family experiences for a pupil with a degenerative physical condition.

The policy background

Every Child Matters (ECM) was announced in 2003 by the UK Prime Minister, Tony Blair, as the government's response to the Laming Inquiry Report (2003) into the death of Victoria Climbié. This tragic death is considered by many to be the catalyst for a change in services for children and young people; however, upon deeper examination we can see that New Labour had already established a track record of reform in this area (Barker 2009).

New Labour was elected in 1997 with an agenda for reform in public services focused upon education (Labour Party 1997). Although schools were the main focus for reform and investment in the first term of Blair's leadership, the remainder of children's services outside of statutory schooling rapidly moved up the political and policy agenda. A plethora of initiatives aimed at addressing wider areas of children's lives had been evident over the period 1997 to 2003. These were largely in response to the number of children and young people living in poverty (Percy-Smith 2005).

Within the context of the wider world, Britain does not suffer high levels of child poverty. However, in the context of Western Europe 23% of children in Britain officially lived in poverty in 1997 set against 18% for the EU members (UNICEF 2005). In order to address this, and alongside an extensive education reform agenda, the Blair government, introduced national policies affecting children from Birth–19, such as the Sure Start Programme, the Children's Fund and the Connexions Strategy. These initiatives reflected the social justice agenda, and were further supported by the targeting of initiatives upon geographic areas of disadvantage through Education and Health Action Zones. Percy-Smith (2005) suggests that the lack of cohesion within these programmes at local level resulted from fragmentation at national level with a range of targets emanating from a range of government departments.

The death of a young girl, Victoria Climbié in 2000 was reported as demonstrating the lack of inter-agency communication, poor integration of services, poor leadership, and funded services that were inadequately staffed. This represented a gross failure of the system at local level (Laming 2003).

ECM: The Green Paper was published in September 2003. It sought to build upon the existing initiatives and strengthen preventative services by focusing upon four key areas: supporting families and carers; early interventions before children reach crisis point; addressing underlying problems, such as weak accountability and poor integration; and ensuring that the people working with children are valued, rewarded and trained.

Following a period of consultation, the government published ECM: Next Steps (DfES 2004) and then legislated later that year through the 2004 Children Act. In our opinion, legislation was necessary but whether the strategy was able to balance the risks inherent in early detection and early intervention approaches alongside intrusion into family life is debatable. This is the ethical tightrope that services and professionals have to walk on a daily basis. Groundwater-Smith (Chapter 8, this volume) refers to Ahmed and Machold's (2004) maxims of no harm, transparency, voice, equity, benefit, integrity, liberty and care as providing a set of domains for ethical accountability. Professionals in education or health and social care, governed by legislation, need to constantly address these in their daily practice to attempt to mitigate the effects of 'one size fits all'.

Towards integrated working

ECM: Change for Children (DfES 2004) signalled government's intention to commence a process of integrating services through a new accountability framework based upon the Local Authorities (LAs) and outlined
the direction for future children and young people's services in England.
Services were required to co-operate and develop new ways of working with
the LAs who now held a new accountability for all children and young
people residing in their area (DfES 2004). Schools were not mandated to
co-operate with LAs with regard to ECM at this point, other than via their
existing role through the 1989 Children Act. Central to this new way of
working was the integration of services aimed at supporting every child,
whatever their background or circumstances to maximise their opportunities through five strands:

- Being healthy
- Staying safe
- Enjoying and achieving
- Making a positive contribution
- Achieve economic well-being
                                        (DfES 2004)

LAs were required to prepare and publish a Children and Young People's
Plan. This was made accountable through the newly established roles of
Director of Children's Services and Elected Lead Member in LAs through
the 2004 Children Act.

ECM guidance followed quickly from cross-governmental policy
makers to support the development of these news ways of working. A review
of the children's workforce commenced at national level with the estab-
lishment of the Children's Workforce Development Council (CWDC).
This new organisation began reviewing the core skills and knowledge for
this future workforce although their remit did not include teachers, the

responsibility for whom remained with another government department – the Training and Development Agency (TDA).

These new ways of working have posed challenges for LAs and those working in children and young people's services. ECM is not prescriptive in its application when compared to most national policy. It provides LAs and professionals with space to design local services to be delivered around the needs of individual children and families (Dyson et al. 2008). Agencies were provided with the opportunity to work together to collectively support children and young people, to respond to the criticisms and debate regarding fragmented services (Percy-Smith 2005) and to the recommendations of the Laming Report (Barker 2009). The intention was to help them to move beyond the 'silo-style' model of working to overcome the isolation associated with pre-ECM policy (Ainscow et al. 2008).

Prescribed requirements, covering significant principles of practice, include:

- The implementation of the Common Assessment Framework (CAF) and associated information-sharing based on the holistic needs of the child. The CAF process provides professionals working across children's services with the ability to form a multi-professional team around the child at a much earlier stage than previously possible. This is due to this principle of earliest possible intervention to result in prevention.
- The development of local integrated working through the Lead Professional (LP). The LP becomes the key element in the role of integrated practice. Any professional can be nominated to undertake this role (Walker 2008). The selection of the LP has to be agreed with the child and parent (DCSF, 2009). The family can nominate their preferred single contact to be their lead contact for this new array of professionals and agencies supporting them.

Dyson et al. (2008) emphasize the opportunities for devising new ways of working that this less prescriptive guidance allows grassroots professionals. However, despite this local freedom to develop new practice and multi-professional teams based upon need, the prescriptive practices outlined above provide fundamental challenges to those working both within schools and in the broader community because their interpretation and application is highly complex, as the forthcoming case study illustrates.

The sharing of information around children and families has become a more common feature of professional life for the children's workforce. ECM had brought a shift in emphasis to prevention and early intervention. These safeguarding principles became further embedded in 2007, when the new Prime Minister, Gordon Brown, re-organised government departments and established a new Department of Children, Schools and Families (DCSF). This new department published the first National Children's Plan in December 2007 which brought together many of the ECM initiatives and brought new responsibilities for schools to become part of the integrated workforce within a ten-year plan (Barker 2009). Within this period of intense innovation, came a need to develop appropriate ethical policies regarding confidentiality of information about sensitive medical and social conditions. This requires service leaders to be clear about 'who needs to know' and how information is recorded and communicated in the context of multi-agency working.

The National Children's Plan builds on five central principles:

- Parents and families in the lead
- All children should go as far as their talents can take them
- Enjoyment of childhood and preparation for adult life
- Services need to be shaped and responsive, not designed around professional boundaries
- Prevention of failure – for children and families

(DCSF 2007: 5)

These are laudable principles but, arguably, many families experience difficulty in achieving them.

Further steps were taken to merge the schools' workforce and the remainder of the children's service workforce by urging schools to become active participants in their local Children's Trust (Balls 2008, DCSF 2008). This was followed in December 2008 by the DCSF launch of consultation on the twenty-first-century school, which proposed that schools become the hubs of communities for the local delivery of services for children and families. One may wonder at the scale and nature of a prescription that covers aspects such as 'enjoyment' in schools where standards have reigned supreme for twenty years. Further prescription envisages a single workforce by 2020 (DCSF 2009), a tall order for the professions involved. One may also wonder how the rhetoric of current policy matches with the reality of life for many staff and children as they struggle to cope with policy overload, heavy workloads and poverty in challenging areas within this rapidly changing world.

Multi-professional working and schools

Anning et al. (2006) argue that ECM has provided a direction through which professionals are challenged to move from their traditional roles within health, social work and education to form multi-professional teams based upon the needs of the child and family. MacBeath et al. (2007: 5) consider ECM to be an explicit acknowledgement that schools cannot meet the needs of all children:

> Change for children signals the need for a new relationship, between schools and other community agencies and in relation to offices of government, as children and young people live out their lives in different sites and in often rapid and discontinuous transition from one site to another.

ECM has challenged schools and agencies – through the sharing of information, assessment protocols and frameworks – to adopt integrated ways of working. They have to consider the holistic needs of the child within the family as reflected in the newly devised and universally adopted Common Assessment Framework (CAF).

There has been a growing diversity of workforce in schools (Ainscow et al. 2008), demonstrated by the increase in Teaching Assistants, the introduction of Learning Mentors and more recently the Family Support Worker.

Schools are now expected to endorse and embrace ECM principles by which they become the host for integrated working and the community hub. School leaders face challenges relating to how the broader issues of childcare, social care, health care, child protection or leisure and play relate to the educational setting. Within a relatively brief period, the schools' remit has expanded substantially, and yet schools are still judged on 'standards'.

Unsurprisingly then, in the current context of ECM, Moss and Haydon (2008) ask: 'what is education'? They conclude that ECM and its relationship to the concept of what education actually is, has resulted in the educational goals of pupils' development being framed within a much wider field and not just as it relates to academic achievement. Kirk and Broadhead (2007), in a paper on ECM and Teacher Education, argue that ECM might mark a return to a broader conceptualization of education after an unacceptable narrowing of the teacher's concern for the 'whole child'; traditionally and previously found in early years and primary settings. ECM has, through its implementation, provided an environment in which the whole of the children and young people's workforce is challenged by change, as it moves towards a single workforce through the newly developed Children and Young People's Workforce Plan 2020 (DCSF 2009). The chapter now moves on to look at a case study school that will illuminate some of these changes and challenges.

One school's experience

X Primary School (XPS) has many interesting features. It was one of the first primary schools in the Private Finance Initiative (PFI) rebuilding programme and gained Pathfinder status, giving it a leading role in the development of PFI schools. The school moved into its new building in September 2001, from one that was run down, old and inadequate. The 500 or so children come from a wealth of different cultural backgrounds: 98 per cent speak English as an additional language. The pupils have predominantly

Punjabi, Urdu, Arabic and Somali as their home languages. In addition, pupils also speak another eleven languages. One of the authors of this chapter, Anne Campbell, has been a governor of the school for nine years. There are sixty-two staff consisting of teachers, assistant and deputy head teachers, head teacher, teaching assistants, learning mentors, bilingual support teachers and instructors, lunchtime organisers, and administrative and clerical staff, but excluding catering and caretaking and cleaning staff who are employed and managed by the Facilities Management Group under PFI rules. Staff members are either called teaching staff or associate staff. There is a good ethnic mix within the staff and governors, nearly half of whom are from minority ethnic backgrounds. Parents are welcomed as partners and support workers in the classrooms. XPS is a busy, vibrant, multicultural, inner city primary school that has many challenges as well as many opportunities. The local area has high levels of deprivation, a high level of crime and poor levels of mental health. OFSTED found the school to be 'outstanding' in 2007.

Interview protocol

After the head teacher consented to interviews, the staff, one pupil and his mother were identified and approached; they were given information about the purpose and content of the interview and asked for consent to participate. The interviews were informal in nature and undertaken in the deputy head's room – a familiar place for interviewees. In the case of Child E, a teacher was present to help him feel at ease. Campbell (conducting interviews) is a governor and a regular visitor to the school and often spoke informally with children and staff about their school life and experiences. Interviewees were fully informed as to the publication of the chapter and were ensured anonymity. The following presents selected verbatim extracts to illustrate the ethical challenges being confronted on a day-to-day basis in endeavouring to become an integrated workforce.

The story of Senior Manager A

ECM is such a huge agenda that we have had to bite off a bit and do it well before going on to another bit. I think it requires a very high level of communication and professional commitment from all staff to be able to work with other agencies effectively. We have organised our Teaching and Learning Responsibility posts to cover the various strands of ECM but that is only a small part of the work, more related to curriculum. It is the family support work that is crucial and that is not only done by the Family Support Worker, but by all teaching and associate staff. Inevitably, senior managers have a huge role to play in all cases and in keeping an overview of how the school is working with all agencies.

We have to be very vigilant in detecting children's needs and protecting them, for example we have had some cases of cyber-bullying in the school. Our Special Educational Needs Co-ordinator is a key person in our policy and practice with regards to ECM. She often initiates the CAF process and occasionally is the Lead Professional in a case. Even when education is not in the lead we often end up doing most of the work.

I have to mention the costs involved in ECM. The cost of a multi-agency meeting is huge. I have had to review attendance at these meetings as it was inappropriate for staff to attend the whole meeting when they only need to contribute about one child. So now we have re-organised these meetings so that people only attend for the numbered item that concerns them. This also increases aspects of confidentiality that we need to ensure.

We are affected by parents' and agencies' attitudes to working with us. They have to be willing to commit to that work. Sometimes this is difficult. We have had to deal with some very sensitive issues involving the police with huge amounts of ethical and confidential issues recently. Most of that work is done by senior managers who are aware of all the ethical protocols and how to limit information being made public and to protect our pupils. It is a great responsibility involving different skills than were previously required of senior managers. Times have changed. I always believe that it is people rather than processes that matter most. It is a balancing act trying to ensure you have the enough of the right, vital people for the good of the child working on each case. Continuity is important too.

The story of the Special Educational Needs Teacher B

In my role at the school I have been used to working in a tightly knit multi-agency team for longer than the ECM initiative. At this school the context is very challenging with a lot of children from families experiencing challenges and difficulties. Of course many schools work in very different contexts and have had few experiences of multi-agency working because it just has not been necessary; the children's needs do not require many other professionals to contact or work with the family.

For me the biggest implication of ECM is the Common Assessment Framework (CAF). It involves a huge amount of work, the meetings, the record keeping and the other paper work. Don't get me wrong, I think the CAF is a very good idea where everyone uses the same method and processes – but there is too much paper work for schools. On top of CAF meetings we still have termly multi-agency meetings to discuss reviews of children identified as in need for some reason or another.

Mostly it is a health or social work practitioner that is the Lead Professional, though sometimes I initiate the CAF process. For example, we had a child who was having problems with English language acquisition and through exploring this problem we discovered a severe health issue. The child's sole parent was unclear as to the nature of the child's illness and rather unwilling to discuss it. She was initially reluctant to give permission for investigation of the health problem. I started the CAF process and enlisted both health and social workers and eventually permission was given and now the parent is working with us to help the child. This is good team working.

The CAF process takes a great deal of my time and requires head teacher support. That is crucial. If your head did not support you by allowing time for the administration it would be very difficult to liaise with other agencies and cope with the administration work. Support from a Family Support Worker (FSW) is also crucial. The FSW and the head have detailed knowledge of the family or care situation and this is essential, especially in Child Protection cases and Looked After Children. Confidentiality can be difficult as you have to be clear about what information can be shared and who can be told. The CAF cuts across Educational Psychologists' work, which is quite diminished in this Local Authority now. We are in the situation where we have to buy in an Educational Psychologist for a CAF meeting so we have to be sure it is worthwhile to do so.

In the end what makes a big difference to implementing ECM is the ethos of the school. Here we work hard to ensure everyone is aware of children's needs, we do lots of therapeutic work in art, yoga, social awareness and emotional well being with all children. We engage in lots of training to make sure we have a high awareness of children in need and we work well as a team. We have to beware of being too intrusive, yet have to be vigilant.

The story of Teacher C

My role is to focus on school-wide initiatives and external links to do with ECM. I've organised Super Learning days and weeks where we try to embed ECM work in enjoyment and learning, healthy school approaches and work with local businesses. We have had an Equality Day where we had a focus on disabilities and had agencies such as Shopmobility in to talk to parents and children. We've had someone from Children's Services too.

I also contribute to Extended Schools activities where we have after-school clubs and work with parents and children. We are in a cluster group of four schools and we have to be mindful of confidentiality when we meet and not discuss individual cases so they can be identified, but it is useful to share practices and approaches.

I've had CAF training but not actually been involved yet. It takes up a lot of time, especially if you are the Lead Professional. There are lots of challenges involved and you need to be able to cope with the breadth of issues that can be covered in the CAF process.

One of the activities we've done for a few years now is a residential visit for older children. This seems to have a very positive impact on child-child and child-adult relationships which we are currently evaluating. Sensitive issues do arise and we have had discussions as a staff on how to deal with them and about confidentiality issues too. We do have a number of children who need support and some quite complex family and cultural arrangements as well as wider community and political issues which affect our school and families.

Our future plans for ECM are to extend the team and establish roles to work in a co-ordinated way, manage the paper work better and evaluate what we do in order to improve it.

The story of Teacher D

My role was established as part of a new government initiative to improve community cohesion. I cover global, national, regional and school level perspectives and try to bring the wider community closer to school. I also contribute to the school Self Evaluation Form which analyses the school context with regard to all the work we do, not just curriculum. Some parents and children have negative perceptions of school life and we hope to improve this by bringing school and community closer together.

One of the activities I've initiated has been the link with a school in Merseyside where the community is very different with regard to cultural backgrounds. We linked children in pairs across the schools and have had an exchange day where children made Identity Boxes as an introduction to each other. This resulted in some work around stereotypes and accepting difference. We have always done a great deal of work in this area of challenging stereotypes in school due to the number of different cultural and language groups in the school, but much less work has been done in other schools. This will require them to examine their attitudes and ethical issues.

We are aiming to help children make their own decisions, develop critical thinking and evaluation and develop mature attitudes and build respect for self and others. Another project we are working on is building bridges with the Jewish schools in our area as a way of developing cultural and multi-faith understandings. We also have a link with a Catholic School in another part of the city. We have linked with a school in Ghana but are experiencing some problems with the technology – from their side, not ours.

All of this work raises sensitive issues and has ethical dilemmas. I often ask myself: are we pushing it too much when looking at cultural, religious and social difference? I think we ought to do it with children to open their minds, but parents often object or do not participate due to prejudices they have developed. It can be difficult work but it is important work to improve communication and understanding of difference.

The story of Pupil E

I have some friends in school and Mr X (his mentor at school) helps me. I have booster lessons with Mrs Y and she helps me read. I have this special chair to help me and I have to do exercises for my back. I come to school in a car and I have a sister in the nursery and a brother at the secondary school. He has the same illness as me. I am going to the secondary school next year and we are doing some visits already. I've been to the taster day at the University and walked round the campus and saw the graduation place.

We did a charity walk called Wobble and Walk – the school sent a person from each class. It was to help people like me. I liked it.

I sometimes have to go to the medical room and to the hospital for X-rays. The doctor comes to visit me at home too.

One thing I would change is to have a better attitude at school and not get into fights and trouble any more. When I grow up I might go to university.

The story of Parent F (mother of Child E)

My child has a severe degenerative disease, the same as my eldest child. My youngest child who is in the nursery does not have the condition. Having gone through the first child's schooling here, we have learned much about how to support the second. I was able to give advance warning to the school so that we were prepared for my son's needs from the beginning, though it was really in year 3 (age 6–7) when more intensive support really began.

My older child has a full statement of Special Educational Needs and has good access to technology such as a voice-activated computer to assist his writing. The younger son (E above) does not have a statement yet, but has support in walking, writing (a scribe), physiotherapy, and nurse attendance at school. He also has an occupational therapist, a community paediatrician, a neurologist, heart specialist, podiatrist, eye surgeon and a spinal surgeon. The Lead Professional is the neurologist. This is an extensive and complex team to relate to as a parent. The school give very good support and I have not been disappointed with their level of support.

I suppose my ability to communicate with the team is a key one and I have a pivotal role in the support organised for my son. The community paediatrician has provided excellent emotional support to me as this has been a very difficult time for our family. She has been someone to whom I can talk to confidentially about problems and know that she will not tell anyone else unless I give permission. I would say that the multi-agency work and team is adequate for now but I am concerned for the future, particularly the transition to secondary school. Hopefully Child E will go to school with his friends. He does not want to be different and that sometimes causes him to be aggressive, get into trouble and argue and fight with other children. We have talked about this with the school and with him. The school are giving him help and counselling.

I think it may be time to review the multi-agency partnership. I have very limited support in the home and have to bathe and bed the children without help.

One lesson I have learned is that early detection and intervention is very important so that the school does understand why my child's motor skills were poor when entering school, even though he was undiagnosed at that point.

New worlds of ethical challenge for schools and teachers

One major aspect arising from these short responses is the commitment of professionals and parents to meeting children's needs at as high a level as possible within the resources available. All these stories report positive points and illustrations but there are undoubtedly other instances where parents or professionals may seem to be less committed than those above for a variety of different, complex reasons. Good effective leadership within the school would also seem to be essential where an overview of cases is maintained and knowledge of professionals working on cases as well as the vital, good family relationships which encourage communication and empathy are developed. Understanding the social and cultural context of the school is important to taking an ethical stance to the challenges that arise. This does not happen easily and this school has had to work hard and persistently at creating common approaches and teamwork to ensure everyone develops an understanding of ethical practice. This is still evolving in the light of new challenges.

One of the tensions relates to who and what specific individuals need to know. Maintaining a professional dialogue with children, families and other agency staff takes time to develop and establish. Administrative staff members are key people as they are often the first point of contact. Their ability to identify and filter confidential information to the relevant person is very important. Some of the school activities undertaken within the implementation of ECM involve risks: residential visits often illuminate sensitive issues which have to be dealt with carefully, such as incontinence or inappropriate behaviour; opening up discussions about cultural and racial difference which may allow children to display prejudice; bringing the community into the classroom may also bring conflicting views that have to be confronted by teachers. Difference is important. Child E does not want to be different, although he is and it is especially challenging for the school to help him understand that being different is acceptable and he is anyone's equal. The school has thought hard about this and it is reflected in their motto – All Different, All Equal. Taking risks is necessary in opening up social learning as well as school learning.

Working in multi-agency teams has become more usual for some teachers, especially those in roles similar to the interviewees. Implicit in their stories are the themes of how times have changed their roles and how they have to be mindful of confidentiality and ethical issues as more sensitive information is provided about children. Being an ethical teacher in 2010 is more challenging than ever before, as the need to work with parents, other professionals, and agencies ranging from health, social work, police, and community, increases the type and volume of information and activity with which schools and teachers are involved. Edwards et al. (2009) argue that distributed expertise calls for the capacity to 'know how to know who' and emphasize the relational aspects of expertise for inter-professional work. We would argue that a school that is good at their own internal relations has a head-start in their relation-building with other agencies. The professionals interviewed above go some way to demonstrating how one school listens to its staff, pupils and parents and so opens the door for listening and talking to other professionals in the pursuit of the best for children.

Not all parents are as articulate and informed as Parent F. She demonstrates a high level of commitment and understanding of processes and procedures and has the ability to talk to a wide range of professionals involved in her children's care. Personal support for individual parents is scarce and Parent F is appreciative of support from the community paediatrician as someone who is an ethical practitioner. For some parents the task might be too daunting or even impossible. One challenge for schools and other agencies is to provide support for all parents at the level they require. Edwards et al. (2010) describe the emergence of a new space of action and new roles on the boundaries of schools in inter-professional collaboration. The new role of welfare manager was identified as important in building new professional networks to support children and parents. Edwards et al. signal some warnings against both marginalising parents during the CAF process and containing teachers within school boundaries while these new roles undertake the multi-agency work within professional networks outside the school. The dangers of separating curriculum and pastoral work may cause schools to remain closed to the wider aspects of pupils' lives and unknowingly exacerbate the social exclusion of children, young people and parents.

ECM is creating environments where professionals at all levels working in children and young people's services face new ethical challenges. The central pillars of the new working practices are early intervention, with the associated requirement to share information in ethical ways.

Historically, integrated or multi-professional working followed episodes in children and young people's lives that moved them through key thresholds. One example was, the Youth Offending Teams, who were deployed to work with young people *after* they have entered the criminal justice system. Social or health care professionals have dominated many of these deep interventions related to the historical forming and deployment of multi-professionals to work with families. The language and settings of these teams have been within areas that can be described as having 'complex needs' or 'vulnerable children' (Atkinson et al. 2002). Anning (Chapter 4, this volume) and Edwards et al. (2010) eschew the use of 'vulnerable' and promote the use of 'at risk', denoting the need for early intervention and prevention rather than remediation techniques.

The implication for all professionals working with children is the need to bring about this early intervention and to open up dialogues and share information and arrangements with a much wider group of professions. Risk is used in its broadest definition. The process makes a judgement regarding 'how well the parents are able to support their child's development and respond appropriately to their needs' or 'the wider family environment elements on the child's development and the capacity of the parents', which are two of the three key themes of the CAF assessment (DfES 2005: 6). This represents a shift in the role of the professional or multi-professional team into new areas, such as the impact of sleep on the child's development, the risk of offending and the ability of the parent(s) or wider family environment to respond to these perceived barriers to the child as it grows and develops. These present ethical challenges for professionals as they work their way through the quagmire of defining which children are at risk and in what ways. Getting it wrong could alienate families and destroy trust.

The permission for schools to operate under these wider ECM principles has resulted in schools taking action outside their traditional role of providing teaching and learning. For example, through the provision of breakfasts for children who are perceived not to be able to learn through a lack of early morning sustenance and through 'wrap around' care initiatives before and after school. Through the CAF process, professionals may intrude into the heart of family life. Early intervention can highlight issues of lifestyles which are considered in value-laden terms such as 'undesirable' in fulfilling outcomes such as being healthy. The introduction of the 'lunch box checks' and additional activities prescribed for children considered at risk of obesity could erode parental responsibility and put professionals in highly judgemental positions.

Contributing to this intrusive nature of ECM is practice developed from the Sure Start Local Programmes where judgements about the suitability of parents to raise their offspring seem implicitly condoned. These judgements move the nature of intervention from the level of protecting from significant harm (Walker 2009) to higher levels of intervention within the family. Does this authenticate action at the earliest possible stages, even though there is no identification of significant harm factors? This is a huge area for ethical decision making.

The introduction of ECM has opened up the door to professionals from a much wider area of children and young people's services intervening in the family when compared to previous legislation such as the 1989 Children Act. It requires professionals in schools to debate and examine their ethical stance with regard to practice, as 'everything's ethics' (Cochran-Smith and Lytle 2007). It also opens up new areas of professional learning for all agencies. Gaining insight into other professional worlds and developing new knowledge and skills, which allow for effective, multi-agency working needs to a top priority for these new teams of professionals as they forge their way in integrated working in schools.

References

Ainscow, M., Dyson, A., Goldrick, S., Kirstin, K., and Miles, S. (2008). *Equality in Education: Responding to Context*. Manchester: The Centre for Equality in Education, Manchester University.

Abbott, D. (2005). 'Multi-Agency Working in Services for Disabled Children: What Impact Does it Have on Professionals?', *Health and Social Care in the Community*, 13 (2), 155–63.

Ahmed, P. & Machold, S. (2004). 'The Quality and Ethics Connection: Towards Virtuous Organisations', *Total Quality Management*, 15 (4), 527–45.

Anning, A., Cottrell, D.M., Frost, N., and Green, J. (2006). *Developing Multi-Agency Professional Teamwork for Integrated Children's Services*. Maidenhead: Open University Press.

Atkinson, M., Wilkin, A., Stott, A., Doherty, P. and Kinder, K. (2002). *Multi-Agency Working: A Detailed Study*. Slough: LGA/NFER.

Balls, E. (2008). *21st Century School: Letter to Head Teachers*. London: DCSF.

Barker, R. (ed.) (2009). *Making Sense of Every Child Matters: Multi-Professional Guidance*. Bristol: The Policy Press.

Brandon, M., Howe, A., Dagley, V., Salter, C., Warren, C. and Black, J. (2007). *Evaluating the Common Assessment Framework and Lead Professional Guidance and Implementation in 2005–6: Final Report*. London: DfES.

Cochran-Smith, M. and Lytle, S. (2007). 'Everything's Ethics: Practitioner Inquiry and University Culture'. In A. Campbell and S. Groundwater-Smith (eds), *An Ethical Approach to Practitioner Research: Dealing with Issues and Dilemmas in Action Research*. Routledge: London.

Department of Children, Schools and Families (DCSF) (2007). *The National Children's Plan: Building Brighter Futures*. London: DCSF.

—— (2008). *Children's Trusts: Statutory Guidance on Inter-Agency Co-operation to Improve the Well-being of Children, Young People and Their Families*, London: DCSF.

—— (2009). *Common Assessment Framework Guidance*, London: DCSF.

—— (2009). *2020 Children and Young People's Workforce Strategy*, London: DCSF.

Department for Education and Skills (DfES) (2003). *Every Child Matters: The Green Paper*, London: DfES.

—— (2004). *Every Child Matters: Change for Children*. London: DfES.

—— (2005). *Common Assessment Guidance*. London: DfES.

Dyson, A., Farrell, P., Kirstin, K., and Mearns, N. (2008) Swing, Swing Together: Multi-Agency Work in the New Children's Services. Paper for *Radical Reform*, 1 September 2008, <http://www.manchester.ac.uk/education> accessed 3 December 2010.

Edwards, A., Daniels, H., Gallagher, T., Leadbetter, J. and Warmington, P. (2009). *Improving Inter-Professional Collaborations: Learning to Do Multi-Agency Work*. London: Routledge.

—— Lunt, I. and Stamou, E. (2010). 'Inter-Professional Work and Expertise: New Roles at the Boundaries of Schools', *British Educational Research Journal*, 36 (1), 27–45.

Kirk, G. and Broadhead, P. (2007). 'Every Child Matters and Teacher Education: A UCET Position Paper' <http://www.ucet.ac.uk/downloads/168.pdf> accessed 10 February 2010.

Laming, H (2003). *The Victoria Climbié Inquiry*. London: HMSO.

Labour Party (1997). *The Labour Party Manifesto: New Labour, Because Britain Deserves Better*. London: Labour Party.

MacBeath, J., Gray, J., Cullen, J., Frost, D., Steward, S. and Swaffield, S. (2007). *Schools of the Edge: Responding to Challenging Circumstances*. London: Sage.

Moss, P. and Haydon, G. (2008). *Every Child Matters and the Concept of Education*. London: Institute of Education.

Percy-Smith, J. (2005). *What Works in Strategic Partnerships for Children?*. Ilford: Barnardos.

Sloper, P. (2004). 'Facilitators and Barriers for Co-ordinated Multi-Agency Services', *Child: Care, Health and Development*, 30 (6), 571–80.

UNICEF (2005). *Child Poverty in Rich Countries, 2005*. Florence: UNICEF Innocenti Research Centre.

Walker, G (2009). *Working Together for Children: A Critical Introduction to Multi-Agency Working*. London: Continuum.

ANGELA ANNING

4 Researching vulnerable people: The importance of sensitivity

Research in interdisciplinary settings

In the last fifty years approaches to research in the social sciences have been 'democratized'. In the 1980s action research began to be used in British educational contexts as a tool for practitioners to improve their own practice – through spirals of planning, acting, reflecting and refining. In the United States, participatory research was promoted as a mechanism for bringing about social change by demystifying research, opening it up to real world contexts (rather than laboratories), and promoting the findings of projects with the aim of giving 'voice' to those perceived to be powerless – for example, those living in poverty or with disabilities. A more radical version has been emancipatory research, whereby researchers immerse themselves in communities and work alongside people who are not 'listened to' in society, because they are outside existing power relationships and structures of social relationships, so as to give voice to marginalized and disempowered groups.

All these approaches have been influential in the field of children's services, and in particular in the desire to give voice to children and so-called 'vulnerable' adults and to the practitioners (predominantly women and traditionally low status) involved in delivering services to them. These historical factors make it important that those working in children's services are alert to the sensitivities of research in the real world of their workplaces. It is also worth spending time and energy unpacking what each of us in a workplace mean by 'vulnerability'. The starting point has to be that vulnerability is a contestable term. Each person's constructs of vulnerability are informed by their personal and professional experiences and may change over time. We need to understand why others in our workplaces, and those outside who influence policy and practice in children's services, view vulnerability differently. We need to acknowledge that constructs of vulnerability influence the nature of daily interactions in the workplace between professionals and children and their parents, and to recognize that our views on vulnerability inform the way we think about and engage in research-based activities.

Applied (often qualitative) research in the social sciences has always had to contend with trying to understand and make sense of the 'messy' and shifting realities of unique settings – that is, particular sets of individuals within settings at specific points in time and in changing contextual circumstances. As Tewkesbury and Gagne (2001: 72), cited in Liamputtong (2006), write:

> Qualitative investigations are not explorations of concrete, intact frontiers; rather they are movements through social spaces that are designed and redesigned as we move through them. The research process is fuelled by the raw materials of the physical and social settings and the unique set of personalities, perspectives and aspirations of those investigating and inhabiting the fluid landscapes being explored.

It is this fluidity that creates unease in quantitative researchers who may perceive explorations of fluidity as being equated with a lack of rigour. And it is the accusation of lack of rigour that makes it imperative for qualitative researchers to *be* rigorous in their methodologies. They need to:

- Set out clearly the nature of the relationships between researchers and those researched
- Clarify how contextual features may have influenced the nature of the evidence they have collected
- Carefully articulate the processes by which they have gathered data
- Document clearly how they have analysed data
- Be transparent about how they have generated results/findings from the data
- Be cautious about generalising from individual or small-scale studies

Multi-agency teamwork complicates research in what is already a complex field (Anning et al. 2010). The speed of changes in UK settings responsible for delivering children's services has been accelerated by a raft of government initiatives since the Labour Government came into power in 1997. Now everything seems to be in a state of flux. Government imperatives to reform children's services into multi-professional (and therefore inter-disciplinary) and multi-agency teams, at domestic and international levels, have created a new set of challenges for research into the lived experiences of those providing and using the services. There are sensitivities to be addressed as power relationships between professionals shift and settle within newly formed teams. There is also much ground clearing of key constructs to be done, such as the causes of problems in families and the appropriate treatments to remediate problems, as workers with different professional backgrounds and experiences negotiate new ways of working and researching as teams.

Qualitative researchers are often professionals seconded to research posts or involved in research projects as a component of upgrading their qualifications. Individuals, now working in teams in the fluid contexts of inter-agency collaboration, have been trained in different disciplines: for example, a nurse's training is different from that of a teacher's, and a social worker's different from a playworker's. Even practitioners with generic childhood studies qualifications will have been taught in discrete modules by tutors with expertise in distinct bodies of knowledge and professional skills. It can be challenging for students to put the parts together into holistic sets of knowledge and understandings. Early work experiences of part-time students, often in single-agency contexts, will have shaped their beliefs and values. The result is that individuals within multi-agency teams are likely to hold distinct beliefs about how to 'treat' their clients, distinct values about families and childhood and different ways of talking about and interacting with children and their parents. The 'baggage' they bring to research impacts upon the way practitioners undertake and interpret research.

Training in research methods is also problematic, particularly when applied to children's services where participants (both traditionally low status workers and the children and their parents/carers with whom they work) may be defined as 'vulnerable'. Graduate programmes tend to focus on the substantive content and methodologies of distinct disciplines (for example, psychology, sociology, education, health and medicine) and the scientific processes inherent in those disciplines. Each discipline has a different approach to research ethics and, even at postgraduate level, training in the values and ethics underpinning research in and across disciplines is given minimal attention – sometimes only 'a nod' towards a subject specific code of ethics for students to reference in their coursework and theses. Yet working with children, families and practitioners – particularly those defined as 'vulnerable' – requires a rigorous approach to ethical issues.

In this chapter I will explore some of the ethical and practical dilemmas we face in our responsibilities towards 'vulnerable' communities involved in research projects.

Some important starting points: Three aspects of transparency

The first issue is to identify the purpose of the research; motives may be mixed. Some researchers claim to be motivated by a passion for social justice, others by an imperative to improve practice, whilst others stress the need to earn a living or gain a qualification. From an ethical perspective it is important for any researcher to be clear and honest with themselves about why they want to do the research. Having thought carefully about motives, it is essential they convey their purpose honestly to the people they want to involve in their projects.

The second area requiring transparency from the researcher is with regard to their personal intent and the influences on this intent. Every researcher should explore and acknowledge the professional and personal baggage they bring to research; but particularly in qualitative research, where the human mind plays a central role in interrogating so-called 'soft' data. My own professional training, experience and research has been in the field of early education and services for young children and their families, mainly in a female-dominated world. I have worked mainly within communities labelled 'vulnerable'. Having raised two children as a single parent, I have first-hand experience of being categorized as a 'vulnerable' subject. I have forged a career in the male-dominated discipline of education, often treated as low-status in universities. I know that these experiences have shaped the lens through which I observe and try to make sense of phenomena when I am being a researcher. When I analyse and try to make sense of data, I have to acknowledge the power of these formative experiences in my personal and working life; by forcing myself to be open to other perspectives, I am able to guard against bias in interpreting the evidence I am interrogating.

A third area of concern is the consideration of how the research will impact on participants. A key imperative is that the research will not do harm or cause stress. Linked to this is the concept of reciprocity; that the outcomes will be of value to participants, as well as to the researcher. These three areas will be revisited throughout the chapter.

Ethics in practice: The concept of vulnerability

The purposes of a research project, and the previous experience/expertise of the researcher as a scholar, professional and researcher, will determine the research paradigm in which they choose to work. Researchers have an obligation to be transparent about which paradigm they are adopting. Their choice will determine their methodologies. It is likely that the research will include predominantly qualitative approaches to data collection such as interviews, observations and case studies, perhaps mixed with some quantitative elements and approaches – including questionnaires. Many qualitative approaches require 'close encounters', forging reciprocal relationships with participants. It is also likely that some participants will be characterized as 'vulnerable'. So what is meant by vulnerability?

Definitions of vulnerability are usually related to social factors, though sometimes the factors may be related to health or other circumstances. The terminology used to define vulnerable people shifts as social and cultural sensitivities shift over time. For example, in research into the impact of the early intervention initiative Sure Start, the term 'hard to reach' was replaced by 'those whom services had not yet attracted'. In other research, 'hidden populations' were rebranded as 'marginalized groups' and the term 'deprived' replaced by 'socially excluded'. The bottom line is that populations or groups who are not in a position to exert power are routinely defined in policy documents as vulnerable: children, families living in relative socio-economic deprivation or in abusive relationships, people from ethnic, racial or religious minorities, those with illegal status such as asylum seekers or refugees or criminals, lone parents, those with chronic health conditions, those with substance addictions, and those with disabilities or additional needs. The important point, however, is that vulnerability is a relative concept – dependent on the cultural norms, socio-economic conditions and expectations/aspirations of host communities and those who serve them.

We know that 'vulnerable' populations, using the definitions above, are disproportionately represented in large-scale research studies. For example, in education children identified as '*at risk of failure*' are more likely to be investigated because they are perceived to be (a) problematic to the smooth running or accountability of educational systems, and (b) expensive in terms of additional costs to the state. In early intervention programmes the children of families defined as '*living in poverty*' – and therefore projected to have poor health, welfare and educational outcomes – are more likely to be targeted because of the projected cost benefits to the state of improving their life trajectories. Examples in the UK have been the Sure Start early intervention programme (Belsky et al. 2007) and, in the USA, Early Head Start (Love et al. 2002). Some might argue that powerless populations are more likely to accept 'being researched'.

When we read articles, books or reports disseminating research, we need to know who funded the studies. Large scale social science research projects may be financed by government agencies, particularly in such fields as anti-poverty, preventative health and social exclusion.

Researchers as individuals may be driven by an underlying passion for social justice, but it is likely that the government departments that commission them will expect a degree of control over the publication of the findings of expensive research projects. Interference at government level is often not so much into *what* the final reports say about their results as *how* they say it. Researchers funded by charities (such as the Joseph Rowntree Trust) or funding councils (such as the Economic and Social Research Council) are not restricted in what they say or how they say it. Since each of these funding agencies have different constructs of vulnerability, some more politically sensitive than others, readers need to be aware of reading between the lines of the research reported in different dissemination systems. Authors of government-funded, research-based reports, for example, will have different constraints than authors funded by research councils.

In small-scale research there is a tendency for inquiries to focus on 'problems', and by extension to focus disproportionately on vulnerable groups. Researchers seem fascinated (or perhaps challenged) by these subjects, even if they are not 'the norm' in their settings. Some researchers have commented on their sense of unease about 'mining misery'. Others have expressed feelings of guilt at using research as a means to their own ends; for example to gain a qualification, enhance their career, or gain another research grant. The ethics of researchers may be questionable if their approach to working with vulnerable communities is to arrive from the safety of their campus, institution or suburban house to do their field work, and then return there to write up their notes, sort their data and publish their papers – thereby enhancing their careers, without giving anything back in return. Giving back could include follow-up work, or feeding back insights from research to communities in an accessible way so that they can use the evidence to improve their own lives and their ability to voice their concerns for wider political purposes.

Problems in research with vulnerable people may also be related to disclosures/discussions about 'taboo' issues such as prostitution, drug and substance abuse, criminality, domestic abuse and child neglect or abuse. Sensitive topics, with vulnerable people as the subjects of their enquiry, present both experienced and inexperienced researchers with particular challenges and responsibilities. Of course it is important that potential researchers get ethical clearance for proposals, but it is equally important that they take expert advice about relevant qualifications researchers should have before embarking on sensitive research. Some dilemmas we might face are rehearsed in the next section of the chapter.

Ethical dilemmas in research with vulnerable subjects

Ethics must permeate all aspects and stages of research in any context or with any participants. The chapter now focuses on four challenging aspects of working ethically with subjects perceived as vulnerable:

- Gaining informed consent
- Ensuring confidentiality/privacy
- Sustaining rapport and gaining trust
- Protecting participants from harm

Gaining informed consent

A prerequisite of any research is to gain informed consent from participants. Informed consent includes:

- Ensuring that participants have sufficient information (in an appropriate language and medium) and are competent to understand the research
- Ensuring that participants understand the implications and potential risks for them of being involved in the research (time, commitment, interruption to their normal routines, possible intrusion into their personal feelings)

- Ensuring that participants give consent that is voluntary (not coerced by a more powerful person such as an employer/manager or parent/partner)
- Ensuring that participants have the right not to take part and to withdraw at any time

Informed consent is particularly challenging with participants who may not be articulate or powerful in expressing an opinion or formulating a view as explored in this example:

A team of researchers want to explore the views of children on the quality of their experiences in a range of education and care settings: pre-school playgroups, private day care provision, childminders, nursery schools and nursery classes/extended services in primary schools. They have already gained consent from the parents and key workers of a sample of children. They feel strongly that they want to gain informed consent from the young children. They realise that they will need to co-operate with the children's key workers in entering into dialogue with the children, but are worried that some of them are sceptical about gaining informed consent from such young children, and in any case are less committed to the research than their managers.

The United Nations Convention on the Rights of the Child acknowledge that it is likely that children will give 'assent' to involvement in research, but that their parents or legal guardians can give consent on behalf of the child (Coady 2001). Researchers have worked hard to establish ways of gaining assent from young children (Armistead 2008). Methods used by Armistead to gain assent from children included immersing herself in the contexts in which she intended to research, establishing responsive relationships with her sample of children and their key workers over time, and creating a 'story' booklet which helped the children to understand what her research was going to be about before she began it. She intended to empower children with the right to say no, and paid close attention to the moods and feelings of children when she worked with them in settings – asking their permission for her to observe and talk with them on a regular basis. She did not assume that one act of assent from young children was sufficient to cover every act of data collection.

In relation to adults giving informed consent, when for example practitioners have been told that the focus of a research project is on the quality of services in a setting, there is bound to be anxiety about the risks to reputations and sense of competence of either individuals or groups of workers. They may have been intimidated by a manager into giving consent despite their misgivings: *'What have you to be afraid of if you think you are doing a good job?'*; *'You'll be letting the rest of us down if you don't agree to take part – the researchers will think we have something to hide'.* Thus, some people who may not be deemed vulnerable as subjects of research may become vulnerable through coercion. In cases where workers have been pressurized into taking part in research projects, anxiety becomes outright hostility to researchers. It takes time, patience and honesty to gain the trust of participants. Researchers need to establish a dialogue with all workers – and not just the manager – before embarking on gaining informed consent in a workplace, so that they can be sure that their consent is willing and that they have been clearly informed of any consequences for them. If researchers find they cannot convince a participant of the worthwhile nature of the research, they must not exert pressure on unwilling participants. However 'inconvenient 'it may be to the design of the research project, they must find alternative sites where participants feel comfortable about co-operating.

Ensuring confidentiality and privacy

The Data Protection Act of 1998 was designed to protect the interests of individuals in our society, ensure their protection from harm and entitle them to privacy. But participants in research must be given rights to confidentiality and privacy beyond this basic requirement. The ethical requirements to ensure confidentiality are subject to particular scrutiny by research ethics committees within the institutions responsible for training students/researchers and within disciplines (Baez 2002). Committees will be extra careful about granting permission if the focus of research is on vulnerable participants.

The ethics of confidentiality require researchers to pay careful attention to data handling and management:

- Data coding (so that the subjects of research are not identifiable)
- Data security (so that notebooks, transcripts, raw data sets are always stored securely)
- Restricted access to data (so that on shared information systems data and field notes are always protected by passwords)

When research findings are disseminated, attention must be paid to preserving the anonymity of participants in writing reports, articles and conference papers. All transcripts of conversations and interviews which may potentially be published must be returned to participants, to provide them with an opportunity to delete content. Maintaining confidentiality can be particularly taxing when researchers are basing their evidence on visual images (photographs, digitial recordings on DVDs) or audio recordings (Prosser 2005), requiring inexperienced researchers to seek out specialist advice.

In practice, the ethics of confidentiality may present researchers with unanticipated moral dilemmas, particularly when their professional roles may conflict with their roles as researchers. Sometimes dilemmas emerge as a project progresses. We know that it can be advantageous to get a 'match' between fieldworkers and the communities in which they are working. This is particularly pertinent when communities are defined as being excluded from mainstream systems and structures: for example, when working with travellers living in close knit communities, families living in economically deprived circumstances or marginalized groups such as racial, religious or ethnic minorities (Munford and Sanders 2001). But consider the consequences of this strategy in the case below:

A fieldworker has been seconded to work on a local authority funded project, whilst contracted to a local university, on the impact of extended services on the children of 'vulnerable' families. Over the two years of the project she has gradually gained the trust of the people she has interviewed. Her ability to have a good rapport with the families arises from her skills as a researcher, but also because as a lone parent who grew up in the community, she has an empathy with the daily lives and priorities of the participants. She is party to open discussions of the strategies local families are currently using to survive the complexities of benefits and entitlements. She discovers that several families have misrepresented their circumstances in order to fit the criteria for free access to the extended services. She is torn between her enduring loyalties to the community in which she grew up, her past role in the local authority, and her current responsibilities as a researcher.

In such circumstances it is important that the fieldworker is able to go for advice to those with overall responsibility for the research project – in this case, the grant-holder of the university research team. If a lone researcher engaged in a programme of study or a fieldworker encountered a similar dilemma, they should also have access to an experienced supervisor. Decisions about conflicts of interests would be shared, discussed and, hopefully, resolved. In the case described above, considerations would include whether the researcher was mandated by her seconded role to report the deceit, whether disclosure of the deceit would result in traumatic results for the families, and whether and to whom the continuation of the deceit was harmful. In short, decisions about what to do in particular situations would have to balance breaching the promise of confidentiality against the risks of disclosure.

Sustaining rapport and gaining trust

Some ethical considerations relate to the procedural aspects of research. As the above example considered, in order to gain good data using qualitative methods researchers must establish rapport with participants. Yet they must also retain an 'objective' approach as they seek to sustain the rapport. Objectivity is not to be confused with disinterestedness. Many researchers have emotional commitments to their work; but they should guard against becoming so emotionally involved with participants or settings that they (a) interpret data in a biased way; (b) doggedly pursue predetermined findings, despite evidence which contradicts their 'preferred' outcome; or (c) lose sight of their responsibilities to others who may be affected by the research.

When a group or community are persuaded to make a commitment to involvement in a project and work with researchers they are likely to build a rapport over time. It is important for researchers to be able to stand outside these personal relationships so that they can take responsibility from an early stage for managing participants' expectations of research. They must explain clearly that the research findings may ultimately be positive or negative, and possibly to participants' advantage or disadvantage as stake-holders. If expectations are not managed in this way, when the time comes to report the findings to those involved – and to others with vested interests in the success or failure of an activity or project – participants may feel a sense of betrayal. Consider the case below:

An evaluation of a family-learning project has been commissioned and funded by a national charity. The aims are to enhance the developmental gains of three- and four-year-olds in language and to enhance parents' capacities to help their children to develop communication skills. The evaluation team has been working closely with parents and professionals involved in the project over eighteen months and they all know each other well. The evaluation methodology includes time bought in for data collection by speech therapists and family-learning support workers. These professionals, who were centrally involved in designing and delivering the initiative, were trained in aspects of data collection; but other data were collected by the researcher.

When they are briefed by the researcher at a feedback session before the report is made public, the workers who had undertaken data collection are shocked by what they perceive to be 'criticisms' of the scheme. Findings include lower than expected levels of impact on the children's developmental gains in language and dissatisfaction expressed by some parents with the way they felt pressurized at home to improve their children's communication skills. There is a stormy exchange at the feedback meeting between the researcher and the workers. The workers want to know what their rights are to demand that some aspects of these 'negative' findings are softened in the final report. They are worried that the project will be shut down if senior officers feel it is 'not working'. They argue that the evaluation report as it stands will threaten their professional beliefs in the efficacy of the scheme and their jobs.

This example shows how constructs of vulnerability can shift. A group of workers whom we might have considered to be powerful became vulnerable, and might almost have been placed in this position because of a good rapport with the parents. Conversely, parents of children with language delay, who might have been considered vulnerable, gained power through trusted participation. Sometimes the emotional response of participants to research findings can take researchers by surprise; but it is important to be sensitive to the feelings of those with whom you are working and to think ahead to what might distress them. Their working lives go on, while researchers come and go. Sensitivity should include:

- Ensuring that participants in research are informed about the possibility of both positive and negative findings
- Being clear at the outset about who 'owns' the outcomes of research and who has the right to control its dissemination
- Managing everyone's expectations of the impact of the research (including those who commissioned it)
- Being flexible and responsive to changing circumstances and pressures on children, parents and professionals in the workplace
- Protecting individuals and groups in the workplace from the repercussions of research findings by being honest about the political implications of reporting both positive and negative outcomes of activities (for example in evaluations of intervention programmes)

Coady, M.M. (2001). 'Ethics in Early Childhood Research'. In G. Mac Naughton, S.A. Rolfe and I. Siraj-Blatchford (eds), *Doing Early Childhood Research*, pp. 64–72. Buckingham: Open University Press.

Gilligan, C. (1982). *In a Different Voice: Psychological Theory in Women's Development*. Cambridge, MA: Harvard University Press.

Gilligan, C. (2003). *The Birth of Pleasure: A New Map of Love*. New York: Vintage.

Liamputtong, P. (2006). *Researching the Vulnerable*. London: Sage.

Love, J., Kisker, E.E., Ross, C.M., Schochet, P.Z., Brooks-Gun, J., Paulsell, D., Boller, K., Constantine, J., Vogel, C., Fuligni, A.S. and Brady-Smith, C. (2002). *Making a Difference in the Lives of Infants and Toddlers and Their Families: The Impacts of Early Head Start Volume 1: Final Technical Report*, <http://www.mathematica-mpr.com/PDFs/ehsfinalvol1.pdf> accessed 5 September 2009.

Munford, R. and Sanders, J. (2001). 'Ethical Issues in Qualitative Research with Families'. In M. Tollich (ed.), *Ethical Issues for Qualitative Research*. London: Sage.

Prosser, J. (2005). 'The Moral Maze of Image Ethics'. In K. Sheehy, M. Nind and J. Rix (eds), *Ethics and Research in Inclusive Education: Values into Practice*, pp. 133–49. Abingdon: Routledge Falmer.

Trimble, J.E. and Fisher, C.B. (2005). *The Handbook of Research with Ethnocultural Populations and Communities*. London: Sage.

5 Pedagogy as an ethical encounter: How does it look in our professional practice?

This chapter reflects on the ethical dilemmas we faced as co-authors and teacher educators, contracted by the Province of New Brunswick to develop an official curriculum framework for early learning and childcare, alongside a mandatory province-wide programme of professional learning and curriculum implementation.

Our commitment to pedagogies which foreground responsibility and relationship to the 'Other' (Dalberg and Moss 2005) is explicit, drawing on Levinas' ethic of an encounter. We recognize that we operate as players in a global neo-liberal policy context viewing early childhood reform via technical practice and performativity, extending implicitly beyond young children to professionalizing childcare educators (Osgood 2006). Having actively resisted this dominant discourse – being firmly committed to democratic practice, a co-constructed curriculum with/in local communities, a pedagogy of listening and openness to diversity and future possibilities – our participation in it is, nevertheless, implicit in accepting a mandate for curricular reform. Particularly poignant and problematic is our work with the provincial aboriginal childcare educators. Consequently, we draw on post-colonial scholarship (Cannella and Viruru 2002 and 2004; Pratt 1997) to discuss the spaces we occupy between the ethics of an encounter and colonial encounters as we enact our professional identities.

Understanding that 'everything's ethics' (Cochran-Smith and Lytle 2007), we choose to focus on challenges relating to the role of language in professional practice and the negotiation of power, position, privilege and politics with/in our childcare community. Messy, multi-layered and context-specific as our practice is, such a discussion can hopefully contribute to professional ethical debate.

The political context of our work

Neo-liberal policy agendas cast young children as the hope for a brighter future, and early childhood services as sites for producing subjects conforming to the demands of globalized economies (Osgood 2005: 298; Duhn 2006; Canella and Bloch 2006) – 'programmed to become a solution to certain problems arising from highly competitive market capitalism' (Moss 2006: 128). Situating the early years as the first steps along a narrow path of 'lifelong learning', policies focus on educational reforms to produce young children as school subjects and prospective global citizens[1] able to contribute to their own nations' economies and potentially cure multiple social problems, including the support of an aging population (Osgood 2005: 298). Such neoliberal rhetoric is proliferated globally through the World Bank and the practice of 'policy borrowing' (Kuehn 2008: 56). In Canada, provincial policy agendas bill the young child as an investment commodity with a high rate of return. The province of Manitoba proposes that:

> The evidence is solid – economists, political scientists, neuroscientists and social scientists have substantial data proving that programs which promote the growth and development of young children (0–5 years) are the best investment for developing the human capital necessary for economic growth. Early childhood development is the foundation of human capital development; has the highest rate of return in economic development; is the most cost effective way to reduce poverty and foster economic growth. (The World Bank 2007, cited in Government of Manitoba 2008)

New Brunswick's 'Be Ready for Success: A 10 year Early Childhood Strategy' notes: 'Quality early childhood programmes are not only good for children and families, they are good for the bottom line. Focused public spending provides returns that outstrip any other type of human capital investment' (Government of New Brunswick 2008).

---

1   The global citizen, Beck suggests, has 'both roots and wings' and 'as author of his or her own economic biography, is capable and willing to wing his or her way across the slippery global in search for job opportunities while feeling rooted in his or her local communities' (Beck 2002: 19, cited in Duhn 2006: 198).

Neoliberal discourse of *human capital development* 'expresses something quite horrific; *the human as capital*' (Rikowski 2006: 258, cited in McGregor 2009: 355). Nevertheless, 'harnessing' early education to economic development has focused political interest on curriculum, pedagogies and assessment (Schweinhard 2002: 1, cited in Ryan and Griesharber 2005: 36). In a field that had seemed safe from 'the terrors of performativity' (Ball 2003: 215), there is now 'increasing steerage from the state' (Osgood 2006: 188). The discourse of child *development*, aligned with *human capital development*, constructs young children in a normative-performative mould, as early years curricula articulate progression to predetermined developmental outcomes in relation to standards which are both curricular objectives and assessment or monitoring criteria: Britain's Early Years Foundation Stage (EYFS), outlines sixty-nine learning goals to be monitored by child-minders and nursery school teachers. Where curricula are not structured along developmental lines, standardized testing – readiness tests, and developmental screening – narrow curricula, as educators teach to the test to produce competitive scores.[2] Embracing diversity is compromized (Cannella and Swadner 2007; Mac Naughton 2007; Rinaldi 2006; Ryan and Grieshaber 2005), ironically at a time when hybridity rather than similarity characterizes global contemporary life (Luke and Luke 1998, cited in Ryan and Greihaber 2005: 1).

Producing the child as a developmental subject and 'redemptive agent' that can solve current problems (Dahlberg and Moss 2005: vii) is, then, used to justify the curriculum as a strategic site for professional reform: a reskilled[3] or re/professionalized workforce can reliably produce the prescribed outcomes. The 'good' early childcare educator is someone who maintains the standards set out officially. That 'someone' is often a woman, whose assumed professionalism is unlikely to command a commensurate

---

2　See, for example, Radhika Viruru's (2006) critical examination of standardized testing as an imperialist product.

3　For a discussion of the role of closely prescribed curricula in deskilling/reskilling educators, see Michael Apple's discussion on curricular form and the logic of technical control (1983).

salary, or opportunities for professional judgement (Osgood 2006).[4] S/he[5] is obliged to produce and, as prescribed, perform regulatory and surveillance functions. In the neoliberal agenda, early learning invariably trumps care,[6] with critical tensions between professional identities, past experience and personal/professional values, rarely acknowledged.

Conceptualizing other possibilities

Recognizing that 'we are all (children and adults) being created as both subjects and objects of [these] narrowed, fundamentalist, global discourses' (Cannella and Bloch 2007: 5), we nevertheless enact our professional lives at the intersection of discourses and resist notions of children as developmental subjects indentured as human capital, with their teachers cast as technicians. The need to challenge neoliberalism's 'perverse ethic ... founded in the laws of the market place' (Freire 2004: 100) has become urgent.

Ironically, our opportunities 'to put a stutter in the dominant discourse' (Moss 2007: 128) have come not so much from our critical standpoint, as via contract work with the New Brunswick Government.[7] With trepida-

---

4   Even in Sweden where professional credentials for the school years and the years prior to school are aligned, salaries in schools are higher than salaries in childcare, with a consequent disparate subscription to the school and prior-to-school programme streams in teacher education programmes.

5   We have used the inclusive s/he throughout, although it must be recognized that internationally early childcare educators are predominantly women and, in New Brunswick, almost exclusively so.

6   In the titles of curriculum documents presently emerging in Canada, the care in child*care* has been systematically erased. The New Brunswick Curriculum Framework for Early Learning and Childcare is the exception. We do recognize, however, that the omission of the word childcare may (sadly) be a deliberate attempt to elevate the status of the field. Our pairing of care with learning was similarly motivated.

7   Pam Nason as project co-director and Anne Hunt as co-director of the programme of professional learning.

tion we submitted a proposal for an official curriculum for early learning and childcare and an associated training programme[8] for the approximately 1,350 childcare educators in New Brunswick's English childcare sector.[9] All state authorized curricula and training programmes partly regulate practice and influence the ways educators construct their identities. So we knew we would risk reproducing '[a] colonizing discourse [that] creates a "subject people" who are described as lacking and in need of control by the people who have generated the knowledge' (Cannella and Viruru 2004). How could we avoid this? We also worried about the constraints of contracted research development on academic freedom.[10] Yet we understood the invitation as a vote of confidence from insiders who knew us well enough to know that we would operate in a critical fashion. In the final analysis, we reasoned that we could open up more possibilities for early childhood education inside a major government initiative than we could from the outside. In any event, we wanted to be a vital part of potentially momentous change.

Opening spaces for ethics as first practice

Our proposal, within the constraints of a government template, excluded discussion of our ethical position.[11] Moreover, it would not have been politic to offer an explicit critique of neoliberalism's 'perverse ethic' (Freire 2004:

---

8   Initially referred to as a training programme, this is one instance of our changing the language to *programme of professional learning* in a bid to construct early childhood educators and education in a professional image.

9   There is a parallel project for the French sector, but none specifically designated for the First Nations.

10 Well documented in the literature. See, for example, Clayton, O'Brien, Vagra-Atkins and Qualter (2008).

11 In accordance with our university policy, we were required to submit for ethical clearance, in line with the *Tri Council Policy Statement: Ethical Conduct for Research Involving Humans.*

100), or challenge the discourse of instrumental rationality and technical practice that de-ethicalizes and de-politicizes practice (Moss 2006b: 37–8). Nevertheless, in our proposal we did begin to argue for 'ethics as first practice' (Moss 2006a: 129) by proposing a social pedagogical approach[12] and warning against the marginalizing effects of being school subjects on minority children and children with special needs (Nason and Whitty 2007: 274). Moreover, by proposing a participatory and collaborative approach for the curriculum process, and foregrounding intellectual dimensions for childcare educators' work, we countered the view that 'creates early childhood institutions as places of technical practices [and their] workforce as technicians' (Moss 2006a: 128). Our commitment to dialogic ethics – open sharing and discussion of ethical codes and issues – could be inferred from our proposed province-wide consultations, reflective practice, local co-construction of the curriculum, pedagogical documentation making the work of children and educators visible and open to interrogation, building professional communities through dialogue and the co-production of framework and support documents with practitioners. We recognized the need for our practice to conform to ethical human discourse: 'in the end we run out of words and meaning is rooted in judgment and action' (Gee 1993: 293, cited in Comber 2005: 52). However, for some time after the contract was awarded, our words probably worked as 'slogans' (Beyer and Apple 1998: 9) that flagged our intentions to proceed with openness to diversity and helped structure our planning.[13]

Aware of the need to pay attention to the complex power relations involved in a government contract while remaining critical of its powerful

12   See Bennett (2004).
13   Although the original proposal was submitted by Pam Whitty and Pam Nason, the research and development team that undertook the work quickly expanded to ten (including the co-author of this chapter, Anne Hunt), and subsequently to twenty-two. This chapter represents the co-authors' views, recognizing that the other members of the team contributed immeasurably to their work and their thinking.

regulatory potential,[14] certain questions have focused our work and our reflections:

- How can we produce an official curriculum document for the province that resists normative-performative constructions of children and childcare educators and celebrates and encourages difference?
- How can a state authorized and mandated course of professional learning explicitly linked with the development and implementation of an official curriculum framework give voice to the diverse experiences and perspectives of childcare educators, and foreground their agency as intellectuals and researchers?
- How can this work be enacted and understood within an ethic of care, responsiveness, and respect for the alterity of the 'Other'?

Opening spaces for dialogue and critique

In Fall 2005, we convened a symposium of people who typically work in separate settings, and variably within departmental hierarchies. We sought opportunities for critical questions and dialogue across the existing education/health/family and community services silos. We wanted to communicate our understandings of contemporary thought and practice in early childhood curriculum studies with a learned, non-authoritarian voice, and begin negotiating the Framework values. To maximize participation, we organized the conversational groupings so as 'to disrupt established power

---

14   See Moss (2006) for a discussion on the need for continuous and rigorous critique to ensure that the 'powerful potential' of a shared orientation and values does not result in stronger regulation and governing of children. According to Levinas, it is necessary to be constantly vigilant for 'the political order of the state may have to be challenged in the name of our ethical responsibility to the other' (Levinas and Kearney 1986: 30).

relations, destabilize emerging dominances and establish a wider communication network'. These practices contributed to a sense of community
over the two days. However, as we noted, 'the participants ... were chiefly
white women, with only one First Nations participant and one male in
attendance'. We recognized that this reflected 'the deeply gendered nature
of the profession and the raced jurisdictional policies that separate out First
Nations Peoples – cultural conditions that we must address as we proceed'
(Nason and Whitty 2007: 277).

Value statements generated in the Fall symposium were subsequently
negotiated and refined within committees and meetings with childcare
educators. One emerged completely unchanged: We value a zest for living
and learning.

Finally, twelve values were articulated (Framework 2008: 6–7).
Making the values explicit opened them to critique, which we considered
our responsibility to precipitate. One avenue has been the introduction to
the programme of professional learning, where we asked childcare educators to discuss how these values are transformed by their practice. Some
values are proving more contentious than others, particularly: We value
the child's right to a restorative spiritual space for enhancement of moral
and ethical development. Spirituality is invariably interpreted by some as
organized religion, and hotly debated. This value was hard-wrought, and
the curriculum was deliberately produced as a loose-leaf binder to allow
for amendments as values and practices change. Hopefully, when the time
for revision comes, rich discussions will have changed the possibilities the
wording affords.

De/constructing the authority of the text

Opening spaces for critical conversations has been our concern throughout.
However, even as we wrote the document we were aware that our province-
wide consultations – intended to generate shared values and create col-
legiality in the early childhood sector – had nevertheless excluded some

perspectives. Some, we knew of (Whitty and Nason 2007), whilst many others were as yet unvoiced or un-thought. This renders such phrases as 'We value ...' entirely problematic. Who are we? How can such a construction, intended to indicate shared values wrought through extensive consultation, respond adequately to the other's uniqueness and singularity? Such a reduction amounts to a kind of subjective colonialism, where all the other's desires are reduced to the desires of the home country (Nealon 1997: 129). We therefore sought to lessen the authority of the official text: we underscored its provisional nature by juxtaposing our purposes with a call for debate.[15] For example, in the section entitled 'Purpose', we propose to:

> Articulate common goals, values and principles for early learning and child care *that are open to ongoing input and change*; ... affirm exemplary practices *while encouraging the ongoing dynamic development of diverse practices*; develop a shared professional language [but] *prompt change by directing attention to questions about our agenda for children and the ways in which we respect children's capacities, ideas and potentials.* (New Brunswick Curriculum Framework for Early Learning and Child Care – English 2008: 3, italics added)

We need now to ask ourselves hard questions about what public spaces we have actually opened for discussion about the purposes of the curriculum – possibly the most dangerous conversations of all, addressing questions such as whose language counts as a 'shared professional language', and how will marginalization and exclusions accrue? Among whom would 'shared values, goals and principles' be shared, and what about those who didn't share them? How would the process of ongoing input and change work? Which practices would be affirmed as exemplary, and by whom? Although we have not avoided such questions,[16] and some of them will only be answered as the project progresses, it is our responsibility in gener-

---

15   We are indebted to Sue Frazer, author of *Authentic Childhood*, for her review, which focused our attention on the need for this specific wording.

16   We commissioned critique from academics and from the field; made public our concerns at academic conferences; and passed on the critical questions arising from our encounters with educators – particularly with regard to what happens to non-compliant centres and individuals – to the Department of Social Development.

ating such critical conversations amongst educators that we would like to stress. The way in which the role of childcare educator has been historically framed within maternalist assumptions and instrumental rationality (Moss 2006b: 37), and the working conditions in many New Brunswick childcare centres, tends to preclude extended professional discussions. Rather than facilitating critical conversations, for some educators the new curriculum proved an added burden, with time pressure repeatedly hindering reflective practices and professional learning. In written evaluations of the Program of Professional Learning New Brunswick Early Childhood Educators wrote, 'Time is the biggest barrier. We work long days, with all other government forms, not just curriculum work each day. Too much documentation. Not enough time to document during working hours'. Our call for critical conversations sounds hollow, and prompts us to consider how our 'open ended responsibility and sense of obligation' (Dalhberg and Moss 2005: 82–3, discussing the work of Levinas) extends beyond this particular project. Acting in solidarity with this predominantly female workforce as they struggle to improve working conditions is one possibility.

Resisting a normative/performative discourse

In establishing as the four goals for this curriculum – Well Being, Play and Playfulness, Communication and Literacies, Diversities and Social Responsibility – we made a conscious effort to depart from historically established disciplinary and developmental categories and hierarchies. Moreover, we dispensed with the language of objectives and outcomes that might lend themselves easily to 'the terrors of performativity' (Ball 2003).[17] Thus, we reasoned, we would be opening spaces for children and educa-

---

17   We appreciated that they could be added with the stroke of a pen, and were relieved when the inter-departmental Advisory Committee recommended approval to the New Brunswick Department of Social Development in March 2008.

tors to participate as active agents in the co-construction of knowledge, unfettered by the old orthodoxies and respectful of the caring heritage of child*care*. However, our alternative construction of knowledge – into *goals, facets, aspects* and *what's involved in learning* proved easier to invent than to use. We were often muddled in presentations and even confused our newly minted language of 'facets' and 'aspects'. Consequently, it should have come as no surprise when the director of one of our pilot projects created 'the curriculum at a glance' to help her staff negotiate the new curriculum framework. In it, she had transposed the content into categories that were already familiar to her – goals, objectives and outcomes.

A framework for co-constructing curriculum at the local level

Mary Louise Pratt (1992) articulates the ways in which writing a depopu-lated landscape enables the inscription of colonizing texts. We were, and are, ethically obliged to do otherwise. We saw the curriculum document as a place to render the existing landscape of childcare in New Brunswick vis-ible and vital – a complex, relational dynamic. We sought to represent the goals of the official curriculum (New Brunswick Curriculum Framework for Early Learning and Child Care) as flexible enough to invite diverse responses to constructing curriculum at the local level: 'In practice the goals are in constant interplay, brought to life by communities of children and adults to constitute the curriculum as an organic whole in which early learning and care are always connected' (4). The curriculum framework includes sample narratives from the childcare educators, and photographs that reveal their ongoing work.[18] We ourselves have repeatedly underscored co-construction as democratizing pedagogical practice and asserted the

18   Ironically, the inclusion of photographs to make their work visible has limited its
     proliferation; some parents gave consent for their children's images to appear in the
     printed documents but not on the web.

authority of children and educators as curriculum makers, emphasizing that the official framework is *only a framework* – the construction of the curriculum itself involves educators, children, parents and other community members as active agents.

We have consistently pointed to the diverse exemplars generated through the work at the pilot project sites, using local examples to illustrate interpretations. Many of the educators know each other, so can verify the provenance of the narratives, and exemplars which are acknowledged by name can thereby infer local input.

Yet, it could also be that these sample narratives make the text seem more, not less, authoritarian. Although collecting them involved reconceptualizing the curriculum framework, now that they appear in print, they might be read simply as evidence of general applicability. However, dialogue over the written text affords both revisiting and re-interpretations. We have used these narratives with the current professional learning cohort as group exercises in reflection, an important part of the pedagogical shift that we were (ironically) imposing on educators. Reflecting on these narratives invariably begets more little narratives, and the critical tension between them prompts further reflection. Like Moyles and Adams, we have found that '[p]ractitioners have revealed themselves capable of significant thought on their own practice once provided with a context in which this is made acceptable, desirable, necessary and inspiring' (Moyles 2001: 90).

Support documents and the mirror dance of transculturation

Working with pilot site educators to co-construct 'professional support documents [that] further elaborate the framework in practice' (4) we have been able to explore deeply the interactive and improvizational potential of the childcare centre as 'contact zone' – a place in which transculturation can take place with the construction of new hybrid texts (Pratt 1992). In truth, the co-construction of these texts involved asymmetrical relations of power: the University of New Brunswick (UNB) team initiated the project;

helped forge connections between the ongoing work in the childcare centres, the draft curriculum framework and new possibilities; and, further, introduced the idea of 'pedagogical documentation as a process to make [their] pedagogical work visible and subject to interpretation, dialogue, confrontation (argumentation) and understanding' (Moss 2006b: 36). We provided information about the techniques of pedagogical documentation and held up as examples carefully produced documentation panels,[19] and digitalized learning stories[20] currently being produced in the UNB Children's Centre. Happily, these were neither imitated nor dismissed, but were quickly appropriated and transformed by a field that has more limited access to digital technologies, money and preparation time. The pilot project educators produced documentation that included handwritten learning stories; photographs quickly 'mounted' under a clear plastic tablecloth to prompt snack-time conversations; handmade books; a cooking project with two year olds, artfully documented using paper muffin cups; photographic essays located in spaces that would catch parents' and children's attention and become a focal point for talking, prompting parents to extend the project with photos from home.

These cultural texts speak to the local realities of diversity and to the resourcefulness of the educators. They have had great allure for the childcare educators attending the curriculum orientation sessions. As co-presenters at these sessions, the pilot educators have elaborated their documentation with verbal accounts of how a particular document evolved, what it tells us about their practice, what discussion it prompted in their centre and broader communities, and what they might do next. Some pilot participants recently presented their work to groups of more than 200. Less than a year previously, our invitations for them to tell their stories to much smaller groups were, more often than not, met with point blank refusals – evidence, perhaps, of their 'fragile self concept and self confidence' (Moyles 2001: 87). Their growing sense of confidence in public forums speaks, we think, of the support and care taken in collaborating.

19   Inspired by Reggio Emilia.
20   Inspired by a trip to New Zealand and the work of Margaret Carr.

Equally important, their documentation is to be published in support documents that celebrate the multiple possibilities for local interpretation. Through the lens of postcolonial theory, the childcare educators have 'in an autoethnographic gesture, transculturat[ed] elements of metropolitan discourses to create self affirmations designed for reception in the metropolis' (Pratt 1992: 143). Taussig calls this the 'mirror dance' of transculturation (Pratt 1992: 140). The documents to be distributed to support the official curriculum will reflect the polyphony and diversity that can disturb its regulatory potential.[21]

As co-production continues, we interrogate the ways in which our editorial filters modify educators' voices (Ashton 2009) and ask *what* and *whose* purposes are these texts serving?.

Making ideas visible and accessible: Troubling the idea of a common language

From the outset we were warned that we would need to use 'plain language'. Allusions were made to the low levels of formal education in the childcare sector and to the jargon of academia and the gap between. Consequently, when we commissioned reviews of the draft curriculum document, we asked specifically about the accessibility of the language. Reviews from the field were mixed, ranging from 'It's great! Don't dumb it down', to a call for more accessible language: 'inaccessible words' included 'confluence', 'reciprocal', and 'interdependency', as well as 'jargon' such as 'heuristic', 'metacognition', 'pedagogies' and 'multimodal'. Flagging the need for 'more concrete examples' and 'road maps to follow the curriculum', 'explanatory side bars', and 'speech bubbles', childcare educators, centre directors and early interventionists encapsulated a critique of our use of language and

21   Eight support documents are published or in process, edited by Pam Whitty, Pam Nason and Emily Ashton.

discourse practices that exclude. In our response to this critique we tried to reconcile the need for a text that might elevate the profile of early childhood education in bureaucratic and political circles, yet be accessible and useful to educators in their professional lives and their work with children and parents. We appreciated that some such educators did not read professional or academic texts; however, we are also aware of the pitfalls of producing infantilized texts – such as the Sure Start materials, critiqued by Jane Osgood (2005), which underwrite the historical construction of women as subjects in need of regulation and surveillance.

We went to press with no speech bubbles or explanatory sidebars, and most of the 'inaccessible' (to us, 'professional') language intact; confident that the 'road maps' discreetly embedded into the colour scheme and fonts, and the dialogue we would prompt in the professional learning programme would serve to mediate the language. A year on, childcare educators who had participated in the programme indicate otherwise: 'We find the phrasing a little complicated. It seems like fancy technical words to say something simple'; 'The people creating the document are submerged in the jargon'; 'To someone on the outside looking in, it's a little confusing, lend your knowledge instead of show how to do it'. One group of educators said: 'We want a workshop on terminology geared toward the curriculum framework binder'.

There are many possible ways to read these comments. Given the 'suturing of curriculum to professionalism' (to use Michael Apple's phrase) they could be read simply as a desire for a more clearly articulated path to access the profession. However, they could also be read as acceptance, acquiescence or resignation – i.e., 'No question that we will have to comply, just tell us more clearly how to do it'. Alternatively, it is simply the illusion of compliance that the childcare educators wish to convey, or perhaps a clearly defined rule is a rule more easily resisted.

All of these possible readings beg the question of whose language is adopted as the 'common language' and point to the need for conversational spaces in which to problematize professionalism and discuss how language both reflects and constructs professional identities and affiliations – how it excludes even as it includes.

Changing professional identities

In New Brunswick, as elsewhere, the call for professionalism in childcare is a compelling call to enhanced salaries and elevated status. However, when curriculum is viewed as a basis for professional reform, the promise of professionalism is also tied to compliance with the official curriculum by the 'good teacher'. Compliance is achieved partly through regulation, surveillance and sanction – into which the language of the curriculum is likely to become 'rigidly stabilised' (Marcuse 1965: 96) – but also by desire. As a new normality is created by the new curriculum discourse, *disciplinary power* is imposed on bodies by creating the desire to be "normal"' (Foucault 1978). Cannella and Viruru note that '[i]ndividuals construct standards by which to judge themselves', citing as examples 'the desire to be a good girl, a good mother, or a good teacher (however these desires are defined)', which 'are all disciplinary technologies imposed on females in Euro-American society' (2004: 63).

Given that professional identities have been historically framed as mother-substitute and more recently as technician, the image of the 'good teacher' as reflective practitioner and researcher that is encrypted in the New Brunswick Curriculum has created tensions that are, for some, quite welcome as catalysts for learning and, for others, decidedly unwelcome. Some expressed their resistance thus: 'As a pre-school we didn't like being roped in with daycare. We are preparing kids for schools and parents' expectations are different than daycare'. The 'new normal' represents for some an undesirable diminishing, not improvement, in status.

Changing, or even adopting, a professional image is always accompanied by some discomfort and is made even more difficult when mandated, as in our province. As one educator said: 'We had no choice in the matter.' During the pilot year, working with forty educators in nine centres, who had *chosen* to participate, we had been able to establish a climate of collaboration and develop responsive relationships with many educators. One-on-one conversations, opportunities to 'work alongside,' and times together to share challenges, concerns and successes were possible. Confronted with the task of providing this programme of professional learning to almost 1350 educators, we struggled to keep conversational spaces open.

Educators experienced varying degrees of support. Some directors had reorganized staffing schedules to accommodate the demands of the new curriculum, others had not – leaving educators with the overwhelming demands of finding time to meet all their challenges. It became impossible to establish the professional identities envisaged. The need for action to improve working conditions is clear. We recognize that '[t]he political order of the state may have to be challenged in the name of our ethical responsibility to the other' (Levinas and Kearney 1986: 30), and are committed to support childcare educators in relation to wage enhancement and working conditions.

Missing voices

> The demand for an invisible silent presence ... is a common colonizing practice, that (1) creates invisible power for those who would demand invisibility, and (2) constructs a group of people ... as marginal and without a voice in a world that demands formal expressive power. (Cannella and Swadner 2006: 87)

It seems ironic that whilst a postcolonial lens can offer up possibilities for de-stabilizing the regulatory potential of the text for the majority English population, it is not so easy with the region's First Nations, the Maliseet, Passamaquoddy and Mi'kmaq. A colonial history of domination, silencing and assimilation into monocultural schooling has left the indigenous languages of our region with no official recognition, and a fragile and precarious existence. Our work is in English only, although there is a French counterpart. What we have not said in the curriculum document speaks volumes. Aboriginal children are caught, often in poverty, between the cracks of Provincial and Federal policy when it comes to early learning and childcare. In theory, Aboriginal education comes under federal auspices with local control accorded to each community. In practice, for First Nations children living 'off reserve', and for childcare centres on reserves that are licensed by the province – a requirement for funding – the English (or French) curriculum is required.

When Andrea Bear Nicholas, Chair in Aboriginal Studies at Saint Thomas University, first read the curriculum framework she told one of the authors – Pam Nason – that it should carry a label, much like the ones you get on cigarette packages: 'This curriculum is hazardous to your health'. Her eloquent postcolonial critique[22] elaborates that in claiming to make our values explicit – 'arrived at through an extensive review of the literature, broad consultation and feedback from reviewers', with 'no single value is privileged over another' (6) – we have written out our fundamental bias, which is the privileging of mono-lingual/monoculture ideology. This, through a text inscribed with 'disingenuous claims for inclusivity' and, 'at several junctures, through the separation of language and culture.'

Andrea Bear Nicholas made clear the urgent need for early immersion to stop the cultural genocide of Aboriginal people, and the failure of the New Brunswick curriculum in this regard. Its pages offer no hope for the disruption of English language education, of – as she puts it – 'submersion education' for Aboriginal children.

Her words resonate hauntingly with our colonial pasts, and with stories of more brutal 'silencings' in residential schools (Chrisjohn and Young 1997) that are being made more public in the current climate of truth and reconciliation.[23] Binding submersion between the brightly coloured covers of an official text renders it no less powerful. In fact, as Canella and Viruru remind us, '[c]ontemporary forms of Empire are much less direct, more seductive' (2004: 59). Ethically, we must continue to acknowledge this and examine our complicity.

We understand the preservation and revitalization of indigenous languages and cultures to be enormously complicated. In practical terms, it is feared that the number of speakers may have already fallen below the critical mass for the survival of some languages. Andrea Bear Nicholas' urgent calls for early language immersion are not alarmist, yet she readily acknowledges

22   Commissioned by project co-directors, Pam Whitty and Pam Nason.
23   See <http://www.trc-cvr.ca> for documentation of this.

that they are not necessarily shared by First Nations communities. English is still recognized as the *lingua franca* by many, the key to a brighter future for Aboriginal children, with the arguments similar to those made for the incarceration of Aboriginal children in residential schools a century ago. As non-aboriginals committed to supporting Aboriginal self-governance, it is difficult to know what to do.

We have chosen, full of hope, the 'possibility of dialogue, not as an exchange but as a process of transformation where you lose absolutely the possibility of controlling the final outcome' (Rinaldi 2006: 184). In pursuit of dialogue, we ask: 'What type of a relationship might both connect but also distinguish between myself and the Other, might assume responsibility whilst maintaining a distance by which difference can be maintained ... [How, in this case, might we enact] open ended responsibility and a sense of obligation?' (Dahlberg and Moss 2005: 82–3).

From that position of open debate we have begun to imagine new possibilities for acting in solidarity with the Mi'kmaq, Maliseet and Passamaquoddy peoples. Collaboratively with the Mi'kmaq community of Elsipogtog we convened a talking circle attended by 30 educators and community members from 12 different Mi'kmaq and Maliseet communities, who raised questions about whether and how a co-constructed Aboriginal Support Document[24] might redress some of the omissions in the Framework, and showcase the work, words and wisdom of indigenous childcare educators and elders. We agreed that – whilst UNB's expertise in compiling and publishing support documents would be useful – the content would need to come from the First Nations communities, as would editorial control. We contemplated a tri-lingual support document in Mi'kmaq and Maliseet, and English (writ small) – to make Maliseet and Mi'kmaq languages more visible and accessible (through translation) to childcare educators who no longer speak their mother tongue, as well as to non-Aboriginals. Childcare educators from eight different First Nations communities immediately

---

24 Provisional title. *First Nations* Support Document has recently been suggested as an alternative to *Aboriginal* as it is particular First Nations – the Mi'kmaq, Maliseet and Passamaquoddy – which will be the focus of this document.

volunteered to sit on an editorial board, characterizing this as 'important work'. One educator voiced the shift of power relations in the moment: 'And we came here expecting you to tell us what to do'.

Our work with these communities has just begun, as it did with the Framework, with a discussion about values. The National Children's Agenda recognizes the distinctiveness of Aboriginal Communities, articulating it explicitly as one of its six values:

> We believe in the importance of parents, elders and extended families in nurturing Aboriginal children. We value the voices of Aboriginal children, and honour their traditional and spiritual significance in Aboriginal Communities. (Government of Canada 2000)

In unpacking this value we must take care to recognize 'opacity' both as 'a necessary condition for relationships to flourish', and 'as a fundamental right, as it is a way in which human beings can resist being categorized and essentialised. Cannella and Viruru point out that 'It is also a way of resisting what Glissant sees as a particularly colonizing concept: "understanding"[,] especially when one recognizes that the root of the French word for understanding (*comprendre*) is the word *prendre*, which means to take' (Cannella and Viruru 2004, 38–9).

Turning the inside out

Whether on the inside or outside of governmental initiatives for educational reform, negotiating the idea of curriculum as fluid, flexible, relational, dynamic, and democratizing engages us – as teacher educators – in complex ethical dilemmas. Whether official curriculum documents are structured as linear texts or co-constructed and produced in more complex postmodern textual designs,[25] and even when critical dialogue over

---

25   Such as those we have chosen for the curriculum support documents.

printed texts is successfully precipitated, 'knowledge that is sanctioned institutionally can produce such an authoritative consensus about how to "be" that it is difficult to imagine how to think, act and feel in any other way' (Mac Naughton 2005). Throughout our careers we have resisted such authoritative consensus, considering it our responsibility to create spaces for polyphony, dissent and diversity to flourish.

Choosing, this time, to be on the inside of reform – by accepting the contract for both the production of the official curriculum documents and the associated programme of professional learning – has afforded us a powerful colonizing potential, a potential which we have struggled continually to resist. Even as we have been complicit in the production of official texts, we have subjected them to interrogation and critique. In a sometimes paradoxical turn, we have enacted our identities in the spaces between an ethic of an encounter and colonial encounters. As we have explored the possibilities of dialogue in the construction and disruption of curricular reform, we have resolved our ethical dilemmas insofar as we have needed to in order to move on. By turning the inside out and making our struggle public, we trust that we have done no more, and no less, than begin to unmask our own agendas and contribute to the ongoing critical dialogue about early childhood curriculum that strives to disrupt marginalizing discourses and open up new possibilities.

References

Apple, M.W. (1983). 'Curricular Form and the Logic of Technical Control'. In M.W. Apple and L. Weis (eds), *Ideology and Practice in Schooling*. Philadelphia: Temple University Press.

—— (2004). *Ideology and the Curriculum*. New York: Routledge.

Ashton, E. (2009). 'Folding Ethical-Textual Tensions: Explorations in Curriculum Writing'. In L. Iannacci and P. Whitty (eds), *Early Childhood Curricula: Reconceptualist Perspectives*, pp. 63–86. Calgary: Detselig Enterprises.

Ball, S.J. (2003). 'The Teacher's Soul and the Terrors of Performativity', *Journal of Education Policy*, 18 (2), 215–28.

Bear Nicholas, A. (2007). *Commissioned Critique of the New Brunswick Curriculum Framework for Early Learning and Childcare*. New Brunswick: Education.

Bennett, J. (2004). 'Curriculum Issues in National Policy Making'. OECD. Keynote address at the European Early Childcare Education Research Association (EECERA) Conference, 2 September 2004, Malta.

Beyer, L.E. and Apple, M.W. (1998). *The Curriculum: Problems, Politics and Possibilities*. Albany: State University of New York Press.

Bredekamp, S. and Copple, C. (1997). *Developmentally Appropriate Practice in Early Childhood Education*. Washington, DC: National Association for the Education of Young Children.

Cannella, G.S., and Bloch, M.N. (2006). 'Social Policy, Education and Childhood in Dangerous Times: Revolutionary Actions or Global Complicity', *International Journal of Educational Policy, Research and Practice: Reconceptualizing Childhood Studies*, 7, 5–19.

Cannella, G.S., and Lincoln, Y.S. (2007). 'Predatory vs. Dialogic Ethics: Constructing an Illusion or Ethical Practice as the Core of Research Methods', *Qualitative Inquiry*, 13 (3), 315–53.

Cannella, G.S., and Swadener, B.B. (2006). 'Contemporary Public Policy Influencing Children and Families: "Compassionate" Social Provision or the Regulation of "Others"', *International Journal of Educational Policy, Research and Practice: Reconceptualizing Childhood Studies*, 7, 81–93.

Cannella, G.S. and Viruru, R. (2002). 'Childhood and Cultural Studies', *Journal of Curriculum Theorizing*, 19 (1), 87–8.

—— (2004). *Childhood and Postcolonisation: Power, Education and Contemporary Practice*. New York: Routledge Falmer.

Chrisjohn, R., and Young, S. with Maraun, M. (1997). *The Circle Game: Shadows and Substance in the Indian Residential School Experience in Canada*. Penticton, BC: Theytus Books.

Clayton, S., O'Brien, M., Vagra-Atkins, T., and Qualter, A (2008). 'Power and the Theory-and-Practice Conundrum: The Experience of Doing Research with a Local Authority. Presentation at CARN Study Day, Glasgow.' <http://www.did.stu.mmu.ac.uk/carnnew/events.php> accessed 7 August 2008.

Cochran-Smith, M., and Lytle, S.L. (2007). 'Practitioner inquiry and University Culture'. In A. Campbell and S. Groundwater-Smith (eds), *An Ethical Approach to Practitioner Research. Dealing with Issues and Dilemmas in Action Research*, pp. 24–41. London: Routledge.

Dahlberg, G. and Moss, P. (2005). *Ethics and Politics in Early Childhood Education*. New York: Routledge.

Duhn, I. (2006). 'The Making of Global Citizens: Traces of cosmopolitanism in the New Zealand early childhood curriculum, Te Whāriki', *Contemporary Issues in Early Childhood*, 7 (3), 191–202.

Freire, P. (2004). *Pedagogy of Indignation*. Boulder, CO: Paradigm Publishers.

Fraser, S. (1999). *Authentic Childhood: Experiencing Reggio Emilia in the Classroom*. Scarborough, ON: Nelson Education.

Government of Canada (2000). 'A Shared Vision for Canada's Children' <http://www.unionsociale.gc.ca/nca/June21-2000/english/sharedvision_e.html> accessed 20 September 2009.

Government of Manitoba. 'Family Choices: Manitoba's five year agenda for early learning and child care' <http://www.gov.mb.ca/familychoices> accessed 30 July 2008.

Government of New Brunswick. 'Be Ready for Success: A 10 Year Early Childhood Strategy' <http://www.gnb/0017/ELCC/strategy-e/asap> accessed 30 July 2008.

Government of New Brunswick. The New Brunswick Curriculum Framework for Early Learning and Child Care. <http://www.gnb.ca/0017/Promos/c003/curriculum-e.asp> accessed 8 September 2010.

Grieshaber, S. (2001). 'Advocacy and Early Childhood Educators: Identity and Cultural Conflicts'. In S. Grieshaber and G.S. Cannella (eds), *Embracing Identities in Early Childhood Education: Diversity and Possiblities*, pp. 60–72. New York: Teachers College Press.

——and Cannella, G.S. (2001). 'From identity to identities: Increasing possiblities in early childhood education'. In S. Grieshaber and G.S. Cannella (eds), *Embracing Identities in Early Childhood Education: Diversity and Possiblities*, pp. 3–22. New York, NY: Teachers College Press.

Grunewald, R. and Rolnick, A. (2007). 'A Productive Investment: Early Child Development'. In M.E. Young (ed.), *Early Child Development from Measurement to Action: A Priority for Growth and Equity*. Washington, DC: World Bank.

Kuehn, L. (2008). 'The education world is not flat: Neoliberalisms global project and teacher unions' transnational resistance'. In M. Compton and L. Weiner (eds), *The Global Assault on Teaching, Teachers and Their Unions*, pp. 53–72. New York: Palgrave McMillan.

Levinas, E., and Kearny, R. (1986). 'Dialogue with Emmanuel Levinas'. In R.A. Cohen (ed.), *Face to Face with Levinas*, pp. 13–35. Albany: State University Press of New York.

Mac Naughton, G. (2005). *Doing Foucault in Early Childhood Studies*. New York: Routledge.

Marcuse, H. (1965). 'Repressive tolerance'. In R.P. Wolff, B. Moore and H. Marcuse, *A Critique of Pure Tolerance*, pp. 95–134. Boston: Beacon Press.

McCain, M.N., and Mustard. J.F. (1999). *The Ontario Early Years Study: Reversing the Real Drain Brainy*. Toronto, ON: Publications Ontario.

McCain, M.N., and Mustard, J.F. (2002). *The Early Years Study Three Years Later*. Toronto, ON: Founders Network.

McCain M.N., Mustard, J.F., and Shanker, S. (2007). *Early Years Study 2: Putting Science into Action*. Toronto: Council for Early Childhood Development.

McGregor, G. (2009). 'Educating for (*Whose*) Success? Schooling in an Age of Neo-Liberalism', *British Journal of Sociology of Education*, 30 (3), 345–58.

Moss, P., Dahlberg, G. and Pence, A. (2000). 'Getting Beyond the Problem with Quality', *European Early Childhood Education Research Journal*, 8 (2), 103–15.

Moss, P. (2006a). 'Early Childhood Institutions as Loci of Ethical and Political Practice', *International Journal of Educational Policy, Research and Practice: Reconceptualizing Childhood Studies*, 7, 127–37.

Moss, P. (2006b). 'Structures, Understandings and Discourses: Possibilities for Re-Envisioning the Early Childhood Worker', *Contemporary Issues in Early Childhood*, 7 (1), 30–41.

Moyles, J. (2001). 'Passion, Paradox and Professionalism in the Early Years', *Early Years*, 21 (2), 81–95.

Nason, P.N. and Whitty, P. (2007). 'Bringing Action Research to the Curriculum Development Process', *Educational Action Research*, 15 (2), 271–81.

Nealon, J.T. (1997). 'The Ethics of Dialogue: Bakhtin and Levinas', *College English*, 59 (2), 129–48.

Osgood, J. (2005). 'Who Cares? The Classed Nature of Childcare', *Gender and Education*, 17 (3), 289–303.

Osgood, J. (2006). 'Professionalism and Performativity: The Feminist Challenge Facing Early Years Practitioners', *Early Years*, 26 (2), 187–99.

Pratt, M.L. (1997). *Imperial Eyes: Travel Writing and Transculturation*. London: Routledge.

Rinaldi, C. (2006). *In Dialogue with Reggio Emilia: Listening, Researching and Learning*. New York: Routledge.

Ryan, S. and Grieshaber, S. (2005). 'Shifting from Developmental to Postmodern Practices in Early Childhood Teacher Education', *Journal of Teacher Education*, 56 (1), 34–45.

Viruru, R. (2006). 'Postcolonial Technologies of Power: Standardised Testing and Representing Diverse Young Children', *International Journal of Educational Policy, Research and Practice: Reconceptualizing Childhood Studies*, 7, 49–71.

BRUCE JOHNSON

6 Maintaining professional ethics during a 'moral panic' over sex education: A case study

Introduction

Professional ethics are frequently represented in statements or 'codes' about the 'ethical commitments, practices and aspirations' of workers who have specialist knowledge which they use to provide a service to members of the public (Tasmanian Teachers Registration Board 2006; Martin 2000). These 'codes' articulate the *standards* of conduct expected of professionals. Yet more fundamental and implicit value agreements exist among groups of professionals, which are often more influential and enduring than the legalistic statements contained in professional codes of ethics. This broader conceptualization of professional ethics draws on a long tradition of *virtue ethics* that emphasises the intrinsic qualities or values that motivate professionals, rather than the rules of conduct that guide and regulate their behaviour.

This chapter offers an analysis of the trials and tribulations of a group of health and education professionals who re-asserted their ethical commitment to secular principles in the face of sustained attack. I explain how these shared beliefs provided them with the moral strength to persist with their reformist project. I present a detailed account of a major clash of values between this group of professionals and a coalition of fundamentalist Christians and opportunist politicians, over the development and implementation of a comprehensive sex education and relationships programme in South Australian secondary schools. I argue that the clash – which played out as a classic 'moral panic' – was a very public collision of competing worldviews and ethical commitments that challenged the taken-for-granted secularism of a modern Western community.

The protagonists were a group of sexuality educators, teachers, and administrators (hereafter referred to as 'the programme developers'), who worked for an organisation called Sexual Health Information Networking and Education South Australia, a non-government organisation which had a forty-year history of providing sexual health advice and services in South Australia. Their opponents (hereafter referred to as 'the traditionalists') were an alliance of Pentecostal, evangelical Christian groups, pro-family and anti-abortion lobbyists, and conservative politicians. The health and education professionals shared many beliefs that had their intellectual and moral roots in secular humanism, while their opponents based their ethical and moral beliefs on a literalist reading of an inerrant and infallible Bible (the Christian fundamentalists), or on traditional patriarchal gender relations, family arrangements, and heterosexual human sexuality (the lobbyists). The ethical and moral bases of their relative positions are outlined to provide the philosophical context for what follows – a detailed analysis of what happened when the traditionalists launched a very strident and public attack on the sex education programme, its developers and their professional ethics.

The programme developers: Champions of secular humanism

The programme developers worked for an organisation that had been established to provide 'family planning' advice in the 'promiscuous' 1960s and 1970s; this frequently involved dispensing the contraceptive pill and providing information about fertility issues including abortion options for women. As a consequence, it was frequently targeted by socially conservative pro-family and anti-abortion lobby groups which vehemently opposed its pro-choice mission. This ethical heritage was deeply felt by those who worked for the organisation; the shared work-place culture was assertively liberal, feminist, and secular. Its claim to be 'the lead sexual health agency in South Australia' reinforced its mission to be 'your source for information to help you enjoy your relationships and sexual health with safety, pleasure and respect' (SHine SA 2004; 2009). Significantly, it espoused beliefs and principles that were consistent with those promoted by the Council for Secular Humanism (Stevens, Tabash, Hill, Sikes and Flynn 2009). These included:

- A 'commitment to the use of critical reason, factual evidence, and scientific methods of inquiry, rather than faith and mysticism in seeking solutions to human problems and answers to important human questions'
- 'A conviction that dogmas, ideologies and traditions, whether religious, political or social, must be weighed and tested by each individual and not accepted on faith'
- 'A commitment to a set of principles which promote the development of tolerance and compassion and an understanding of the methods of science, critical analysis and philosophical reflection'

In practice, this meant embracing a range of professional ethics that promoted the interests of those they 'served' as professionals within the organisation, rather than the interests of the state or other social and religious institutions. It meant that they actively promoted individual autonomy and self determination ('individual choice'), an acknowledgement and acceptance of difference ('tolerance of difference, and mutual and reciprocal respect'), and a commitment to rational, evidence-based information generation and dissemination ('scientific veracity').

The sex education and relationships programme they developed reflected these ethical commitments. The programme was

- Research-based, having drawn on evidence from evaluations of comprehensive sex education and relationships programmes in northern European countries, as well as local surveys of parents, students and teachers
- Highly explicit, with detailed descriptions and diagrams of human sexual anatomy and, more controversially, human sexual behaviour
- Accepting of sexual diversity, including homosexuality

- Focused on respectful sexual relationships rather than on social and religious conventions like marriage

Perhaps most importantly, the programme assertively promoted the view that *all* humans are sexual beings who have the right to express their sexuality in a variety of ways, and that the pursuit of sexual pleasure was a legitimate human goal.

Given the explicitness of the programme, its direct challenge to many social taboos and religious edicts about human sexual behaviour and the strident advocacy of its developers, it is not surprising that it attracted the attention of groups in the South Australian community whose worldview and belief structures were antithetical to secular relativism.

The traditionalists: Champions of Christian fundamentalism and/or 'family values'

The identity of those who opposed the programme is on public record, as these groups and individuals openly published their objections. The majority made no secret of their membership of a socially conservative, pro-family, fundamentalist Christian coalition that opposed the erosion of 'traditional values'. The key opponents were:

- Right to Life, an anti-abortion lobby group
- Australian Family Association, a pro-marriage, pro-abstinence lobby group
- Festival of Light (re-named Family Voice Australia in July 2008), a Christian fundamentalist advocacy group promoting 'true family values in the light of the wisdom of God'
- Family First Party, a conservative pro-family minority political party
- Assemblies of God Church (re-named Australian Christian Churches in 2007), an evangelical Christian organisation with over 1,200 churches across Australia

- Hills Parent and Friends Group, a specifically formed opposition group
- Advocates for Survivors of Child Abuse, a support group for victims of child sexual abuse
- The Liberal Party, a socially conservative political party which formed the Opposition in the South Australian Parliament. The chief protagonist for the Liberal Party was its Shadow Minister for Education and Children's Services.

While this was a loose coalition of conservative traditionalists, the dominant ideology was Christian fundamentalism. Vorster has identified the following 'core characteristics of religious fundamentalism':

- Scriptualism: 'fundamentalism designates a form of conservative, evangelical Protestantism that … lays exceptional stress on the inerrancy and infallibility of the Bible as the absolutely essential foundation and criterion of truth … Scripture is verbally inspired, inerrant and in toto the source of principles and norms applicable to modern-day life.' (2008: 45–6)
- Traditioning: 'tradition is expanded into a relatively systematic and consistent social critique and theory of history, society and salvation. It glorifies the positive and outstanding events of its past and this glorification becomes simultaneously a foundation and guideline for modern-day intensions.' (2008: 49)
- Casuistic ethics: 'Casuistic ethics points to a legalistic ethical system that is not controlled by applying principles and norms in every new situation, but provides a fixed recipe for moral conduct. Casuistic ethics aims to control life with moral laws and to deny the individual the right to freedom of choice when it comes to the management of their behaviour and conduct.' (2008: 50)
- Oppositionalism: 'Religious fundamentalism is usually caused by the fear of a perceived enemy. Fundamentalists define themselves in large by what they are against. It is, therefore, reactionary in nature …. (Preachers) nurture the faith of their adherents by

pointing to the constant dangers threatening true believers and the appeal to be steadfast in the face of all onslaughts on the children of God.' (2008: 51–2)

These elements of Christian fundamentalism were evident within the evangelical communities that opposed the sex education programme. As I demonstrate later in this chapter, their actions in resisting the implementation of the programme were justified by literalist readings of selected passages from the Bible, invocations of past examples of sexual transgressions and God's responses, the re-statement of absolutist moral rules about sexual behaviour, and the demonization of the programme developers. Moral certainty was a feature of their position.

Before describing and analysing the 'moral panic' that ensued, a word about the role of the conservative political parties is needed. When the sex education programme was released to be trialled in selected secondary schools, a minority Labor Government had just been formed with the support of several socially conservative independent members. Because of this, the Government was perceived to be unstable and vulnerable to attack from the Liberal Opposition, particularly on issues of social concern like law and order, education, and the wellbeing of children and adolescents. The public disharmony over the sex education programme was seized upon by an opportunistic Opposition as an example of Government support for a morally questionable initiative that threatened social and religious conventions about human sexuality, and undermined the role of parents in educating their children about sexual matters. Due to these local idiosyncrasies, the political responses to the 'moral panic' over the programme can be seen to be more concerned with party politics than with the clash of worldviews between secularism and religious fundamentalism. However, Parliament provided a very public stage for this clash of views to be played out.

Sources of insight into the clash

Most of the public responses of both groups of protagonists were available in local newspapers, transcriptions of talkback radio conversations, press releases, and official records of Parliamentary debates (Hansard). However, I was interested in the perspectives of the group of health and education professionals who developed and trialled the programme and then had to defend it against sustained attack. As a consequence, I conducted:

- Individual interviews with six programme developers
- Two focus group interviews with fourteen senior teachers from the four schools which trialled the programme
- Individual interviews with ten teachers and five school leaders in the four trial schools
- An individual interview with a senior official of the Department of Education and Children's Services who liaised with the programme developers and the trialling schools

I also accessed:

- Curriculum documents and support materials
- Internal reports, memos and correspondence relating to the development and implementation of the programme

What is a 'moral panic'?

Most analyses of contemporary 'moral panics' cite Cohen's opening paragraph of *Folk Devils and Moral Panics*, the first and most influential explanation of collective alarm over perceived social problems:

Societies appear to be subject, every now and then, to periods of moral panic. A condition, episode, person or group of persons emerges to become defined as a threat to societal values and interests; its nature is presented in a stylised and stereotypical fashion by the mass media; the moral barricades are manned by editors, bishops, politicians and other right-thinking people; socially accredited experts pronounce their diagnoses and solutions; ways of coping are evolved or (more often) resorted to; the condition then disappears, submerges or deteriorates and becomes more visible. Sometimes the object of the panic is quite novel and at other times it is something which has been in existence long enough, but suddenly appears in the limelight. Sometimes the panic passes over and is forgotten, except in folklore and collective memory; at other times it has more serious and long-lasting repercussions and might produce such changes as those in legal and social policy or even in the way society conceives itself. (Cohen 1973: 9)

The emergence of 'the problem'

The sex education project was perceived to be a threat to societal values because its opponents claimed that it promoted homosexuality, was too explicit about human sexuality and did not promote sexual abstinence or the institution of marriage. Curriculum materials were selectively quoted to show how the project threatened 'traditional' sexual values and regulatory processes:

> The teachers' resource manual, not only avoids discussing thoroughly at-risk sexual behaviour and life styles, but openly endorses, if not encourages, a number of these. And ... the resource deliberately avoids discussing marriage, fidelity, parenthood and abstinence. (Hills Parent and Friends Group, Press Release, 3 December 2003)

By drawing attention to the features of the project that challenged the hegemonic position of 'family values' in society, opponents of the project explicitly targeted the programme as socially dangerous and a source of moral threat. The 'problem' was named.

The form of 'the problem': Exaggeration and distortion

Critcher maintains that in the early stages of a moral panic, 'exaggeration and distortion, of the seriousness of events, the numbers involved, the extent of violence and damage' (2003: 12) is common. This serves to alarm people and mobilise their support for actions directed against the moral threat.

In the case of the sex education project, alarmist claims were commonly made in the media in an organized and coordinated campaign to alert the parents of students undertaking the programme of its moral dangers. Exaggeration was common. For example:

> [The program] centres on homosexuality, group masturbation and licking of body parts, use of sexual aids and mind/thought manipulation by telling students to 'imagine' themselves in these situations. (Advocates for Survivors of Child Abuse – SA, Press Release, 28 April 2003)

> Theft of children? Some Government Educators want to steal your children's values and thinking away from you. How? The new ... Sex Education course deliberately seeks to normalise and popularise homosexuality and bisexuality. Don't let the Education Department steal your children's innocence or your family's values. (Advertisement, *Port Lincoln Times*, 18 September 2003)

Even politicians from 'mainstream' parties helped to construct elements of the sex education programme as problematic and dangerous by repeating the highly selective and overstated claims of opponents of the project:

> Aspects of the curriculum which have generated the most concerns are so-called 'intimacy cards' which teachers are told to display on the floor for all students to see which canvass issues such as licking parts of the body, sucking breasts, and masturbating each other.
> Concerns were also raised about a series of 'safe practices' cards which students are asked to organise into safe and unsafe practices including 'using a sex toy' and 'using a devise for sexual arousal'. (Shadow Minister for Education and Children's Services 2003a: 2)

By extrapolating from a narrow range of activities, overstating their significance, exploiting their 'shock value', and repeating their shared 'concerns' about them, opponents of the programme were able to increase community anxiety about the threat the programme might cause, to levels 'above and beyond that which a realistic appraisal could sustain' (Goode and Ben-Yehuda 1994: 36). From a moral panic perspective, the 'problem' posed by sex education programme was deliberately exaggerated and overstated.

Opposition strategies and tactics

There is considerable evidence to suggest that the opposition groups were well organised and used very similar strategies and tactics in different locations.

At the local school or community level, multiple 'attacks' were mounted against the programme. This was done through letters to the editors of suburban or regional newspapers, paid advertisements in those papers, email campaigns, the distribution of pamphlets, and significantly, by conducting public meetings of 'concerned parents' in local areas.

One pamphlet produced by the Australian Family Association contained advice about how to initiate individual and group actions, including writing letters to MPs, local and state papers, forming delegations to visit schools, and calling talkback radio programmes. Activists were encouraged to inform local 'group coordinators' of their plans (Australian Family Association 2003).

Community meetings were held in trial school areas. Posters, brochures and newspaper advertisements announced the meetings and invited community members to attend. One teacher describes how these meetings were used by opponents:

> I can remember that there was a lot of controversy, mainly through religious groups, Family First probably, holding meetings in [a SA regional city]. There'd be a lot of people who'd arrive – anywhere between fifty and a hundred – a big turn-out considering you'd only get four or five parents to a parent information night.
>
> They'd have a couple of spare chairs out the front as well, and on one of them would be a big placard or cut-out of the high school teacher involved who didn't come, another placard or cut-out would be of the SHine representative who was invited but who didn't come. And so that sort of message was a little bit negative for us.

Similar accounts were provided by other teachers.

While these local activities were occurring, higher profile initiatives at the state level were being pursued by the Liberal Opposition, and members of the loose coalition against the programme. The Shadow Minister for Education and Children's Services distributed a series of press releases in April 2003 that were critical of the programme. She 'called for a commitment from the government not to proceed with the introduction of its controversial sex education programme until public meetings with parents have been held' (Shadow Minister for Education and Children's Services 2003b). The press release explained that, '[the Shadow Minister's] comments follow an outcry from many parents and others in the community about the explicit nature of aspects of the programme which parents were not fully informed about by the Government'. Her other concerns were that:

- Parents had not been properly informed about the programme
- *Teach it like it is* [the main teacher resource] had not been publicly distributed
- The programme could put young people at risk
                    (Shadow Minister for Education and Children's Services
                                                          2003a; 2003b)

The Shadow Minister continued her campaign making two major speeches in Parliament in September and December 2003. On this latter occasion, she moved the following motion:

> That the House urges the government to immediately withdraw the trial Sexual Health and Relationship Education Program developed by SHine from all 15 participating schools pending professional assessment and endorsement. (South Australian Parliamentary Debates 2003: 1107)

Against this backdrop of political activity, 'behind the scenes' lobbying took place mostly through 'form' letters sent to the state education department and the Minister for Education and Children's Services. Hundreds of letters were delivered to these offices. A senior official commented:

We dealt systematically with letters of concern and complaint that came in from the community. Every letter. A lot of the 'form' letters were tragically misinformed about the programme. We really saw it as an opportunity to inform people about what was actually happening, so we always responded in a respectful way.

The education department's approach was measured, careful and discriminating. It was aware that there was 'a loose coalition of people with similar interests' which was orchestrating a campaign of opposition but that not all of the 'concerned groups' were extremists or fundamentalists:

I thought that it was an important distinction, to work out who your friends are in this kind situation and not unnecessarily alienate people over relatively small points, when we're in broad agreement with a whole range of other points. (Senior Official)

The final tactic used by some opposition groups and individuals involved the personal intimidation of local teachers, the programme developers, education department senior officials, and in one case an Independent Member of Parliament. These fear-inducing methods were mentioned by several interviewees:

So the campaign wasn't about people just going in the media. It was also about them trying to do something to scare us and so, very early on, there were the incidents of windows broken, eggs thrown at the windows here. I was followed home and then I had three young people with a gun outside my place at home. There was the abuse of clinic staff by women from a church, you know, down south. I mean it was awful. And people were abused in shopping centres and stuff like that. (Programme Developer A)

Perhaps the most vitriolic personal attack was made in a letter to the programme developers. Among other things, the leaders were accused of being 'enemies of God'. The letter contained the threat that, 'You'll be crushed and destroyed by God's almighty power, you abhorrent Satanists, you evil doers'. The letter was addressed to 'SATAN'S DEN'.

These extreme measures represent the worst manifestations of a litany of oppositional strategies and tactics designed to mobilise political and community opinion against the sex education project and to weaken the resolve of those who were promoting it at the policy and organisational level, and at the local school level in community secondary schools.

One of the reasons for analysing, in some detail, these aspects of the opposition campaign is to point to the sources of quite difficult and serious 'tensions and dilemmas' experienced by teachers, school leaders, programme staff, and education department officials. How they responded to, coped with, and/or resolved these extraordinary demands is discussed in the remainder of this paper.

Initial responses to the traditionalists' opposition

Surprisingly – in hindsight – the key actors in the project had not anticipated the nature and extent of the opposition that emerged. The programme developers, for example, placed great faith in the capacity of parents, teachers, and members of the wider community to 'look at the evidence' – both local and international – in support of comprehensive sexual health and relationships education. They were convinced that their stance, which was grounded in a set of professional ethics that promoted the primacy of informed individual choice, was unassailable. They admitted taking some time to understand the dynamics of an opposition campaign that seemed to defy the ethical and moral strength of their position. As one leader recalled:

> It took us about three months really to start to realise what was going on. When we actually launched the programme in March we had at that stage no reason and no concrete evidence to believe that there would be the level of opposition that we subsequently experienced.
>
> We started to understand quite early on that the opposition wasn't grounded in fact, but that it was actually grounded in religious ideology and that it was [linked] to the anti-sex education movement in America that had been going on for about a decade before. (Programme Developer A)

They weren't alone in being surprised by the opposition – a key education department official admitted that his organisation wasn't prepared for what was to follow the release of the project. He described trying to establish clear protocols with the programme developers about 'responding to the media, about maintaining a flow of communication' while 'on the run' and under 'extreme pressure'. He candidly reflected that, 'We built all those structures on the run – the database of participants, communication protocols and so on' (Senior Official).

These initial reactions to the first wave of concerted opposition to the sex education programme have all the hallmarks of what Cohen calls ways of coping that those under attack frequently resort to because they are largely unprepared for the scope and intensity of the moral panic enveloping them. In other cases of moral panic (see Critcher 2003), startled and worried politicians and community leaders have resorted to legislative action to address the perceived threat posed by so called 'deviant' groups and their behaviour. In the case of the sex education programme, this didn't happen; the programme was successfully defended and promoted by a range of advocates who re-grouped after the initial onslaught of criticism. As an education department official said at the conclusion of his interview, 'this is a story about a significant triumph of good over the forces of social control' (notes of interview, 3 February 2006). It is also an example of significant professional groups maintaining their focus on what they believed to be in the best interests of young adolescents in the community. What follows is an analysis of how these groups recovered from the early days of the moral panic to re-state their raison d'être for developing and implementing the programme. That is, how they re-asserted their ethical commitment to secular principles in the face of sustained attack.

Re-stating the programme's essential rationale

While the developers of the programme were shaken and distracted by the campaign against them, they were not 'broken' by it. They spoke of getting 'back on track' once they had worked out what was happening and what was still important to them. They articulated an unusually strong resolve to remain committed to the principles and values that had motivated their development of the project in the first place:

> We were very clear and very determined that this would happen and nobody, nobody would cause us to go off the rails. Because what we were trying to do here was what our core business was about in this organization and that's about improving sexual health and wellbeing. (Programme Developer A)

Another programme developer invoked the sentiment behind the classic Latin dictum *ad adstra per aspera* ('to the stars through difficulties'). She talked about her colleagues stoically gaining moral strength by not succumbing to pressure to change or dilute the programme.

These developers resisted the framing of their project as 'controversial', 'marginal' or 'contested' by the media and its opponents:

> People talk about our programme as being controversial but we're saying, no we're not controversial, the programme is not controversial ... I try to get away from that idea and the chaos around what happened. I just focus on the fact that we're trying to deliver best practice relationships in sexual health in schools and not bring that stuff up again. (Programme Developer C)

Not only did the project leaders return to their essential reasons for developing the programme to restore their sense of moral purpose and determination, school teachers and leaders also re-articulated their educational rationale for teaching the programme to justify their continued commitment in the face of opposition.

Acting centrally and professionally: The developers mobilize their defence

After the initial shock of opposition, the programme developers embarked on its spirited defence. This involved:

- Directing a media officer to provide advice on how to engage the media in the defence of the programme
- Writing media releases rebutting erroneous and/or exaggerated criticisms of the programme
- Writing letters to the editors of local and state newspapers

- Writing to Members of Parliament to counter misleading and exaggerated claims made by the coalition of opponents of programme
- Participating in talk-back radio debates with opponents of the programme
- Advising schools about how best to cope with criticism
- Engaging other professional groups and encouraging them to publicly support the programme

The involvement of 'experts' in the defence of the programme is noteworthy, particularly from a moral panic perspective. As occurred in the moral panic over AIDS in the late 1980s, medical opinion was highly valued and considered in the debate over the worth of the programme. While a few medical arguments were cited in opposition to the programme (see Grace 2003), the weight of medical and health evidence was strongly in favour of comprehensive sexual and relationships education of the type promoted by the programme. As a consequence, the local support of organisations like the Royal College of Nursing Australia, the Australian Medical Association (SA), Council of General Practice, and Health Promotion SA in particular, was critical in establishing the credibility of the programme's defence. To paraphrase Critcher (2003: 39), the programme became a medical and health issue and eventually the views of health experts prevailed – 'high in status and credibility, their expertise was not easy to dismiss ... Expert opinion was clearly weighted against a moral panic'.

Acting locally

Not all responses to the moral panic were reactive, immediate, or driven by 'expert opinion' in sexual health. Several schools, for example, bided their time and waited for a strategic moment that advanced their cause. They unobtrusively continued teaching the programme, collected various forms of feedback from key stakeholders in the school, and then carefully used the local media to craft a 'good news story'. A teacher in the focus group describes his school's approach:

> Well we thought we'd wait until a semester in and then get some responses back through feedback sheets, class discussions, parent feedback and all that sort of stuff, and see how positive it was ... we have a good relationship with the local media up here so we collated it all, then got an overwhelmingly positive front page story about the course.

Other schools reported similar examples of 'using' local media to counter negative criticism. Rather than casting teachers and schools as passive 'victims' of a relentless, orchestrated campaign of opposition, these anecdotes of local action re-position them as quite 'savvy' community campaigners who knew how to passively resist outside criticism ('we thought we would wait until a semester in') and strategically use the media, at a time of their choice, to disseminate *their* story.

The moral panic subsides

One of the mysteries of moral panics is how and why they seem to 'fade away' (Critcher 2003), 'disappear', 'submerge' or 'deteriorate' (Cohen 1973). One explanation is that the main purveyors of moral panics, the news media, apply 'news values' – 'journalists' rule of thumb about what does and doesn't not make a good story' – to decide when to 'tune into', and 'tune out' of, the debates that provoke moral panics (Critcher 2003: 132).

However, perhaps more salient than the actions of the local media was the behaviour of the vast majority of parents (variously estimated to be 95–98 per cent of parents) who gave their active and continuing consent for their adolescents to participate in the sex education programme. The clear message these parents gave both supporters of the programme and those who opposed it was that the moral panic had no base in public opinion. They clearly refused to share or contribute to the social anxiety about the programme promoted by its critics.

Conclusion

This depiction of the 'clash' between the programme developers and the traditionalists raises interesting issues about how professional groups can and should act in ways that are consistent with their professional ethics when they are challenged, questioned, confronted, and attacked by dissenting interest groups. In many ways the developers were unprepared for the nature and extent of the attack on them and their ideas as their secular worldview and ethical commitment was so dominant and 'taken-for-granted' that it seemed beyond reproach. They had to quickly come to grips with the stark realities of fundamentalist opposition by re-stating their philosophical and ethical principles and drawing on long-standing, historical and populist support for their views. Yet it was insufficient for the developers to be ethically principled during this time as the powerful political and media strategies that were used by the traditionalists needed to be countered; the developers had to be 'politically savvy' as well. They realised that they could not remain aloof from the everyday *realpolitik* of opposition, but had to embrace a range of political strategies and tactics that were not part of the usual repertoire of actions undertaken by health and education professionals. Finally, they found that the need to 'play politics' sometimes compromised their deeply felt ethical principles about respecting diversity and tolerating difference; the dilemmas they faced were palpable and caused them personal and professional concern.

These issues will have relevance in other places and at other times, when the lure of fundamentalism challenges the secular principles on which the professional ethics of most teachers, social workers, and health workers are based. Hopefully, in these instances, the 'use of critical reason, factual evidence, and scientific methods of inquiry' will prevail over 'faith and mysticism in seeking solutions to human problems and answers to important human questions' (Stevens, Tabash, Hill, Sikes and Flynn 2009).

References

Advocates for Survivors of Child Abuse – SA (2003). Press Release, 28 April 2003.

Australian Family Association (2003). *Sex Education: Group and Individual Action on the SHine SA SHARE Program*. Brochure. PO Box 460, Fullarton SA.

Cohen, S. (1973). *Folk Devils and Moral Panics*. St Albans: Paladin.

Critcher, C. (2003). *Moral Panics and the Media*. Buckingham: Open University Press.

Goode, E. and Ben-Yehuda, N. (1994). *Moral Panics: The Social Construction of Deviance*. Oxford: Blackwell.

Hills Parents and Friends Group (2003). Press Release, 3 December 2003.

Martin, M. (2000). *Meaningful Work: Rethinking Professional Ethics*. Oxford: Oxford University Press.

Patton, M. (2002). *Qualitative Research and Evaluation Methods*. Thousand Oaks, CA: Sage.

Shadow Minister for Education and Children's Services (2003a). 'Back to the Drawing Board'. Press Release, 8 April 2003.

Shadow Minister for Education and Children's Services (2003b). 'Opposition calls for commitment from Education Minister'. Press Release, 10 April 2003.

SHine SA (2004). *Teach It Like It Is: A Relationships and Sexual Health Curriculum Resource for Teachers of Middle School Students*. Kensington, SA: Sexual Health information networking and education SA.

SHine SA (2009). 'Mission Statement' <http://www.shinesa.org.au/go/our-services/about-us> accessed 21 October 2009.

South Australia Parliamentary Debates (Hansard) (2003). 'Debate on the Sexual Health and Relationship Education Program', 4 December, 1107–24.

Stevens, F., Tabash, E., Hill, T., Sikes, M. and Flynn, T. (2009). 'What is Secular Humanism?' Council for Secular Humanism. <http://www.secularhumanism.org/index.php?page=what&section=main> accessed 21 October 2009.

Tasmanian Teachers Registration Board (2006). 'Code of Professional Ethics for the Teaching Profession in Tasmania'. <http://www.trb.tas.gov.au/TRB%20Code%20of%20Professional%20Ethics.pdf> accessed 21 October 2009.

Vorster, J. (2008). 'Perspectives on the Core Characteristics of Religious Fundamentalisms Today', *Journal for the Study of Religions and Ideologies*, 7(21), 44–65.

BRIDGET COOPER

7 Valuing the human in the design and use of technology in education: An ethical approach to the digital age of learning

Globalization, society and learning: The ethical challenges for technology

Ethics is a complex and evolving area, engaging with fundamental questions about what constitutes a 'moral' society and a 'desirable' education. If education is to have a worthy goal, it must aspire to enhancing human skills such as imagination, creativity, intellect, empathy and communication, all of which can be multiplied through the collaboration of conscious minds across the globe. Internet users can rapidly access vast electronic databases of knowledge, research and experience. As bandwidth improves, individuals and groups create and share vast libraries of video, film and photography with real-time debate, utilizing an ever-extending range of data capture and communication tools, embedded with artificial intelligence. Multi-modal tools (Kress and van Leeuwen 2001) enable us to know distant human beings more intimately, to enter each other's worlds and share understandings. Some might say that furthering wisdom through technological interaction has never been easier. However this chapter will consider some of the moral and affective issues in learning with technology, the challenges faced by designers and how empathic design might positively or negatively impact on the creation and deployment of educational technology for the benefit of human kind.

The internet, which supports global communication, learning and research, is taken for granted, yet has been commonly available for less than twenty years and is only easily available to around one fifth of the global population. However, developments in nano- and bio-technology will result in total interaction, where everyone and everything becomes an integrated part of the 'infosphere' (Floridi 2007). This pace of change can have ethical advantages, because developing countries can leapfrog swiftly over outmoded developments, creating 'compressed modernity' (Law and Chu 2008). The rise of India, China and Brazil are examples of this, and Africa may follow.

Technology can be used unethically. The speed and convenience of the internet for learning or research is as astounding as the availability of child pornography is terrifying. Although technological design raises exciting possibilities, educationalists need to be critically aware of its impact on learners, especially the most vulnerable. The pace of invention can militate against thoughtful human-centred design and favour some values above others which may hinder rather than enhance human development. Some human values may be lost in the race for technological innovation or the pursuit of power and wealth. Technology can encourage collaboration, intellect and empathy; it can also promote propaganda, greed, deceit, abuse of power or intolerance. Ethical issues must be central to the design, development and deployment of technology if aspirations to an educated and virtuous society are to be realized. This chapter considers theories of learning and moral development to help understand approaches which can support the ethical design and use of technology in education and identifies key challenges.

Understanding learning: The importance of the affective and links with the learning environment

Humans are highly complex and capable of multi-sensory interactions. Across disciplines and time, from Rembrandt to Darwin, the importance of non-verbal signals has been recognized with over ninety percent of communication in this category (Mehrabian 1971). Multi-sensory processing is how humans comprehend their environment. More brain capacity is used through the employment of all human senses and this enhances engagement and enjoyment; a sense of personal value is embedded in social interactions (Cooper 2004). The valuing of others through face-to-face interaction is a process which begins at birth (Leal 2002) and remains significant in well-being and development throughout life. Learning and interaction created through human communication is socially constructed and the understanding of non-verbal signals highly dependent on context (Eckman 1997). Lack of face-to-face interaction can be detrimental to relationships (Klein 1956), leading to alienation. When technology utilizes a multi-sensory approach and supports real–time, mutually respectful human communication, with non-verbal as well as verbal or textual interaction, it is likely to be more effective than transmissive approaches.

Educational technology now needs to reflect developments in learning theory which focus on the intrinsically affective nature of learning (Cooper 2004; Narvaez 2008) and the significance of human relationships for learning. Rapid developments in neuroscience (Damasio 1999; 2003) are reinvigorating research into emotion and learning which reaffirms previous psychological research on affect (Aspy 1972; Rogers 1975). Vygotsky (1986) argued that the separation of cognition and affect was one of psychology's biggest failings and evidence suggests that an important aspect of a teacher's role is emotional scaffolding (Purkey 1970; Long et al. 2007). This is a challenge in large classes, where children compete for attention and teachers struggle to respond to individual needs; there are organizational dimensions to the deployment of technology in schools.

Learning environments can produce alienation, with students as recipients of knowledge and teachers as technicians, floundering beneath the burden of endless initiatives, curricula and targets which numb the mind and inhibit creativity. In such circumstances, teachers and children forfeit self-esteem and pleasure in learning which limits development. The quality of learning could be improved if historical prejudices about emotion are challenged (Damasio 1999) along with academic traditions and subject divisions (Vygotsky 1986). A more creative and affect-based approach has potentially huge implications for the values implicit in the design of learning technology and the technological environment.

Identifying problems in educational systems and educational research

Many education professionals understand the importance of affect and relationships in learning but, as indicated above, work within traditions and systems which do not (Long et al. 2007; Cooper 2005). The mechanistic approach embedded in many virtual learning environments means that educators have seen their well-honed skills and expert understanding degraded by a technicist process for the delivery of a transmissive curriculum despite the fact that modern students are more likely to require qualities of autonomy, empowerment, flexibility and adaptability (Williams 2005). Traditional hierarchies of academic, financial and political power have influenced perceptions of learning and consequently have also influenced the design and deployment of technology to support learning. Hence we have virtual learning environments designed around learning 'objects' for students to experience alone, or laboratories with rows of computers non-conducive to human interaction.

Consequently, human relationships, despite being at the heart of the learning process are frequently ignored in educational research. Measurable factors within the curriculum and its assessment attract substantial funding. Many research projects investigate programmes in which fractions of percentage points in test results are valued more highly than the interactions between actors involved in the process. It is more straightforward to analyse language, than the more elusive use of intonations, gestures and body-language (Broadfoot 2000). Factors with greater affective impact potential, such as tutor/student ratios, informal settings or activities which equalize power relationships, are seldom researched. Universities which might be conducting cutting-edge research into humane, affective aspects of learning, conduct large-scale testing, to secure funding, regardless of the outcomes for children – of itself, a serious ethical issue.

Sensitivity to human qualities in the ethical design of systems and software

If learning is conceived of as an affective process, developed through complex and caring human relationships (Clark 1996; Gibbs 2006) rather than only being the rational acquisition and manipulation of knowledge, this alters the underpinning principles for technological design and development. An understanding the mind and body union and the importance of emotion to all interaction and sense of self needs to be built into the design of hardware, software and learning environments for maximum communication and impact. Designers may assume that individuals should accommodate themselves to technology rather than the reverse and, although some academics do investigate the emotional aspects of human computer interaction, too often design-thinking is subsumed into the overarching hegemonic values of rationality, seriality, auditing and control.

Technology needs to facilitate and expand the multi-sensory approach to learning in humans to produce systems that enable communication which is as close as possible to face-to-face presence rather than forcing people through unforgiving, serial and digital pathways. Systems and software which enhance humanity will be innately more ethical because they value the higher level attributes of humans, rather than an essentially mechanistic and emotionless agenda. Developments which objectify humans and their knowledge and devalue human interaction may limit learning. Terms such as 'knowledge transfer' and 'learning objects', epitomize the challenges for computer scientists, because ultimately they depict a lack of understanding of human learning processes.

Profound empathy between individuals (Cooper 2004) enables maximum communication and shared understanding. These qualities are needed to facilitate global understanding and enable people to both model and engender morality in their relationships. Non-verbal communication is central to the creation of profound empathy and involves the recognition and development of the whole person. Through continuous dialogue, empathy ensures continuous formative assessment which enables both cognitive and emotional scaffolding and supports creativity and imagination, enhancing positive attributes of humanity (Cooper 2004). Learning engendered through human values of care and personal interest is of the highest order and includes spiritual and moral learning as hidden by-products of other learning. Of course, such learning is hard to measure; it is often covert, often long-term, manifesting itself as motivation and desire to learn for its own sake. Students first learn through interaction with others and then internalize their thoughts and feelings (Vygotsky 1978). High quality human relationships can have rapid transformative effects on students. Technological design which incorporates such understanding is more likely to succeed and the design process should emulate an empathic approach by focusing on the needs of the user – utilizing techniques such as listening, dialogue and collaboration with users – throughout the design process.

Technology is often developed in relative isolation, by programmers with limited knowledge of learning process or developed for business and then inappropriately transferred to educational settings. Consequently the values imbued in the design and nature of the technology may be very different from those which educationalists would aspire to. Even if educationalists choose to develop a more human approach to education and technology, the values of a wider society are embedded into culture, thinking and practice. Educationalists need to courageously defend quality experiences and not allow market values to dominate learning and technology inappropriately (Sandel 2009).

Worlds apart: Designers and learners

Some ICT systems are unfathomable because the developer's own technical experience produces designs which work for them. If software is challenging, it excites them; whereas programs that are easy for the average user, the developers may find mundane. For many programmers it can be more important for a program to run without technical faults, than it is for it to work intuitively for the user. It is difficult for technical experts to create intuitive software because mentally they may differ substantially from some users, especially in educational contexts. Equally, designing for interaction is quite different from designing for transmission, but the latter is more likely to match the programmer's and the company's perception of learning and – as indicated above – the transmission mode has prevailed in many educational settings. However, much software is inadequately tested *in situ*, perhaps working well in an exchange between several people in the workshop but failing when user numbers rise as with school-based and university software.

In addition, the ubiquitous nature of computing requires each system to communicate with many others and if this interaction fails, all systems may under-perform. If a student registration system in higher education should link to a virtual learning environment (VLE) but struggles, the VLE can be ineffective and frustrating. Negative experiences of systems and software render users less adventurous (Cooper 2005). Educators need time and easy access to high quality machines and software to create enthusiasm for ICT (Mukama and Anderson 2008; Cooper 2005). Whereas robust intuitive technology is liberating, poorly designed technology is annoying and users often blame themselves and lose self-esteem. Systems and software designers focus on the delineation, fragmentation and sequential, rather than the integration of the whole. The culture experienced by many software developers, encourages them to be efficient, mechanical and systematic rather than human and sensitive in their design. Empathic design requires effort, dialogue and consultation.

The competitive structures of academic disciplines, coupled with the relative exclusion of women from the higher levels of the technological field (Gillard et al. 2008) prevents holistic theory from advancing and limits major shifts in the nature and ethics of design. Co-operative multidisciplinary work is required, involving psychology, education, neuroscience, sociology and the many branches of computing, in order to effectively couple a profound understanding of learning to the design process.

Ironically, many virtual learning environments were built precisely to reduce the need for human contact – to enable university students, in particular, to learn independently. This is despite the fact that research (E-novate 2003) shows the significance of human contact favoured by tutors and students, making blended learning more successful than purely online. Currently education policy demands that technology is overused for auditing and monitoring and the transmission of a rigid curriculum, at the expense of expanding learning possibilities through creative interaction, exploration and dynamic research (Williams 2005). In order to make good decisions, leaders at all levels need to understand the human, affective and moral issues in learning generally and how that applies to learning technology.

Good technology can affirm and enhance humanity

Some theoretical and empirical research does pursue more empathic, user-centred design from infant classrooms to artificial intelligence. The European Union encouraged futuristic research in the 1990s, funding ten projects in education with young children (Siraj-Blatchford 2004). These emphasized affective issues – including enjoyment, curiosity and engagement – rather than teaching, testing and basic skills. Powerful arguments have been made for including children in the design process for hardware and software (Druin 1999; 2009) and for the embedding of specific cultural aspects in design (Young 2008) to meet the needs of diverse audiences.

The significance of the affective is recognized in human computer interaction and in artificial intelligence (Self 1999; Sloman 2001; Cooper 2003a). The Massachusetts Institute of Technology (MIT) is one of the foremost examples of research into affective issues in the design of technology aiming to bridge the gap between human beings and technology. Neural networks have been a major development in computing and mimic the multi-sensory, parallel processing and impressionistic approach which the human brain uses, as opposed to the serial, sequential model of traditional machine-processing. Some of the most successful recent software is intuitive and multi-sensory. Apple has led the way with intuitive, graphical user-interfaces and applications. Young children could easily create animations on the standard Apple machine long before PCs managed an equivalent. Currently the iPhone is having a powerful impact, with an interface which is sensory and sensitive. The explosion of the use of social networking software and visual media such as YouTube and virtual worlds like Second Life has occurred because they appeal to the affective through the use of picture, video, animation or interaction.

Technology can be excellent for differentiation, both in terms of content and process. It endows the untidy with presentation skills and can support early creativity and higher order skills for children who are just becoming literate. It can guide, repeat sounds and show pictures for early readers, creating music and voice and offering intense interaction at an appropriate level and feedback where none would have been available. It can create enjoyment and fun in areas of the curriculum renowned for dullness. It can offer scaffolding for the imagination through the use of photography and film and animation, bringing pictures from outer space and around the world into the classroom. Technology could facilitate the personalisation of learning (Rudd 2009), and indeed is excellent for personal research and motivation.

Some technologists and educationalists are considering what technology should and could be used for, such as helping to understand and solve global problems (Lima and Brown 2007) or to improve development and reduce poverty (Franklin 2007). They consider the hidden issues of exclusion, for example in terms of gender (Gillard et al. 2008) or the digital divide (Rudd 2001). Technology clearly does have many humanitarian applications when so designed.

The next section returns to ICT integrated classrooms where software has been designed to increase empathy, improve relationships, aid communication and enhance learning (Cooper and Brna 2004; 2003; Cooper 2005). The theoretical and practical findings could be embedded in future educational technology to enhance human interaction.

Creating and sustaining empathic and ICT integrated classrooms

The Networked Interactive Media in Schools project (NIMIS) was an international, European Union funded project which applied theoretical understanding about the importance of frequent and positive interaction to the design of a futuristic classroom (Cooper and Brna 2004). Using the participant design process (Chin et al. 1997), a highly interactive year one classroom (five and six year olds) was created in the UK, in which computers with child-friendly tablets and a large interactive board – embedded thoughtfully in the classroom environment – enabled frequent, high quality interaction through increased collaboration. Video analysis revealed twice the levels of positive emotion and engagement than in the normal classroom. Empathic participant design had ensured consultation with children and teachers about what kind of equipment, layout and software might assist these very young children to write stories. Paper and pencil versions of the software were tried in the classroom before iterative versions were tested and improved *in situ*. An empathic intelligent agent was created, in the form of an older child, to support creative writing.

The integrated and multimedia nature of the interaction was important. The class learned intensely together in a shared space with a sense of common interest, the human and the computer interaction complementing each other. Children were delighted and engaged by the colours, sound, size and interactivity of the large screen. This was apparent in the video analysis and the interviews. Whole–class sessions became more interactive and fun. The children could explain why they liked the big screen, whilst the teachers were also aware of its power to engage and how it facilitated teaching (Cooper and Brna 2004).

The success of the project, nominated for a European prize, led to several others. Ten years later, large interactive screens can now be found in most British classrooms, although less emphasis has been given to access for students themselves – a concept central to the theory behind the original project. Many primary schools function with one computer lab, a weaker way of introducing technology because logistics mean it is used sparingly by any class and is detached from the normal work and interaction of the classroom. The large interactive screens are often the preserve of teachers, resulting in whole class teaching and reducing levels of empathy from a profound to a functional level (see Chapter 8). Though the original system was designed ethically, over time the values of finance and transmissive learning prevailed. In the project, the shared space in which all interaction occurs, contrasts sharply with the virtual learning environments students use in universities, which are often dull, disjointed and predominantly text-based. Even when podcasts are available, the ability to immediately reflect on the content with others is challenging and the possibility of tutors valuing students' understanding is difficult with multiple large groups on line.

A subsequent project, 'The ICT and Whole Child Project (Cooper and Brna 2003), funded by the Nuffield Foundation and Leeds University, extended the work of the NIMIS project. It built another computer integrated classroom for year two students (six and seven years old) using participant design and compared the ICT-embedded classroom with a normal one over the course of two years. A range of cross-curricular software and internet access was installed on the machines. In addition to the interactive whiteboard and round table with four small tablet computers, the classroom had a scanner, digital camera, remote keyboard and electronic microscope.

The project revealed that teachers work to engage students and focus their attention in a multi-sensory and varied way, allowing them to be absorbed and emotionally involved in the learning process. Self-esteem was considered to be vital to positive emotion and interaction and teachers invested considerable thought and effort into raising esteem through sensitive interaction and positive reinforcement and through building on student's own interests. Affective issues were revealed to be at the heart of learning and quite distinct from the emphasis on transmission mode prevalent in the application of the English National Curriculum. Subsequent initiatives such as 'Excellence and Enjoyment' (DFES 2003) are now recognizing the role of enjoyment in learning and the link to achievement and may be bringing about changes in classroom ethos in England.

Positive emotion was generated in the computer-embedded classroom (Cooper and Brna 2003), where teachers and students collaborated around the machines, ensuring one to one conversations and positive interaction. Teachers felt that good facilities enhanced teaching and learning, suggesting that the quality and quantity of ICT provision is vital to its optimum use. High quality ICT, which is designed to meet needs and provide continually reliable responses, adds to the positive atmosphere and engagement in the classroom; both teachers and children rapidly experience success, which improves self-esteem and skills. The technology supports students and gives them pleasure and new challenges, mathematically compounding their positive sense of self and improving teacher-pupil relationships.

Despite initial anxiety, the class-teacher, close to retirement, saw the benefits this classroom brought both to her own and to the students' learning. She became a convert, changing her attitudes towards technology, and developed strong opinions about how computers should be deployed in school:

> But I do think there's great, great value in having them in the class, rather than having a suite … Because if they are in the classroom it's hands-on, they can go to it … because it covers everything, so you can use it in every subject and therefore when it's in the classroom it's there, if it's in a suite they are going to do it for half an hour. And I've changed my mind over that.

She felt computers supported students with special needs by increasing their concentration span, excitement and self-esteem, thereby improving the classroom atmosphere. Affective issues were central: *'The most important thing is your self-esteem'.* The computers promoted positive emotions:

'As a tool I would just use it more because they enjoy it, you know, it's all about – enjoying the thing'. She felt the big screen supported literacy and she used role-play to make the students the expert in front of the screen, thus equalizing relationships and empowering these young children who worked collaboratively and confidently.

After two years, achievements were higher in the computer-embedded classrooms than the ordinary ones, as was self-esteem (Cooper and Brna 2003). Students had twice the computing skills and were able to use five times as many programs as students in the comparative class. Students in the ordinary classroom used only two basic programs and were very insecure, even in basic tasks. They had insufficient access to use ICT across the curriculum and the teacher could not model ICT skills or benefit from the multi-sensory features of an interactive board. The project class achieved more highly in standardized tests on average, despite having lower starting levels and more special needs students.

The nature of the design process was key to the success of these two projects. Empathic participant design (Scaife et al. 1997; Cooper and Brna 2004) ensured that the computer integrated classrooms were appropriate to the needs of the teachers and students and supported human interaction and collaboration alongside human computer interaction. However, as the giant screens were introduced more widely, their function became distorted by a blanket curriculum dominated by teacher-led activities. The engaging qualities of multimedia are often used by the teacher for control and students often have very limited daily access, either to large or small screens.

The Ripple Project (Cooper 2003b), funded by the British Educational and Communications Technology Agency (Becta), looked at the impact of the two previous projects on all the staff in the school. It identified the importance of positive affect in the learning of adults also, and the importance of embedding ICT in the curriculum in well designed classrooms with high quality hard and software – rather than teaching technology as skills in separate suites, away from normal classroom. Teachers preferred personalized support in school, on their own equipment as and when they needed it. Blanket training sessions, in distant institutions with different equipment and software, were not considered useful. National schemes of work did not enthuse students or teachers. However, daily cross-curricular use of ICT, embedded meaningfully in subjects and themes, did enthuse teachers and children. Interestingly, older and more experienced teachers were more able to integrate ICT effectively across the curriculum, while younger teachers and teachers with larger classes tended to adopt a skills-based approach which was less enjoyable. Good equipment, in carefully designed rooms, all day every day, helped teachers and children to learn and to appreciate ICT. Teachers with poorer equipment, with less opportunity to observe the benefits of ICT or to use it themselves, remained more sceptical about its benefits and more anxious about its use. Like traditional literacy, computer literacy benefits from frequency of practice and self-esteem rises accordingly.

As with the previous project, powerful emotions were associated with teachers' ICT learning, which confirmed the central nature of affect in learning and the importance of supportive and timely relationships, as well as practice opportunities to support learning (Cooper and Brna 2003). Real understanding emerged about the complex causes of staff motivation, interest and learning in ICT. Teachers are essentially pragmatic people with a complex task to fulfil. If resources are helpful to teaching and learning they will use them – if not, they consider their effort wasted. Equipment and software must enhance provision and support the learning process to be adopted enthusiastically. This requires ethical and humane design of ICT.

The importance of positive emotions in creating atmospheres which optimize learning seems to be crucial for staff and student development. Poor ratios and curriculum rigidity, which deaden the learning atmosphere for pupils, do the same for staff. Staff, like students, need learning tailored to their specific needs and context, in an emotionally sensitive climate. They require sufficient high quality equipment, well maintained and with an appropriate range of quality software, to enable them to meet pupils' needs across the curriculum. They need practice, and equipment to practise on. Above all, they need to enjoy their teaching and to have success using ICT. Moreover, if positive emotional exchange lies at the heart of interaction and learning, then teachers must model enjoyment to inspire the same in students.

Conclusion

There is considerable evidence to show the importance and potential of adopting an ethical approach to the design of educational technology based on the significance of affect in learning relationships, a factor which has many potential benefits for human society and in particular for supporting learning. Technologies could be developed which utilize many more human skills in positive environments. As a species we might then be engaged in higher levels of interaction in our technological environments and thus potentially able to learn faster, more pleasurably and more widely. Technological design for learning should be both by humans and for humans, whether designing pencils or sophisticated software. This chapter argues that the limitations of the values in traditional business and education systems have held back the provision of high quality technology in educational environments, a situation which needs to be remedied. The success of social software which does value complex human interaction clearly indicates important ways forward for educational applications and, given the advent of unparalleled changes to come with future generations of technology, we must build these ethics and knowledge into systems development.

Learning holistically and interactively can potentially enable individuals and groups to behave morally by listening to others, valuing others' perspectives, showing mutual respect, taking note of others' feelings through attendance to non-verbal signals and sharing understanding more equitably and more rapidly. This wider application of these approaches to learning could enable rapid intervention in global problems, using advances in technology and research to respond to needs and to facilitate the sharing of rapidly evolving knowledge more swiftly. Valuing and extending the expert human skills of sensitivity, compassion, creativity and imagination – qualities which make the human species unique – we could conceivably engender new levels of learning and development within society. The joint knowledge and skill created could raise the quality of the lives of all people and discourage the less desirable traits of individualism, greed and cruelty which divide us and restrict human development.

References

Aspy, D. (1972). *Towards a Technology for Humanising Education*. Champaign, IL: Illinois Research Press.

Broadfoot, P. (2000).*Culture, Learning and Comparison: BERA Stenhouse Lecture 1999*. Southwell: BERA.

Chin, G. Jr., Rosson, M.B. and Carroll, J.M. (1997). 'Participatory Analysis: Shared Development Requirements from Scenarios'. In S. Pemberton (ed.), *Proceedings of CHI'97: Human Factors in Computing Systems*, pp. 162–9. New York: ACM Press/Addison-Wesley.

Clark, D. (1996). *Schools as Learning Communities: Transforming Education*. London: Cassell.

Cooper, B. (2003a). 'Care – Making the Affective Leap: More than a Concerned Interest in a Learner's Cognitive Abilities', *International Journal of Artificial Intelligence in Education*, 13 (1), 3–9.

——(2003b). 'Emotion and Relationships at the Heart of Learning with ICT – For Children And Teachers: The Ripple Project'. Paper presented at BECTA Annual Conference, 13 June.

——(2004). 'Empathy, Interaction and Caring: Teachers' Roles in a Constrained Environment', *Pastoral Care in Education*, 22 (3), 12–21.

——(2005). 'Learning to Love ICT: Emotion and Esteem in Learning for Teachers and Children'. Paper presented at AERA Annual Conference, Montreal, 11–15 April.

——and Brna, P. (2003). 'The Significance of Affective Issues in Successful Learning with ICT for Year One and Two Pupils and Their Teachers: The Final Outcomes of the ICT and the Whole Child Project'. Paper presented at BERA, Heriott-Watt University, Edinburgh, 10–13 September.

——and Brna, P. (2004). 'A classroom of the future today'. In J. Siraj-Blatchford (ed.), *Developing New Technologies for Young Children*. Stoke-on-Trent: Trentham Books.

Damasio, A. (1999). *The Feeling of What Happens: Body, Emotion and the Making of Consciousness*. London: Heinemann.

—— (2003). *Looking for Spinoza: Joy, Sorrow and the Feeling Brain*. London: Heinemann.

Department for Education and Skills (DfES) (2003). *Excellence and Enjoyment: A Strategy for Schools*. London: DfES.

Druin, A. (ed.) (1999). *The Design of Children's Technology*. San Francisco: Morgan-Kaufmann.

—— (2009). *Mobile Technology for Children: Designing for Interaction and Learning*. Cambridge, MA: Morgan Kaufmann/Elsevier.

Eckman, P. (1997). 'Should We Call It Expression Or Communication?', *Innovations in Social Science Research*, 10 (4), 333–44.

E-novate (2003). SOLT – *A training guidance Project lessons for the future* –some findings of the SOLT project, <http://www.solt.info/project/SOLT%20main-streaming%20findings%20doc%20final%20version%20e-novate.pdf> accessed 10 September 2009.

Floridi, L. (2007). 'A Look at the Future Impact of ICT on Our Lives', *The Information Society*, 23, 59–64.

Franklin, M. (2007). 'The Pursuit and Development of Poverty Reduction through Information and Communication Technology (ICT) in Trinidad and Tobago', *Journal of Eastern Caribbean Studies*, 32 (2), 23–49.

Gibbs, C. (2006). *To Be a Teacher: Journeys Towards Authenticity*. Auckland, New Zealand: Pearson Education.

Gillard, H., Howcroft, D., Mitev, N. and Richardson, H. (2008). 'Missing Women': Gender, ICTs and the Shaping of the Global Economy', *Information Technology for Development*, 14 (4), 262–79.

Klein, J. (1956). *The Study of Groups*. London: Routledge & Kegan Paul.

Kress, G. and van Leeuwen, T. (2001). *Multimodal Discourse: The Modes and Media of Contemporary Communication*. London: Edward Arnold.

Law, P. and Chu, W.R. (2008). 'ICTs and China: An Introduction', *Knowledge, Technology and Politics*, 21, 3–7.

Leal, M.R.M. (2002). 'The Caring Relationship'. Paper presented at the Ninth Annual International Conference on 'Education Spirituality and the Whole Child', Roehampton, London, June.

Lima, C.O. and Brown, S.W. (2007). 'ICT for Development: Are Brazilian Students Well-Prepared to Become Global Citizens?', *Education Media International*, 44 (2), 141–53.

Long, L., MacBlain, S.F. and MacBlain, M.S. (2007). 'Supporting the Pupil with Dyslexia at Secondary Level: An Emotional Model of Literacy', *Journal of Adolescent and Adult Literacy*, 51 (2), 124–34.

Mehrabian, A. (1971). *Silent Messages*. Belmont, CA: Wadsworth.

Mukama, E. and Anderson, S.B. (2008). 'Coping with Change in ICT-based Learning Environments: Newly Qualified Rwandan Teacher's Reflections', *Journal of Computer Assisted Learning*, 24, 156–66.

Narvaez, D. and Vaydich, J.L. (2008). 'Moral Development and Behaviour under the Spotlight of the Neurobiological Sciences', *Journal of Moral Education*, 37 (3), 289–312.

Purkey, W.W. (1970). *Self-concept and School Achievement*. Englewood Cliffs, NJ: Prentice-Hall.

Rogers, C.R. (1975). 'Empathic: An Unappreciated Way of Being', *The Counselling Psychologist*, 5 (2), 2.

Rudd, T. (2001). *The Digital Divide*. London: Becta. Crown.

Rudd, T. (2009). 'Rethinking the Principles of Personalisation and the Role of Digital Technologies'. In R. Krumsvik (ed.), *Learning in the Network Society and the Digitized School*. New York: Nova Science Publishers.

Sandel, M. (2009). 'The Reith Lectures, 1: Markets and Morals', BBC Radio 4, 9 June 2009.

Scaife, M., Rogers, Y., Aldrich, F. and Davies, M. (1997). 'Designing for or Designing with? Informant Design for Interactive Learning Environments'. In *CHI'97: Proceedings of Human Factors in Computing Systems*, pp. 343–50. New York: ACM.

Self, J. (1999). 'The Defining Characteristics of Intelligent Tutoring Systems Research', *International Journal of Artificial Intelligence in* Education, 10 (3–4), 350–64.

Siraj-Blatchford. J. (ed.) (2004). *Developing New Technologies for Young Children*. Stoke-on-Trent: Trentham Books.

Sloman. A. (2001). 'Varieties of Affect and the CogAff Architecture Schema'. Paper presented at AISB'01, Symposium on Emotion, Cognition and Affective Computing, York University.

Vygotsky, L.S. (1978). *Mind in Society*. London and Cambridge, MA: Harvard University Press.

——(1986). *Thought and Language*, trans. by Alex Kozulin. Cambridge, MA: MIT Press.

Williams, P. (2005). 'Lessons from the Future: ICT Scenarios and the Education of Teachers', *Journal of Education for Teaching*, 31 (4), 319–39.

Young, P.A. (2008). 'Integrating Culture in the Design of ICTs', *British Journal of Educational Technology*, 39 (1), 6–17.

PART 2

Striving to be ethical:
Engaging with children and young people

SUSAN GROUNDWATER-SMITH

8 The dilemmas we face: Designing a curriculum for vulnerable children in short-term care

This chapter will consider the ways in which a school designed to support vulnerable children in short-term residential care (a two-week period) has set about framing a curriculum that can have meaning and relevance and be connected to the students' lives and experiences. I will first reflect upon the ways in which schooling can be characterized as riddled by dilemmas and then render the concept of 'curriculum' as problematic, particularly so in a challenging environment, taking it beyond the commonplace definition. I will characterize it in relation to three embedded areas: the complex context; the substance to be considered along with the media to be employed; and, the reasoning that lies behind the choices that are made.

I will argue that to design a curriculum framework that has meaning for a range of students who know little of each other or their teacher requires careful attention, so that fundamental touchstones can be found to which all can relate. Two strong trajectories have been identified as needing to inform the framework. The first of these employs accelerated literacy, a process based upon a teaching and learning scaffold that develops skills through the reading and analysis of a shared text that is engaging and age-appropriate. Its roots are to be found in Indigenous education within Australia. Accelerated literacy is considered to be highly adaptable to the two week intensive residential nature of the programme, with links being made to shared student experiences in the local metropolitan area. Texts are carefully selected on the basis that they can be connected to various sites that the students can visit – for example, the zoo, or a local surf beach. The second trajectory to inform the framework nurtures emotional literacy and resilience. It will be seen that there could exist a tension between the two trajectories and that this tension requires the generation of a coherent and manageable pathway. In considering the nature of the dilemmas faced in this specific case of professional practice, I shall conclude by appealing to a framework of ethical maxims that remind us to: exercise care; do no harm; be open and transparent; and, give students agency and voice in authentic ways (Ahmed and Machold 2004).

Thinking about dilemmas

One way to imagine a dilemma is to think about it in terms of being trapped between a rock and a hard place. From this standpoint, whichever way one turns one is beset by unimaginable difficulties and the choice is that of the lesser of two evils. If this were so, then teaching in challenging environments would be well-nigh impossible. Rather, I wish to construct dilemmas as complex situations where the choices have to be unravelled and the consequences for taking particular paths weighed up, balancing the costs and benefits. For example, does one establish oneself as entertaining, setting small and trivial tasks, or does one seek to inculcate in students a sense of effort, that learning effectively may be hard work? Does one praise a student for her effort or for her achievement? Similarly, students also are making operational and personal choices: does one adhere to the notion that it is 'cool to learn' or believe that it may be better to be one of the 'lads and ladettes' of this world, with little commitment to school-valued learning as described by Jackson 2006?

It has been argued by Groundwater-Smith, Ewing and Le Cornu (2007: 12) that the emphasis in relation to dilemmas in schooling rests upon the moral questions surrounding rights. Whose rights need to be considered? The students' rights to control their own work? The teachers' rights to make judgements about student competence? The state's rights to regulate teachers' professional decision making? The parents' rights to have their children educated in a fashion of which they approve? Different stakeholders in education have different rights and each impact upon the other. To discuss rights is to discuss dilemmas.

Arguably the most comprehensive and enduring work that has been undertaken with respect to dilemmas in education has been that which Berlak and Berlak (1981) engaged with in their study of British classrooms in the early 1980s. They developed a theory about dilemmas in schooling by closely observing practice. The Berlak dilemmas have been organised into three sets: control, curriculum and societal (1981: 22–3).

> *Control set:* whole child versus child as student; teacher versus child control of time; teacher versus child control of operations; and, teacher versus child control of standards.

> *Curriculum set:* personal knowledge versus public knowledge; knowledge as content versus knowledge as process; knowledge as given versus knowledge as problematic; learning is holistic versus learning is molecular; intrinsic versus extrinsic motivation; each child is unique versus children have shared characteristics; learning is individual versus learning is social; child as person versus child as client.

> *Societal set:* childhood continuous versus childhood unique; equal allocation of resources versus differential allocation; equal justice under law versus ad hoc application of rules; and, common culture versus subgroup consciousness.

Such a comprehensive and inclusive set of dilemmas challenges us all to recognise the intricacies of the schooling enterprise as a complex social ecosystem.

Curriculum – Text, context and pretext

Some years ago I suggested that we could conceive of 'curriculum' as an 'educational geography' comprising of overlapping and interacting morphologies: text, context and pretext (Groundwater-Smith 1988). By text I suggested the formation included not only the explicit artefacts of curriculum, but also those which were implied or hidden and embodied in written, visual and spoken media. Context was taken to mean the settings, ranging from the micro to the macro in which the text was enacted. Pretext, meanwhile, embodied the reasoning that lay behind the many choices that could be made by all who participated in the enterprise. Such a means of understanding curriculum takes us far beyond the common-sense understanding of the term – which normally includes that which is taught in schools, sets of subjects, sets of materials, performance outcomes and the like – and moves us towards acknowledging schooling, as I have proposed above, as an ecosystem (Barab and Wolff-Michael 2006).

Using a somewhat different metaphor and thinking broadly about educational practice, Kemmis writes of 'practice architectures' that embrace the sayings, doings and interactions that take place within specific sites. He argues that 'practice is always shaped and oriented in its course by ideas, meanings and intentions' (2009: 22). These, in turn, are influenced by values, preconditions, cultural mores, and are socially and historically formed.

From these two complementary perspectives it is possible to see that in discussing the case that follows it is critical first to understand the particularities of the context and the ways in which these shape the curriculum dilemmas that will be discussed.

A case for study

Before setting out the nature of the setting that will serve as the case study for this chapter, I wish to say what it is not. It is not an observational case intended to create generalisations; it is not an evaluation; and it is not an instrumental one where there was a degree of control over what would be examined and why. Rather, it is a case deserving of study that we might learn from – learn something of the ways in which practices result from solving the daily challenges faced by the practitioners. In Simons' words:

Case study is useful for exploring and understanding the process and dynamics of change. Through describing, documenting and interpreting events as they unfold in 'real life' settings, it can determine the factors that were critical in implementation of a programme or policy and analyse patterns and links between them. (2009: 23)

Maryanne Lodge[1] is a long-standing facility that acts as a respite care setting for young school-age children (aged 5–15 years) who may be facing particularly difficult circumstances at home due to conditions associated with, among other things, family illness, poverty, sudden bereavement and/or Indigeneity.[2] Groups, coming from regions across the State, are brought to the Lodge for a two week period. For many it is their first time away from home and their first visit to a large metropolitan city beside the ocean. The building, which is over eighty years old is perched above the sea with ready access to the beach below. Some youngsters have never seen such a large body of water before.

It is a warm and welcoming place for young people who not only experience a curriculum aimed at enjoyment and co-operation, but also learn to live alongside each other in dormitory style accommodation. While in residence the children undergo health, medical, dental and optometry screening that will stand them in good stead when they return home. The power of the experience is represented through the enduring memories held by those who may have attended Maryanne Lodge many years before. Former residents can send in their memories to a dedicated website, such as this one from Maureen:

---

1   The name of the residential care facility has been changed and details of the particular Australian state or territory omitted in the interests of confidentiality. Few such facilities exist and the greater detail would allow it to be quickly identified. Two leading participants in the setting have read and agreed to the account.

2   Indigenous people in Australia are taken to include Aboriginal people and Torres Strait Islanders.

Thanks – 22 years on

'I was only thinking today and speaking with my Mum about my wonderful experience at Maryanne Lodge in 1984, age 8. We were talking about Maryanne Lodge today because I had an Optometrist appointment and it was whilst I was at Maryanne Lodge that my eye problem was discovered. At the time my parents had just split up, my sister had moved inter state for a year (we are close), we were quite poor, I had learning difficulties, I had never really had a holiday, I was acting out (stealing etc), the list could go on. My favourite memories at Maryanne Lodge were swimming at the beach, getting the yummiest desserts from the leftovers from a bakery, getting to order my lunch, doing fun things and meeting new people. I am now a mother of three, University educated, Justice of the Peace (so I must have stopped stealing – no criminal record!!) etc. I am okay. I just wanted to say thanks for the work you do I still vividly remember my experience, it was much needed, much fun and much appreciated.'

Over the years a range of curriculum strategies have been developed; however, it would be fair to say that until recently the programme was seen to be one more associated with rest and recreation rather than attempting to build skills. It was seen that the shortness of the stay made for difficulties in developing and implementing more formal studies. Also, there was a considerable challenge to the teachers to find ways of better knowing their students and providing worthwhile experiences for them beyond those where they visited various local sites as day-long excursions. Not that such experiences should be discounted. Teachers reported that the informal nature of excursions that are treated as 'down time' allowed them to often have sustained and revealing discussions with the children. As one observed, 'I hear more about home and how things are on a half-hour bus journey, than for a whole week.'

Changing curriculum texts

Recent years in Australia have seen federal programmes which have emphasized the enhancement of what has become known as 'quality teaching', with additional resources being made available for teachers' professional learning in specific areas. Included in these are literacy and technology development. Under one such programme, Maryanne Lodge successfully applied for funds to enhance skills in these areas – albeit within the constraints of a short timeframe.

The first initiative to be undertaken was to examine the ways in which young people, in different age cohorts, were familiar with the ways in which reading was undertaken and understood. Often struggling within larger classes the time at Maryanne Lodge enabled students to function in smaller groups, paying particular attention to explicit features of text as enacted through 'accelerated literacy'.

In their submission for funding the school outlined, among other things, the following intentions:

Through action learning teachers will:

- Maximise their own and student learning experiences by explicitly addressing the engagement of students on a number of curriculum levels (e.g. story telling, oral literacy, visual art representations, understanding of human society in its environment).
- Expand their pedagogical; repertoire to encompass all aspects of Quality Teaching and Learning and as a result raise student engagement, learning outcomes and increase literacy skills for all students based on their individual learning styles.
- Developing a concise Accelerated Literacy Unit using a different text for each class. This will ensure sustainability of the program as staff complete their 3 year tenures. Accelerated Literacy has been identified through the New South Wales Department of Education and Training as an effective strategy to increase the engagement of Indigenous students. Due to the limited classroom time spent at

Maryanne Lodge to measure the success of these units each teacher will conduct a KWL (Knowledge, what do they want to know and what they have learnt) with their class. By informally questioning and discussing, prior to the unit and at the completion, the teacher can gather data regarding the knowledge gained by the students.

At the core of accelerated literacy lies the notion of developing a literate orientation to text. As Gray (2007) argues, it permits students to be 'apprenticed' into ways of talking, viewing and thinking that are part of a literate discourse in Western Culture. Accelerated literacy was originally developed to assist Aboriginal students in remote Australian communities and designed to equip them to engage with text more successfully than had hitherto been the case. It was also seen as a means of enhancing social inclusion. While a number of students at Maryanne Lodge have an Indigenous heritage, not all of them do so; the programme, however, was seen as one that they might all enjoy. Clearly it would not be possible to fully engage with such a substantial pedagogy in two weeks; however, it was seen that a discrete unit of work could be built around specific age appropriate texts. One such example will be offered here.

All students at Maryanne Lodge can be seen to have come from another place. Being 'out of place' requires both emotional and physical adjustments. The text chosen for the junior class was one that narrated the story of a young boy visiting the local zoo. It was a Big Book, *Nan, Dad and Me at the Zoo* (Russell 2004), and one that was designed for shared reading. The zoo is a special place for Dylan, a young Gamillaroi man. In this story he shares with the reader a happy, special day at the zoo with his Nan and his Dad. The book would be read a number of times with advanced organizers and follow-up activities. It was intended to connect not only to the children's sense of place and that of the animals in the zoo, but also to their emotions and their own narratives.

In my own role as a 'critical friend' to the project I kept an electronic journal from which I composed short 'think pieces' that I shared with the teachers. Below is an extract from one such entry describing the ways in which the teacher oriented the children to the text and the ways in which it would connect to the visit to the zoo:

'A. did not initially read the Big Book, but rather familiarised the children with its content and used it as a means of anticipating the various encounters they might have at the zoo. He explained they would be arriving by bus rather than ferry, but would still be excited about anticipating what they might find. He suggested that some might be rather "scared" on the sky safari, but it was a great adventure. Throughout he used colloquial and relaxed language and in spite of only having met the children the day before appeared familiar with them as they were with him.

A. used humour to draw the children in and connected the experiences of zoo animals with their own – for example the elephant was missing a tusk and this was just like one of them missing a tooth. Similarly, Clementine the Pig needed a "bucket of suncream" just as they needed to protect their own skin. He pointed out surprises, such as the lions flicking their ears to rid them of insects. He teased them with the bird show and a bird who "steals dollars" but for them to wait to find out what happens after that. A. appeared to be very conscious of engaging all of the younger students and ensuring that they understood the concepts and vocabulary.

As a follow up to the visit I sat in on A's class while they revisited the Big Book and connected it to their experience. He read them the text and pointed out the features of the book without over-labouring things. He explained that he would be reading it a third time and would intersperse the reading with direct questioning. In this way the young children would be continuing to develop their literacy skills.'

Along with skills associated with accelerated literacy, students were also enabled to develop their technological skills, including being introduced to a simple animation program, *Marvin*, that uses customized 3D animated characters to communicate to community- and school-based audiences through the integration of voice, computer-generated voice, written text, images, video and Microsoft Power Point presentations.[3]

---

3   See <http://www.marvin.com.au/marvin/>.

As a result of their engagement with technology, each cohort worked to create a DVD that would record their experiences and that they could take with them on their return to their home schools and also share with their families.

Thus a curriculum, based on literacy and technology was being designed and enacted at Maryanne Lodge.[4] However, there remained a number of other areas of concern based upon considering student wellbeing. In effect the accelerated literacy programme, referred to at this beginning of this chapter, went a long way to satisfying one of the curriculum trajectories in terms of enhancing student literacy skills *in situ*, but there remained the challenge of nurturing emotional literacy and resilience. A number of readings were presented to the staff for discussion, for example Wyn (2007: 35) where it was posited that:

> While older educational agendas such as literacies and numeracy remain significant, it is argued that education is increasingly important for its role in assisting young people to develop the capacities and skills that will enable them to live well and that will enhance social cohesion.

Cummins and Laue's *Personal Wellbeing Index – School Children* was tabled. The seven domains: happy with life as a whole, standard of living, personal health, achievement in life, personal relationships, personal safety, feeling part of the community, and future security, were seen to be simply and clearly expressed.

Attention was also drawn to the Ministerial Council on Education, Employment, Training and Youth Affairs (MCEETYA) commissioned paper undertaken by The Australian Council of Educational Research (ACER) prepared by Julian Fraillon (2004). The Mission Australia 'snap-shot', *Developing Resilience at Every Stage of a Young Person's Life*, was presented, as was the newsletter for schools from the Centre for Health Promotion, Women's and Children's Hospital, *Resilience and Optimism Promote Students' Learning.* Thus it may be seen that an emerging curriculum

---

4   Of course there were other key learning areas also being addressed, such as those associated with healthy living and personal development.

text was being considered one that would enhance social and emotional literacy, wellbeing and resilience.

Of course, it was not seen that the previous work on accelerated literacy was incommensurable with this new direction, but rather it became a matter of which should have priority. The year 2009 not only saw a new direction being taken, but also a staff turnover with three new teachers joining the staff.

A significant initiative was the involvement of senior students in engagement with the Effective Lifelong Learning Inventory (ELLI) (Deakin Crick, Broadfoot and Claxton 2004) that aims to develop 'learning power' among students. As a self-assessment instrument that allows students to identify and develop enhanced learning strategies that will enable effective learning – changing and learning, critical curiosity, meaning-making, creativity, resilience, strategic awareness and learning relationships – the inventory was believed to have great potential. Students undertaking the inventory can construct profiles that are seen as 'spider graphs' that provide a picture of them as learners, feedback against each dimension, insight into student motivation and a diagnostic tool for examining self-perception. By completing the inventory on more than one occasion students can plot their own growth as they develop their 'learning power'. However, there are some challenges for employing such a tool at Maryanne Lodge. The inventory is undertaken electronically and is coded by the Lifelong Learning Foundation. Thus, each time a student uses it there is a cost involved. Since the students are only in the facility for two weeks it is neither feasible nor desirable to undertake it on multiple occasions.

More profitably, the school has chosen to have several cohorts of students use the inventory so that class profiles might be developed that would indicate patterns of learning capacities, skills and awareness that could be used to nurture and sustain growth and development in terms of student learning engagement, not only for senior students but also for those who are younger. Thus, for 2009 it was decided to continue the work of accelerated literacy and use it as a springboard into more explicit attention being paid to social and emotional literacy using a range of tools. In the Junior classes there was to be an emphasis upon the text, *In My Backyard* (Spudvilas and Hilton 2001), which allows discussion of narrative structure, the use of meta-language and links to concepts of place and identity; clearly an ongoing theme for these young people.

The senior students were to work through a text created by Indigenous students from a regional High School that raises questions and issues relating to being in and out of 'place', and the consequences for identity and self-esteem – issues that correspond closely with the dimensions of the ELLI learning profile. It has been argued that the characters in the student-created text symbolically align with a given learning-disposition and that by closely examining and discussing the text students would also be employing the language for learning. Thus, these students were effectively engaged in a curriculum that attended to both literacies and emotional and cultural wellbeing.

Conclusion – Dilemmas revisited

This brief case study brings into sharp relief the ways in which a curriculum to meet the needs of vulnerable young people is a work in progress that is beset by dilemmas in relation to the extent to which one emphasis or another is placed upon the processes and procedures that will be involved. Just as the study cited earlier (Berlak and Berlak 1981) brought into sharp relief the dilemmas within the curriculum set – i.e. personal knowledge versus public knowledge, knowledge as content versus knowledge as process, knowledge as given versus knowledge as problematic, learning as holistic versus learning as molecular, intrinsic versus extrinsic motivation, each child is unique versus children have shared characteristics, learning is individual versus learning is social, child as person versus child as client – so too might it be argued that for Maryanne Lodge there is an abrasion between hurrying up and slowing down learning. The school deeply desires to make a difference in the lives of these young people, but it only has two weeks in which to realise this ambition.

As has been reiterated, Maryanne Lodge only has a short time to make an impact upon the learning of the young people in its care. In the conclusion to his book *Designing Learning for Diverse Classrooms* Paul Dufficy makes a plea for us to 'slow down the learning':

> The conversations and tasks that I have described in this book could be seen as one take on a slower approach to teaching. Such an approach does not mean that some things are not done quickly, but it does mean that learning and development trajectories of children and young people are not ignored in a rush to complete the task, finish the lesson or cover the curriculum. The old adage to make haste slowly is relevant here. (2005: 148)

Slowing down the learning does not only apply to the students. Faced with the challenge of making significant adaptations to her teaching led R. (a newly appointed teacher) to slow down her own professional learning based on her growing experiences:

> I decided I was not going to try to, as you might say 'move mountains' until I had made some observations. I wanted to consciously spend a term just making close observations of the students' behaviours while teaching. This would then help me to ensure my teaching was of a high quality and addressing the needs of all my students as best I can for the short stay they have at Maryanne Lodge.

Making decisions about curriculum texts in context is first and foremost an ethical concern. The pretexts that are adopted must be addressed to the mental, social and physical health of the students, many of whom have come from the most challenging of circumstances. Those responsible for their wellbeing at Maryanne Lodge face a constant struggle to provide an experience that is of the highest quality and has the potential to be life-changing.

In their account of the connection between quality and ethics, Ahmed and Machold provide us with a set of domains for ethical accountability as a form of moral responsibility; these are voiced as maxims:

- The maxim of no-harm (as far as is possible and predictable)
- The maxim of transparency
- The maxim of voice

- The maxim of equity
- The maxim of benefit
- The maxim of integrity
- The maxim of liberty
- The maxim of care

(2004: 539–42)

By attending to these maxims it is possible to better weigh up the curriculum dilemmas that are faced. First and foremost the staff are concerned to do 'good' and make a difference; they do so in a very public light as they engage not only with each student, but also with their home schools and in their conversations with many who have an interest in their work. They seek to benefit each individual student by providing them with tools that they can take back with them to sites where, in the past, they may have experienced difficulties, even failure. Importantly, they care about instilling enduring competencies that may take the young people forward encouraging them in a sense of their own positive identity as learners, not only in the short-term but into the future.

References

Ahmed, P. and Machold, S. (2004). 'The Quality and Ethics Connection: Towards Virtuous Organisations', *Total Quality Management*, 15 (4), 527–45.

Barab, S. and Wolff-Michael, R. (2006). 'Curriculum-based Ecosystems: Supporting Knowing from an Ecological Perspective', *Educational Researcher*, 35 (5), 3–13.

Berlak, A. and Berlak, H. (1981). *Dilemmas of Schooling*. London: Methuen.

Cummins, R. and Lau, A. (2006). *Personal Wellbeing Index – School Children*. Melbourne: Deakin University.

Deakin Crick, R., Broadfoot, P. and Claxton, G. (2004). 'Developing an Effective Lifelong Learning Inventory: The ELLI Project', *Assessment in Education: Principles, Policies and Practices*, 11 (3), 247–72.

Dufficy, P. (2005). *Designing Learning for Diverse Classrooms*. Sydney: Primary English Teachers Association.

Fraillon, J. (2004). *Measuring Student Well-being in the Context of Australian Schooling: Discussion Paper*. Hawthorn: Australian Council for Educational Research.

Gray, B. (2007). *Accelerating the Literacy Development of Indigenous Students*. Darwin: CDU Press.

Groundwater-Smith, S. (1988). 'The Interrogation of Case Records as a Basis for Constructing Curriculum Perspectives'. In J. Nias and S. Groundwater-Smith (eds), *The Enquiring Teacher: Supporting and Sustaining Teacher Research*, pp. 93–105. Lewes: The Falmer Press.

Groundwater-Smith, S., Ewing, R. and Le Cornu, R. (2007). *Teaching Challenges and Dilemmas*. Melbourne: Nelson Australia.

Jackson, C. (2006). *Lads and Ladettes in School*. Buckingham: Open University Press/ McGraw Hill Education.

Kemmis, S. (2009). Understanding Professional Practice: A Synoptic Framework. In B. Green (ed.), *Understanding and Researching Professional Practice*, pp. 19–38. Rotterdam: Sense Publishers.

Russell, D. (2004). *Nan, Dad and Me at the Zoo*. Rockdale: Indig Readers.

Simons, H. (2009). *Case Study Research in Practice*. London: Sage.

Spudvilas, A. and Hilton, N. (2001). *In My Backyard*. Port Melbourne: Lothian Books.

Wyn, J. (2007). Learning to 'become somebody well': Challenges to Educational Policy, *The Australian Educational Researcher*, 34 (3), 36–52.

DOROTHY BOTTRELL

9 Shifting perspectives, representations and dilemmas in work with young people

This chapter explores ethical dilemmas that arise in everyday situations in youth work programs and work with individual young people, and which represent conflicts between emancipatory aims and elements of social control in youth work. The meanings of and responses to dilemmas include and go beyond those anticipated in codes of conduct, statements of professional principles and agency policies and procedures. They are shaped by practitioner knowledge of individual-community-societal relations and conflicting representations of young people. The dilemmas arising out of contested public space and young people's access to education are thus also at times conflicts of procedural and positioned ethics embedded in the location of youth work with disadvantaged young people at an intersection of social, economic and institutional inequities. The reframing of specific instances of youth work as more than local and individual situations relies on fundamental principles of social justice for animating ethical commitment, centred in the youth work relationship with young people and most significantly the commitment to listen.

The scenarios discussed are not direct recounts of my work; they are fictional, though representative of the kinds of work and issues arising in the author's practice over many years as a teacher, youth worker and researcher working with disadvantaged young people. Excerpts from the doctoral research I undertook while working at an inner-city youth centre in Sydney are distinguished from the scenarios by references to publications where further details are available. The centre provides individual support work, recreational and educational programs for young people aged 12–24 from the local public housing estate.

Emancipatory aims and social control functions of youth work

While her toddler sleeps in the stroller, the young woman talks about losing her job and not being able to make ends meet. The restaurant was not doing well enough to keep her on in her casual waitress position of the past eighteen months. The little one needed new shoes and then there were unexpected expenses of medicine when he was sick and the laundromat because the washing machine broke down. It was just a 'one-off' to pay the phone bill so it wouldn't be cut off. She says she hates asking for help, has always made it 'off my own bat' and doesn't want to 'owe anyone'. 'I've been looking after myself since I was thirteen. I'm not a bludger'. She asks if I will speak to the emergency relief agency on her behalf. We talk about other things while she fills out the 'Consent to share information' form. How fast the baby is growing, his new words, how he loves to dance, the difficult access handovers, 'but his dad is really great with him; all the family fuss over him.'

This scenario may be familiar to youth workers in a range of different organizations, settings and services. Individual support work can be straight-forward: the young woman asks for assistance, the youth worker actions it. Procedures are simple, a conversation, a form and a phone call. In ethical terms, however, such routine procedures are anything but 'routine'. The experienced youth worker may not think twice about the consent form, yet it is an artefact of youth work that signifies the importance of privacy and confidentiality. These are universal ethical principles in human services, the procedural ethics enshrined in duty of care, the policy and practice guides of organizations and professional associations. It is an historical artefact of ongoing dialogue and debate concerning the relationships and professionalization of youth work (Bessant 2004a; Sercombe 2007) and the rights of its young constituencies (Sercombe 1997b). Procedural and professional codes of ethics for working with young people enshrine legal and moral requirements for child protec-tion and recognize young people's vulnerability to potential exploitation in relationships of unequal power and in which young people are reliant on the facilitating role of youth work for access to resources they need.

Ordinary routines articulate the youth work relationship. The scenario exemplifies the very personal nature of issues presented in youth work. Confidentiality is often the premise of young people's engagement with the youth service because they want their troubles and concerns to remain private. Listening is central to maintaining ethical commitments to young people, respecting their decisions and including the silences that respect privacy in not asking for more information unnecessarily. We listen not only for the substantive concerns but to know (better) the young person and strengthen the trusting relationship that is at the heart of youth work. Ordinary routines indicate the emancipatory aims of youth work. Providing assistance to young people in securing access to social goods such as income support, accommodation, health, education, recreation and employment is premised on social justice principles, directed towards the personal and social development of young people, their wellbeing and participation in society.

Signifying the 'failure of mainstream institutions' (Sercombe 1997a), youth work has traditionally articulated the significance of social arrangements for understanding young people's problems. Asserting this perspective is increasingly challenging against dominant risk management accounts of 'problem youth' (Bessant 2004b). Associated with policy reforms, particularly contraction of the welfare state, local and global economic forces and the social categorizations of youth, the risk paradigm reframes unequal access as the individual problems of 'disengaged', 'unemployed' and 'offending youth' or their families, collectively designated 'at-risk'. As a metaphor for unruliness, trouble, dangerousness and anti-sociability as well as vulnerability and dependency, youth is a differentiating political and moral category in which those who are unable to access mainstream institutions or normative life pathways are designated 'other' and in need of preventive, protective and regulatory interventions (Brown 2005); Ginwright, Cammarota and Noguera 2005; Griffin 2004; Wyn and White (997). Emphasis on re-integrative intervention de-legitimates other activities and spaces that young people may choose in pursuing their own interests (Bottrell and Armstrong 2007). While youth workers may subvert the legitimacy of pejorative categorizations and focus on positive development and participation, youth work is increasingly incorporated, through funding agreements and hegemonic models of targeted casework, programs and outcomes into the project of social control. The notion of youth workers as 'soft cops' (Poynting and White 2004) is now more than ever embedded in systemic policy rationales and expectations of prescriptive outcomes that are the hallmarks of neoliberal responsibilization.

Ethical dilemmas concerning the issue of social control in youth work are recognized as the conflict of external pressures and internal principles, generally framed as issues of professionalism and the ideological contexts of practice. The more mundane exemplars of the 'soft cop' role in the everyday operations of youth services are given little attention. Sometimes, however, it is the 'small stuff' incidental to running programs and providing services that challenges principled practice and is most revealing of issues outside our primary youth work relationships. In the following section I reflect on some of the 'small stuff' in my experience as a youth worker that exemplifies ways in which work with young people inevitably involves exerting control and how its community context requires engaging with dominant norms and discourses and consequent 'positioned' ethical dilemmas.

Managing young people: Correction or connection?

In the main hall, less than the size of a half-court, young people manage to play basketball, touch football and cricket. The games often evoke the sense of community that young people associate with *their* youth centre as others gather to watch, cheer and tease their mates. Today it's basketball and the play is enthusiastic, spurred on by the centre's 'Koori youth' team's win last night in the local competition and the backdrop of their favourite upbeat music.

One game finishes and new players take to the floor. On the 'stage' area of the hall, a local volunteer leads the older boys in a card game; girls have taken over the computers upstairs; and a group are working on the mural. A young man who has been to court earlier in the day arrives with his cousin's baby. His gentleness with her is the other side to him the magistrate may never see. A trio of girls show me pictures in *Koori Mail*, explaining who's who and their connections. Gathered around the play station

> another group are intent on the competition, interspersed with laughter and friendly pummelling.
>
> The ambience of drop-in is sometimes ideal; at other times, far from it. Yelling across the hall at young people, I sound like the fishwife: 'Don't kick the basketball at the lights!', 'Don't swing off the goal ring!' My concern is for their safety and for equipment that we don't have a budget for repairing. And after a food fight: 'Now you guys clean up that mess!' There's not much finesse in the tone of these demands and I'm annoyed that we will be left to do the mopping up.

When principled commitment to young people is juxtaposed with the reality of managing twenty or fifty young people at after-school 'drop-in', my track record is less than pristine. I hear myself 'disciplining' individuals, calling out reminders of the centre rules, and I understand in those moments why some services and youth work theorists are opposed to drop-in. Its fluid 'structure' places demands on both workers and young people that may threaten the primary relationship of mutual respect that is at the heart of youth work whereas working one-to-one with young people may present other challenges but rarely involves authoritatively directing behaviour. However, to relegate drop-in and only provide individualized youth work because drop-in creates the challenge of managing behaviour and the latter has more impact in meeting needs and interests may be pertinent in some contexts but may also align practice more closely with governmental responsibilizing agenda. In addition to devaluing programs that respond to young people's present needs and interests that are not interpreted as contributing to transitions and future 'becomings' (Spence 2004), to focus only on prescribed outcomes would, in this centre, mean discarding the principle of listening to young people. The continued provision of drop-in is a response to young people voicing that they want the safe space to meet with mates and make new friends, to access recreations, the daily meal and support work as needed. Respecting their input to planning service provision has over the years initiated various new projects and programs and productive adaptations in scheduling.

Ensuring safety and intervening in conflicts do not directly present ethical dilemmas; exercising control in these ways is a duty of care. Our role in social control in the everyday sense of managing young people is not an issue of incorporation into systems of targeted intervention but a form of regulation inherent in supervision that is every youth worker's responsibility. Managing behaviour can involve interactions between staff and young people that are in the moment anything but emancipatory. But we rely on the positive relationships we have with young people and their agreement to centre rules. The quality of relationships formed out of everyday listening, support and encouragement alongside young people's connectedness to the centre as their place override the minor 'stoushes' over behaviour that is usually over and done with quickly.

Control in context: Community and other interests

There is for me an ethical dilemma that derives from awareness of the overlap between the socializing function of group supervision and broader social processes of responsibilization. Arising out of work in a community context, it is a concern about what may be experienced as more of the same 'correction' that young people already incur through formal and informal policing. Within a virtue ethics framework, the everyday 'social pedagogy' (Coussee, Roets and De Bie 2009) of youth work emphasizes young people's positive development or 'flourishing'. It also includes explicit messages about appropriate behaviour and actions that are moral codes for fostering 'good habits and dispositions' that strengthen 'the capacity to exercise good judgement' (Bessant 2009: 429). Encouraging responsible action in this sense is not a response to 'problem youth' but consistent with enhancing young people's self-determination beyond invoking rules and appealing to fair play. This framing of the regulation of young people in youth work may nonetheless at times be at odds with more utilitarian community demands for social order.

The management of young people's behaviour outside the centre elaborates the dilemma, beyond fourteen-year-old Alex's contestation of where centre rules apply:

A group of about eight girls and boys are standing on the footpath outside the youth centre. They're talking, laughing, taking up the space so that pedestrians have to walk along the edge of the road to pass by. Fourteen-year-olds Alex and Benji are riding their bikes, racing to the corner and back, weaving through the other young people. Alex drops his bike and runs across the road dodging traffic to meet up with a mate, then both race back over. Youth worker, Roger, has a word to the boys about crossing the road, asks Benji and Alex to move their bikes and others to move aside so that there's some space for others to use the footpath. Instead, Alex tosses a handful of stones onto the road and yahoos as they just miss the passing cars. Roger tells him to drop the other handful which Alex promptly throws. 'Okay, enough. On your bike!' says Roger. 'That's it. Come back tomorrow if you want to come in but no more of this. You know you could hurt someone.' 'Don't give a stuff', says Alex, 'and anyway you can't tell me what to do, I'm not in the youth centre.' 'On your bike,' repeats Roger. Alex grabs his bike, tells Roger to f... off and hurls a rock through the front window before racing away.

From a procedural perspective, banning Alex is a straightforward matter of imposing consequences, accepted by Alex and expected by others. In a day or two Roger will visit Alex at home. Discussion of the incident will be brief. Alex describes what happened as 'just stupid. I was pissed off but I shouldn't have done it'. Our ethical commitment is to ensure that Alex maintains access to support work even while his recreations at the youth centre are curtailed in the short-term, that his 'place' is reinstated when the ban expires and former positive relations with his peers are resumed.

However, there is a positioned ethical dilemma concerning complicity in keeping young people 'off the streets'. In the mainly commercial area, the visibility of young people out the front of the centre is seen by some proprietors and residents as detracting from the streetscape. Incidents like the stone throwing, hassling passers-by or loud altercations are taken up as justifications for their claims that 'youth are intimidating' or 'delinquents'. The very presence of young people as non-consumers in a busy commercial strip evokes fear or condemnation as 'the other'; made up of a majority of Indigenous participants, the young people stand out in the predominantly white precinct – with their loud talk, laughter, 'mucking around' and taking up space on the footpath, they are readily associated with the 'criminal' and 'problem youth' discourses that circulate through informal networks, local media and community forums.

According to the young people, the reputation of crime and drugs in the area merges with social problems of the estate, attaching to all young people who live there (Bottrell 2009: 494). Young people's accounts associate street culture including drinking, smoking 'pot', fighting and petty crime with traditions of the local youth network and youth culture more generally, as 'something to do' and 'just what everyone does'. In part, however, this tradition is perpetuated out of resistance to the labelling of young people. Because illicit recreations are common and a minority of young people are known to be involved with juvenile justice for violent or repeated offences, being 'targeted' (Patsy) in proactive policing, pejorative discourses that 'put you into a category' (Sarah) and by those who 'look at us kids like scum' (Rebecca) constitutes marginalization and effectively reinforces the importance of the youth network for its social, emotional and practical goods (Bottrell 2008: 42, 46, 55; Bottrell 2009: 489). The targeting of the young people I worked with is directly related to their visibility in the community and differentiates the young people of the estate from other young people whose lifestyles are more private. Those whose families are able to resource participation in sports clubs, music or academic tuition and commercial recreations are less likely to be on the streets after school. Sharing a cafe table with school friends or browsing in the mall they are unremarkable 'private' groupings because they merge with the consumer-role that predominates in the precinct. The types of activities, who provides them, and the social norms embodied in participation, thus differentiate young people – rendering those from the estate more subject to public scrutiny and exclusion from 'public' space.

Although discrepancies in representations of young people in need of welfare or correction often reflect the socioeconomic divisions of the area, the correspondence is not complete. The youth centre has always received strong support from some businesses, private residents and local councillors in the form of sponsorship, volunteering, advocacy in forums and for funding. Even so, the discourse of problem youth dominates, fuelled by periodic reports in the local press of the 'youth crime wave', 'riots' and 'gangs'.

When we see young people getting into trouble because the domains they choose coincide with surveillance and policing, youth work intervention may be deemed at odds with respect for young people's privacy and control over their own decisions but is warranted and in their interests when we are in a position to foresee the likely harm they will incur by being outside legitimated domains. The social pedagogy here may be interpreted as complying with the most powerful voices of the community and the represented normative moral order. However, it also contributes to young people's empowerment through learning to better negotiate 'community standards': young people want to enjoy living in their community, to elude oppressive reputations and be in control of their identity. However, such regulation cannot ethically extend to community demand for keeping young people off the streets.

Participating in community forums and engaging in conversations with local residents and shopkeepers, youth workers inevitably field complaints and pejorative judgements about young people as 'other' than well-behaved citizens in the making (Lister 2002). Listening to stories of residents being woken at 3 a.m. by young people smashing bottles and shopkeepers' complaints about car break-ins that are deterring customers from their small businesses are reasons for dialogue with young people about considerate and responsible behaviour. It is also an opportunity to challenge the dominant discourses through which members of the community's personal stories are reconstituted. Conflated and generalized marginalizing discourses reflect the conflicting interests of social positioning and relations to resources that enable dominant claims to moral grounds for social control interventions. There are hidden agendas here in issues largely absent from these discourses. Young people are discursively quarantined as a significant commercial problem with little attention to other issues impacting on small businesses such as competition with the shopping malls in surrounding suburbs, unfavourable traffic and parking conditions and disproportionate rent rises that have all contributed to closures or turnover in recent years. Similarly, there is an absence of critique with regard to proactive policing that moves on young people sitting on the footpath outside their home with mates, 'doing nothing', and its direct link to the claims of a few businesses that 'youth gangs' are 'out of control' (Bottrell 2008: 45). This targeting elicits the antagonism of young people who have never been in trouble and largely undermines the attempts of youth liaison police to establish more positive relations for example through youth centre-police sports events and open forums with young people in educational programs. These are typically personality-driven efforts that are unable to affect the institutional culture of aggressive law enforcement and crime prevention that disproportionately targets young people, and particularly Indigenous young people, which – in the context of conflicting community interests and social divisions – exerts a key role in the stigmatization of targeted social groups (Cunneen and White 2002).

Entering into dialogue is part of the community development role in youth work (Westoby and Dowling 2009). However, it is important to be clear about who are the primary constituents of youth work even while there are implicit accountabilities to other constituencies (Sercombe 1997b). Ethical commitment to young people requires challenging claims for keeping young people off the streets as in the interests of the community when 'community' is defined in ways that exclude the young people (and their families and neighbourhoods) as 'not community' and make invisible the social inequities within which they are positioned. Resisting incorporation into inequitable unifying discourses of community interests is enabled by grounding practice in the shared knowledge of young people and their families, the perspective of the least advantaged that anchors the principles of social justice (Connell 1995).

The ethics of pathways and social control

Managing young people's behaviour presents no apparent procedural ethical dilemma but there are clearly positioned dilemmas as the operations of the youth centre spill over into public space and are met by hegemonic discourses of problem youth. Local constructions of problem youth in part derive from the public articulation of social policy that within a dominant risk paradigm reframes unequal access to social goods as the individual problems of 'disengaged', 'unemployed' and 'offending youth' or their families, collectively designated 'at-risk'. Officially sanctioned interventions for youth at risk constitute 'hidden' processes of 'civilisation' that reconfigure marginalization as the problems of deficit young people, ideologically connected with their perceived threat to social order (Coussee et al. 2009).

It is in the knowledge of young people's marginalization that dilemmas arise concerning responses to their relations to schooling. When I first started working at the centre there were many young people who, through sequences of suspensions and changing schools or truancy, drifted out of school without credentials; and being out of school often meant 'hanging around' with other young people and getting into trouble. With relatively high levels of truancy, suspensions, involvement with juvenile justice and welfare systems and unemployment, our approach was to encourage school attendance by providing weekly outreach to the local high school, after-school homework help, programs (approved by the authorities under statewide initiatives) for year 6 to 7 transition support and community-based arts, media and life skills two days per week for students at risk of dropping out of school. Encouraging individuals' school attendance sometimes amounted to 'hassling' them by always asking 'why aren't you at school?' and maintaining the centre's schedule of only offering support work or specific programs during school hours – not allowing 'drop-in' to creep back earlier than the 3 p.m. start. Although it was recognized that young people would be better off inside the centre playing basketball than sitting at the bus stop or drinking in derelict houses, as they sometimes did to fill the day, it had always been policy at the centre to not provide recreational alternatives to school and I also supported that response – knowing that many would choose the alternative were it offered.

This kind of youth work intervention seems self-evidently justifiable when educational credentials are central to employment and other life opportunities. However, critiques of targeted work with 'youth at risk' refer to its narrow conception of youth participation with emphasis on directing young people into mainstream pathways of education, training and work and assuming a person-change focus without challenging the exclusionary or marginalizing effects of mainstream institutions that in young people's experience account for their 'disengagement'. For youth workers incorporated into these processes, there are ethical dilemmas of participating in a 'hidden civilization strategy' and infringement of the principles of young people's voluntary participation and making their own decisions. However, there is no voluntarism in their not obtaining credentials and being unemployed. To not embrace those 'targets' would be to strengthen the institutional processes that actively reproduce marginalization and the social inequities that youth work critiques. Encouraging young people to talk about how education could serve them, their aspirations and plans is a potentially emancipatory mode of social pedagogy that enables us to 'challenge young people's thinking without being moralistic or disapproving' (Coussee et al. 2009: 435).

There remain, however, inevitable tensions in working with individuals for their re/engagement in school because it aims for their access to social goods that are potentially emancipatory but with little scope for transforming the social and institutional conditions that produce their marginalization, particularly when young people are suspended because they have been in fights or have threatened or sworn at teachers. In these circumstances there is an emphasis on person-centred adaptation to the requirements of the institution that are morally reasonable, encapsulating principles of respect and beneficence. However, listening to and understanding reasons for resistance to school shifts that emphasis to decoding oppressive elements of schooling practices (Freire 1972). The ethical tensions here concern holding the knowledge of structural odds against young people's success through marginal positioning, yet encouraging their aspirations and validating their experience by supporting them to cope with the objects of their resistance.

Although young people had articulated some of the difficulties at school that were their reasons for staying away, it was not until I undertook my doctoral research at the centre that I understood the links between tru-anting, getting into trouble and the contexts of schooling and community. It was clear that the young people value and want education as instrumental to life-skills and employment; while taking responsibility for their own oppositional behaviours as inappropriate, their resistances are also based on a rejection of boring curriculum, petty rules, the lack of adequate help with schoolwork, subsequent failures that de-motivate them, and teachers who don't care about them or their results (Bottrell 2007). The strongest theme of their resistance to school, however, was being spoken down to and stereotyped by virtue of where they live. Ascribed pejorative identities are evident in messages they receive from those teachers who consider them 'not worth bothering about' or 'going nowhere' and peers' insinuations that they must be delinquent if they live in an area where crime is a problem. The experiences of stereotyping and stigma are deeply felt and deeply impact on young people's sense of who they are. In these circumstances, positive identity is chosen in identifying with the emotional and practical support they find in their families, neighbourhoods and in the local youth network, including participation in illicit activities like drinking, using drugs and fighting, which alongside the sense of belonging, recognition, loyalty and practical resources of the network constitute social rewards and confer a status unavailable to them at school (Bottrell 2009).

Young people's ethics of care and loyalty in their networks and emanci-patory identity work are political and moral lessons that shifted the basis of my ethical dilemmas. On the one hand, their experience deeply challenged my belief that keeping them in school was justified in terms of the princi-ple that education is a social good. The young people's resistant responses to schooling are authentic in the Freirean sense of action grounded in a critique of the 'de-mythologized' oppressive realities of schooling (Freire 1972: 56), and are morally justified in the choice for acquiring social goods through peer and neighbourhood networks. On the other hand, advocating for viable alternatives to mainstream schooling raises issues of complicity in structuring young people's secondariness as outside the mainstream and the perpetuation of marginalizing schooling practices. The latter are perhaps in-progress towards some resolution. The research provided the impetus for establishing a centre-based education program that enables young people to obtain the school credential they want through distance education. In the five years since its inception it has continued to develop, currently led by colleagues from the university faculty in which I now work. The faculty's community development program enables me to maintain an advocacy standpoint grounded in social justice and it in turn keeps my research similarly grounded.

Placing young people's perspectives and shifting others

The ethical dilemmas concerning elements of day-to-day youth centre operations and support work towards young people's participation in education alike are embedded in discursive, cultural, political and societal relations in and through which individual and local community experience are constituted. Local understandings of 'problem youth' are constructed out of more than personal experience, directly linked to media, political and public discourses of moral panic concerning 'almost every aspect of the lives of young people, at the same time expanding the catchment age of 'problem youth' downwards to encompass ever younger age groups' (Brown 2005: 58). The demonization of young people targets particular social groups and locations associating them with social problems such that the most vulnerable and disadvantaged communities and groups are stigmatized. Merging with these representations other dominant discourses of risk and law and order, justify and hegemonize interventionist youth governance. In this sense there are social goods attached to different social identities within public space and location, and ethical positions grounded in the social and discursive 'places' young people occupy.

A commitment to shifting perspectives that reinscribe and target 'problem youth' invokes the fundamental youth work principle of listening to young people. The collective insights of the young people with whom I worked and researched constitute their own social pedagogy that is rooted in a vernacular ontology and epistemology of the everyday. Listening to young people's accounts of their lives through individual support work, in stories over a card game or on the way to the movies, in crisis, boredom, celebration or anger, is an ethical process that necessitates practical response and advocacy – and in the process shifts the meaning of ordinary routines in recognition of how the 'smallest stuff' is ethically substantive. Relationship in listening draws on the depth and breadth of practice knowledge mapping connections and extended relations through meaning-making in the process of understanding 'otherwise'. In this sense 'ethics arises from listening' (Lipari 2009: 45), who we listen to and whose voices we would prefer to not to hear, who we relegate indoors, off our streets and out of our classrooms. Listening to young people's experience reveals important personal, cultural and social meanings of 'targeting', 'intervention' and social problems as well as the construction of oppression. Their positioning within community relations and institutional practices is an indication of collective ethical commitments as 'the ultimate test of morality resides in what a society does for its children' (Giroux 2008). The status and treatment of young people equally reflects the nature of democratic commitment in the primacy of social control or social responsibility.

The importance of dialogical ethics (interactive, responsive ethics) applies equally to the community development role of youth work which assumes a commitment to promoting 'the common good'. Finding common cause is a challenge when 'the good life' has multiple meanings embedded in socially positioned interests and unequal resources, and when community and young people's narratives are embedded in local but also constructed out of dominant societal relations and discourses. As problematic as it may be to participate in community processes alongside our primary focus on working with young people, it is in such work that the individualization of 'problem youth' may be reinstated to its social context – with greater potential for 'assuring social rights and collective provisions for young people' (Coussee et al. 2009: 435), because although complex there are common interests that belie the divisions inherent in communities. In this context the 'social-pedagogical' role may be more effectual in the community development aspects of youth work where youth participation includes the kinds of forums through which communities aim to articulate common cause. The ethics of listening to young people warrant extension rather than confinement of their domains of participation in recognition of the inherent social good of young people sharing their knowledge, ways of knowing and implications of them as perspectives of the least advantaged.

These aims resonate with the 'ethics of care' (Noddings 1984) and the notion of beneficence that in reference to work with marginalized groups and framed as social justice practice entails making a positive difference. To do otherwise would be to perpetuate the harmful consequences of oppressive conditions. The faculty's community development project is a form of mobilization that indicates how institutional power may operate in other than marginalizing ways. Working 'within the system' with teachers, interagency colleagues, residents and young people instantiates a community of practice for emancipatory purposes through small projects of transformative social justice. At the heart of this work is the fundamental premise of listening to young people and taking seriously their concerns, critiques and insights. In this move we simultaneously effect a counter-hegemonic shift in the discursive framing not only of marginalized young people but also narrow views of 'the community' and relationships with young people from social responsibilization toward practices of social responsibility.

Conclusion

The ethical dilemmas outlined are shaped by consciousness of individual-community-societal relations and conflicting representations of young people. As youth workers we come to know the complex lives of young people in their own words and perspectives. But we contextualize individual stories as more than personal experiences and thus ethical dilemmas are circumscribed by power relations that effect the legitimization of problems. Whose conceptualization of 'the problem' counts in the public domain is largely indicative of the power of resources and the power to define. The assumption that young people need to learn appropriate behaviour and responsible decision-making and that fits with 'community standards' or a normative moral order may have fairly straightforward implications for issues such as sharing the footpath outside the centre and fair enforcement of centre rules. However, it is problematic when issues are connected to divergent community interests or bounded by social structures that are inherently inequitable.

There are no straightforward resolutions to the ethical dilemmas arising out of the positioning of young people, community-based youth work and social control exerted through the regulation of young people in public space. In my own experience, such conflicts form an ongoing negotiation, with a focus on listening to and advocating for young people. While being acutely aware of the regulatory functions of youth work, reasserting social justice principles aims for distinction from the governmental aims of targeted responsibilization. Situated in the community, listening to residents and acknowledging shared concerns for young people's safety and wellbeing is accompanied by challenging oppressive representations. Listening to young people and engaging in the dialogical process in community development aspects of youth work shifts emphasis from changing young people to changing the dominant narratives towards more emancipatory perspectives for those young people (Cousse et al. 2009; Ungar 2004).

References

Bessant, J. (2004a). 'Risk Technologies and Youth Work Practice', *Youth and Policy*, 83, 60–77.
—— (2004b). 'Youth Work. The Loch Ness Monster and Professionalism', *Youth Studies Australia*, 23 (4) 26–33.

——(2009). 'Aristotle Meets Youth Work: A Case for Virtue Ethics', *Journal of Youth Studies*, 12 (4), 423–38.

Bottrell, D. (2007). 'Resistance, Resilience and Social Identities: Reframing "Problem Youth" and the Problem of Schooling', *Journal of Youth Studies*, 10 (5), 597–616.

——(2008). 'TGG: Girls, Culture and Identity'. In A. Harris (ed.), *Next Wave Cultures: Feminism, Subcultures, Activism*, pp. 37–62. New York: Routledge.

——(2009). 'Dealing with Disadvantage. Resilience and the Social Capital of Young People's Networks', *Youth & Society*, 40 (4), 476–501.

—— and Armstrong, D. (2007). 'Changes and Exchanges in Marginal Youth Transitions', *Journal of Youth Studies*, 10 (3), 353–71.

Brown, S. (2005). *Understanding Youth and Crime. Listening to Youth?*. Maidenhead: Open University Press.

Connell, R.W. (1995). *Schools and Social Justice*, Philadelphia: Temple University Press.

Coussee, F., Roets, G. and De Bie, M. (2009). 'Empowering the Powerful: Challenging Hidden Processes of Marginalization in Youth Work Policy and Practice in Belgium', *Critical Social Policy*, 29 (3), 421–42.

Cunneen, C. and White, R. (2002). *Juvenile Justice. Youth and Crime in Australia*. Melbourne: Oxford University Press.

Freire, P. (1972). *Pedagogy of the Oppressed*. Harmondsworth: Penguin.

Ginwright, S., Cammarota, J. and Noguera, P. (2005). 'Youth, Social Justice, and Communities: Toward a Theory of Urban Youth Policy', *Social Justice*, 32 (3), 24–40.

Giroux, H. (2008). 'Disposable Youth in a Suspect Society: A Challenge for the Obama Administration', *Truthout*, 25 November 2008.

Griffin, C. (2004). 'Representations of the Young'. In J. Roche, S. Tucker, R. Thomson and R. Flynn (eds), *Youth in Society*, pp. 10–18. London: Sage/Open University Press.

Lipari, L. (2009). 'Listening Otherwise: The Voice of Ethics', *International Journal of Listening*, 23, 44–59.

Lister, R. (2002). 'Investing in the Citizen-Workers of the Future: New Labour's "Third Way" in Welfare Reform', Engendrer La Cohesion Sociale/Fostering Social Cohesion, Working Paper 5, prepared for the Annual Meeting of the American Political Science Association, Boston for a panel entitled: Redesigning Welfare Regimes: The Building Blocks of a New Architecture (August 2002).

Noddings, N. (1984). *Caring: A Feminine Approach to Ethics and Moral Education*. Berkeley: University of California Press.

Poynting, S. and White, R. (2004). 'Youth Work. Challenging the Soft Cop Syndrome', *Youth Studies Australia*, 23 (4), 39–45.

Sercombe, H. (1997a). 'The Contradictory Position of Youth Workers in the Public Sphere', *Youth Studies Australia*, 16 (1), 43–7.

—— (1997b). 'The Youth Work Contract. Professionalism and Ethics', *Youth Studies Australia*, 16 (4), 17–21.

—— (2007). '"Embedded" Youth Work. Ethical Questions for Youth Work Professionals', *Youth Studies Australia*, 26 (2), 11–19.

Spence, J. (2004). 'Targeting, Accountability and Youth Work Practice', *Practice*, 16 (4), 261–72.

Ungar, M. (2004). *Nurturing Hidden Resilience in Troubled Youth*. Toronto: University of Toronto Press.

Westoby, P. and Dowling, G. (2009). *Dialogical Community Development. With Depth, Solidarity and Hospitality*. West End: Tafina Press.

Wyn, J. and White, R. (1997). *Re-Thinking Youth*, Sydney: Allen and Unwin.

EMMA RAMSDEN AND PHIL JONES

10 Children as active agents in gaining and giving assent: Involving children as co-researchers

This chapter presents an approach to recognizing and supporting children's competence in giving assent within research. It examines the tensions and opportunities within current approaches to child consent and assent, drawing on an ongoing research project involving therapy with children with social, emotional and behavioural difficulties. Areas considered include: how the terms 'consent' and 'assent' are defined and used in practice; the power dynamics at work between adults and children involved in research together and the challenges offered by the new sociology of childhood to traditional approaches to permission-giving and to ways of viewing children's competency and decision-making. Vignettes from research with children involved in therapy within a school setting illustrate aspects of the process of negotiating assent, and are used to examine practices that involve children as active decision-makers in giving assent.

Ethics, permission, consent and assent in research with children

Informed consent in relation to participating in research has been defined as an authorization given, voluntarily, by an individual who has the capacity to understand the aims and nature of the research and to decide whether to participate (Fader et al. 1986). A core element of consenting rests on the premise that any 'prospective research participants should be given as much information as might be needed to make an informed decision about whether or not they wish to participate in a study' (Bryman 2004: 540). Joffe et al. have described informed consent as being considered as 'valid' if the following elements are included in any consideration and implementation of the consent process: the participant's capacity to understand the nature of the research and the concepts and implications of voluntariness, permission and disclosure (2001: 139). Assent has been described as a term used to express willingness to participate in research by 'persons who are by definition too young to give informed consent but who are old enough to understand the proposed research in general, its expected risks and possible benefits, and the activities expected of them as subjects' (Medtran 2009). Assent alone is not deemed adequate as an agreement to participate: informed consent is still needed from parents or guardians (Broome and Richards 1998; Bryman 2004; Field and Berman 2004). Decision-making about a child's involvement and permission to participate has, in the past, often rested *solely* in the hands of adults. The traditional procedure to 'protect' the rights of children involved in research has been to obtain the consent of the children's parents or legal guardians. This position is being challenged by new understandings of children's capacities and the nature of their involvement in agreeing to participate in research.

The concept or practice that children should be involved in deciding about their involvement in research has, until recently, rarely been given attention (Hill 2006; Kellett 2010). Cultural assumptions that children were not competent to make decisions were reflected in codes of practice and guidelines that required only adult consent for a child, as described above. Field and Berman discuss the relationship between consent, assent and research in a way that illustrates current cultural tensions around children's agreement to participate in research (2004: 147–8). They observe that the 'ethical principle of respect for persons underlies the obligation of investigators to treat individuals as autonomous actors who must provide their informed and voluntary consent to participate in research'. This is followed by a summary that reflects a contrary position more commonly taken within research concerning parents or guardians, children and consent, which is that: 'requirements for parental permission serve the ethical obligation of investigators to respect and protect vulnerable individuals' (Field and Berman 2004: 147–8). Children are not treated to the same 'ethical principle of respect' as adults (Field and Berman 2004: 147–8). In Field and Berman's summary, current approaches to consent and assent in research are shown to reflect a division connected to ideas about capacity and autonomy, and whether an individual is deemed worthy of ethical respect. A divide occurs between an adult state – where the capacity to make legally recognized, informed, voluntary consent is located – and that of the child, which is described as a contrary position: as 'vulnerable', not worthy of respect, and not capable of giving consent.

Changes in the ways children are seen, particularly here in relation to research, are a result of disciplines coming into contact. Fasoli for example, positions tradition and development by relating them to the impact of inter-disciplinarity:

> Traditionally, children are considered too young to understand or notice what is going on, and so have often been provided with very few resources to make sense of the research context in which they are expected to participate. Early childhood research has drawn heavily on psychological and scientific views of children and learning in constructing research designs and in interpreting data produced by and about young children ... Gradually this orientation has shifted as early childhood researchers adopt more socio-cultural views of childhood, of children and of learning. (2003: 27)

These comments reflect the need for changes in the way children are seen, and involved, by researchers in areas such as guidance and resourcing to enable them to provide children with information to make 'sense' and to fully consider the nature of their participation. This is illustrated by Twycross's review (2009) of the current research guidelines of organizations such as the British Psychological Society (2009), the British Sociological Association (2004) and the Royal College of Nursing (2004). She concluded that specific guidance on children giving assent or consent is either not referenced, is considered in a way that assumes parental consent for children to be adequate, or mentions any engagement with children through a lens of 'vulnerability' rather than 'involvement'. Challenges from the fields of child rights and the new sociology of childhood (Jones and Welch 2010; Kellett 2010; Moss 2005; Prout et al. 2006) ask whether children are best served by such ideas and practices concerning permission and adult decision-making and by the *divisions* present in the 'traditional' approach?

They question whether the established separation of adult and child in the position summarized above concerning parental consent is still an adequate response for ethical requirements and obligations in relation to children. When looked at in the light of the issues raised by this review, parental consent alone cannot be sufficient when researching with children. In the current cultural climate challenges are being made to traditional approaches to research that do not give attention or status to children's agreement to take part in research. Kellett reflects this flux in the following way:

> The debates rage on about the age at which children are deemed responsible enough to give their informed consent and about when this should be a requirement in addition to any consent given by their parents, irrespective of age ... From an ethical point of view, as opposed to a purely legal point of view, it is desirable for all children to be approached about giving consent. (2005b: 33)

Powell and Smith (2009) argue that, in the current state of flux in relation to consent and assent, children's participation rights are especially compromised when all children are stereotyped as vulnerable, as this can result in inappropriate gate-keeping procedures that prevent some children from participating. They propose that children should be viewed as social actors who can play a part in the decision to participate in research; such a shift would result in more attention being given to communicating with children about research in order to inform their own decisions regarding participation.

The foregrounding of children's agreement raises challenges concerning how children are informed and involved in aspects such as being given information about research in a way that is meaningful to them, and in ways that address the complexities of the relationship between participants concerning power, dynamics and status. Looked at in this way, the child's voice – whether this is considered as 'consent' or 'assent' is one of the most urgent contemporary ethical agendas in the research process. Only in this way can research truly comply with the hallmarks of ethical practice, which aims to 'improve the world' and which 'should do no harm, should be respectful of the persons choice about participation, and should ensure that the benefits outweigh the costs' (Cuskelly 2005: 99).

A key question emerges from this position: how best to engage with children in relation to their assent or consent? The foregrounding of children's agreement raises challenges concerning how children are informed and involved in areas such as being given information about research in a way that is meaningful to them, and in ways that address the complexities of the relationship between participants concerning power, dynamics and status. Here the emphasis traditionally placed on parents as sole gatekeepers shifts to foreground the need to find ways in which researchers can engage meaningfully with children in negotiating areas such as permission or agreement to participate in, or withdraw from, research.

The following draws from ongoing research to address this emerging view of the child as an able meaning-maker and considers the key question of how best to engage with children in informed decision-making about participation.

The research

The research is a study of children's voices in dramatherapy sessions. It arose from Ramsden's work as a dramatherapist in a mainstream, inner-city, primary school serving an area described as having 'high levels of social deprivation ... and ... a higher proportion of pupils with learning difficulties than in most schools.' (Ofsted 2009). Working as a practitioner-researcher, Ramsden aimed to explore with the children the impact of the dramatherapy intervention on their lives. Data were captured by engaging with the participants in a variety of creative, expressive and playful research methods. Practitioner or action research is 'grounded in lived experience, ... addresses significant problems, works with ... people, develops new ways of seeing/interpreting the world (i.e., theory) and leaves infrastructure in its wake' (Bradbury and Reason 2008: 156).

Following ethical approval within Leeds Metropolitan University's procedures, from the Board of School Governors, and having gained parental/guardianship consent, the children were invited to participate as co-researchers rather than subjects or participants. Working with children and young people as co-researchers is a '... continuous developmental process' (Groundwater-Smith 2007: 125). Co-researching acknowledges that 'by working with the children as collaborators, seeking to follow their agendas and facilitate their exploration of their own experiences ... one attempts ... to make a relationship that is equal and active' (Leeson 2007: 139–40). The ethical framework used the term 'assent' in relation to the involvement of children, reflecting Leeds Metropolitan University's policy, and this is the term used below.

Gaining assent, considering some complexities

As discussed above, gaining assent or consent is no simple task of merely asking children if they would like to participate. Complex issues such as understanding and meaning-making, voluntariness, influence, bias, power, control and environment must be taken into account, including psychological considerations relating to the child's potential. This potential could, for example, be expressed in a need to please the researcher or, conversely, a need to act out as a healthy expression of a disempowered life situation.

The presenting challenges concerned how to explore the assent process, in a way which enabled the children – who were already engaged in individual dramatherapy interventions because of individual difficulties and circumstances – to experience their own power and authentic freedom, to foster independent growth and build self-esteem as well as enabling each child to decide whether or not to engage as a co-researcher. A key element of this involved acknowledging that, when working with children, the power of the researcher is a major ethical issue (Morrow and Richards 1996). Each child needed to make her/his choice from a place of safety and trust, without fear of adults usurping their wishes or using coercion, or withdrawing consent once assent had been granted. This latter point must be considered within the context of the school and not legislated for on the part of the practitioner-researcher, as legally it was the parent/guardian's right to withdraw from the research project and/or therapeutic intervention at any point over and above the wishes of the child.

The challenge was to develop methods of assent gaining which enabled the use of 'ethical guidelines' to which Morrow and Richards (1996) refer:

> Which ... call on researchers to avoid undue intrusion, and using ... methods which are non-invasive, non-confrontational and participatory, and which encourage children to interpret their own data ... and is suggested ... might be one step towards diminishing the ethical problems of imbalanced power relationships between researcher and researched at the point of data collection and interpretation. (100)

Gaining permission from children to participate

Drawing upon the action method framework of dramatherapy, in which 'action is a central element' (Langley 2006: 7), the assent-gaining sessions were creatively devised to focus on eliciting a mutual understanding between the co-researchers of the concepts of 'yes', 'no' and 'making a choice', by utilizing a range of methods from visual questions to having 'play breaks'. The session was devised from a child-centric perspective, taking into account concentration span and a child's need to be free to move around the room and to communicate through play as well as words. These considerations led to the risk of the potential power of the use of adult verbal language being minimized and also the pressure the children may have felt to find a 'correct answer' to the questions around becoming a co-researcher.

The assent session lasted fifty minutes and consisted of two parts. In Part 1 the child engaged with a series of questions from categories devised by the researcher/therapist (such as have you got a left and a right hand) to create a language and space to explore issues related to assent. Implicit choice played a part from the outset, as each child first chose whether to engage with the question (whether to sit listening or whether to indicate in some way that they did not want to engage, by moving away from the researcher/therapist or by verbally informing her that they did not want to listen) and further, whether to then answer the question. Firstly came questions to which the evidence was based in the child's experience of themselves, such as 'did you have breakfast today?' Next came questions which elicited visual evidence – 'are you wearing socks/shoes/a jumper?' This was followed by questions about actions – 'would you like to jump up and down/move around the room like an animal?' Each set of questions brought greater choice, both the opportunity to answer or not, and then to embody the action being offered or not.

After about ten minutes of child and researcher/therapist mutually playing with the sequence in Part 1, the 'findings' were established by the researcher/therapist asking 'what did we just find out about you and saying yes, no and making a choice?' During this short discussion each child reflected upon their responses and then had these responses verbally and visually mirrored back. For example if a child had expressed no by shaking their head, this was reflected back. The use of language and the potential bias of choices in phrasing questions or statements in particular ways was considered. For example informing a child that they can 'say yes or no' could be seen as holding a bias towards 'yes' this being placed first in the sentence. The preparation of the researcher/therapist's language prior to the assent gaining session was therefore structured to enable options which placed different concepts at the start of explanatory sentences to provide a balanced use of conceptual language. A further consideration centred on non-verbal influence via the body. An example of this would be if the researcher/therapist asked a child for their answer whilst looking at them with a smile. The child may interpret this to mean there to be an expecta-tion or a 'right' or 'wrong' answer. In order to negotiate this potential bias, a puppet was introduced. Reggie is a 'research frog' hand-puppet made of felt. Reggie the (anthropomorphic) research frog is green, with two large eyes and wears a blue tunic with a badge on that says 'thank you for your decision'. Each child was introduced to Reggie during the 'yes', 'no' and 'making a choice' creative sequence. They were informed that no matter what choice they made when the time came to decide whether or not to participate in the study – that Reggie (who could not speak) would nod his head twice by way of thanking the child for their communication, regardless of the answer. This explanation was then realized in action method terms, by way of demonstration, and the creative sequence of establishing a mutual understanding of the concepts followed.

In Part 2 of the fifty-minute assent session, the child established with the researcher/therapist if they were ready to make their decision about joining the project and, secondly, they were asked to make their decision known to Reggie. An example of this comes from James, a ten-year-old boy who looked directly at Reggie and gave his answer 'yes' then waited for Reggie to acknowledge this by nodding twice, as had been demonstrated earlier in the session. Whilst answering these questions the researcher/therapist focused her attention towards Reggie, using role modelling to encourage the child to do the same. In doing so, the risk of influence via facial expression was minimized. In Part 2 the children who had agreed to become co-researchers then looked through the project paperwork and assent form.

Responses from the children

Adults must believe in and promote attitudes that acknowledge and support the individuality of the child, irrespective of their seeming conformity or likeness to other children and/or other ideas and attitudes. The following vignettes illustrate this by detailing responses to elements of the assent process, carried out with all children invited to join the research. All seven children approached in these assent-seeking ways gave their permission to become co-researchers and find out more about what this entailed. Towards the end of the data collection cycle, each child was given the opportunity to create their own pseudonym. Where referred to by name in this chapter, these names are those chosen by the co-researchers.

Assent-gaining sessions with children took place in the dramatherapy room, once parental consent had been obtained. After focusing on establishing a mutual understanding of 'yes' and 'no', which was developed by individual children to include 'maybe', 'ask me later' and 'don't know', an overview of the research project was explored with them. Employing Reggie, the children were asked whether they would like to become co-researchers. Giving their answer to Reggie, the children then went on to explore related paperwork before making an overall final decision to continue in the project, having now heard more about it, and sealing their affirmative decision with a signature on the assent form, whilst also with the knowledge that they could withdraw from the study at any point without explanation or recrimination. Below are examples from some co-researchers on how they interpreted and engaged with these assent-related processes.

Vignette 1

When asked if he was ready to make his assent decision Rocksus, an eleven-year-old boy, said that he was. The researcher/therapist re-introduced him to Reggie. Rocksus stood up and went to the collection of hats behind him. He selected a fedora and put it on. The researcher/therapist asked 'What have you decided about joining the research project?' Rocksus – now seated on the rocking chair – closed his eyes. He rocked backwards and forwards before opening his eyes and saying: 'I have decided yes.' Both the researcher/therapist and Rocksus were looking towards Reggie at this point. Reggie nodded twice to indicate 'thank you for your decision.' Together we undertook an explanation and exploration of the assent and information forms, which used words and pictures. Rocksus appeared keen to look at the paperwork but on the way to sitting at the table to do so, he went via the gun box and took out a pistol and began shooting it. It made a sound each time the trigger was pulled. The researcher/therapist established with Rocksus that every time he did not understand any of the statements or explanations on the paperwork he could shoot his gun in order to stop and gain a clearer understanding. However, as Rocksus was keen to shoot the gun, he appeared to find this restrictive as he expressed an understanding of most of the points. This agreement was then re-negotiated to enable him to shoot the gun when he did understand, which worked much better.

Rocksus' focus was supported by his need to engage with the play materials in the dramatherapy room. Using materials was familiar to him and enabled him to express and explore his experiences. Using the gun and establishing communication with it meant that Rocksus could internalize new information in an enjoyable way whilst also having his play needs met through his choice of activity.

The next two vignettes illustrate how particular connections to the material and its contents can influence both engagement and the decision-making processes.

Vignette 2

Lava, an eight-year-old boy, was in a lively and energetic mood during the assent-gaining session. He displayed confidence and clear and quick thinking when asked to make choices – such as raising his left or right leg from the ground – and answering questions relating to 'yes' and 'no'. He arrived speedily at a decision about joining the research project and said 'yes' whilst nodding his head towards Reggie, eager and impatient to get this answer out and speaking over the calm and slow asking of the question by the researcher/therapist. Again with energy he moved from sitting on chairs to sitting at the table with an outward sense of curiosity to find out more. When presented with the information and assent forms he remained focused and interested until the researcher/therapist read out the word 'University' which appeared at the bottom of the first page. Lava shook his head and said 'Urgh – I don't like University!' The researcher/therapist asked him 'Why?', to which he replied that he had to explain it in class and he could not do it and it was hard. The researcher/therapist asked him if he'd like to continue and reminded him that he didn't have to. Lava said he did want to continue. However, when the word appeared on the next page he once again exclaimed 'Urgh! University!' Again he was asked if he would like to stop or continue to which he replied: 'I don't mind carrying on.' The exploration continued and when the word appeared towards the end of the document Lava did not make any outward sign of recognition. He then went on to give his assent to become involved in the study.

Lava was able to express his negative association with the word 'University' and make a choice about continuing to explore or not. He was listened to by the researcher/therapist and was able to tolerate continuing. By the end of the document he no longer needed to express his negativity towards the word and it had not prevented him from making a decision to engage with the research.

Vignette 3

Stargirl, an eleven-year-old girl, also expressed a connection to 'University' by identifying the institution's address contained in the project information document. Unlike Lava, this connection was positive from the outset as it was in a city with strong family connections for her and where she spent school holidays with extended members of her family – times she considers as being happy and fun. Seeing the address written on the paperwork added to her sense of joy at exploring the information. A competent reader with a rich and inquiring imagination, Stargirl read through the assent form and project information with ease and understanding. Before signing her assent and having ticked boxes to demonstrate her understanding of each statement on the assent form such as 'I understand that no one outside of the room will ever know who I am and anything that we make or write about me will have a pretend name'; 'I understand that if I do want to do the research I will be called a co-researcher and will wear a badge for part of each session'; I understand that if I do not want to join in with this research I can still come to dramatherapy sessions', Stargirl asked: 'How will we get there each week?' The researcher/therapist asked 'Where?' 'To the University' came Stargirl's reply. Her understanding was that she would be taken there each week to participate in the research. The researcher/therapist's task was then to establish that the assent being sought was in the knowledge that the research would be taking place in the dramatherapy room where they were and not in a university. Once established, Stargirl gave her assent by signing the document. She did not seem disappointed by the news that she would not be travelling to a university.

Adults may take signature-giving for granted. However, the research uncovered a trend that had not been anticipated; most of these child co-researchers had never written their signature before. Signing names on the assent form was an important and notable feature of the assent-gaining process. They each interpreted this task in unique ways. Below are Lady Gaga's and James's perspectives on providing signatures:

> Lady Gaga, an eight-year-old girl, having ticked all the boxes indicating she agreed with the statements on the assent form (some of which are written above), was asked if she should sign the form. The researcher/therapist informed her it was her own decision and that she could not help her make that choice. Lady Gaga chose the pen that the researcher/therapist had held in her hand whilst going through the documents. She then said 'I'll sign it here.' She then printed her name. She then paused as if to compose herself before signing her name in the space for a printed name. The process appeared to be empowering for her, as she sat up in her chair and smiled. The researcher/therapist's impression was that this was the first time Lady Gaga had been given the opportunity to sign her name. Lady Gaga and the researcher/therapist were probably experiencing a new discovery – what a signature feels like to write for the first time.

These non-verbal communications in the signing of names were significant and new voyages of discovery for both co-researcher and researcher/therapist. An important feature of all these vignettes was the enabling of creative expression and freedom of the children to explore their understandings of assent with the flexibility of movement and play that is a consistent feature of their individual dramatherapy work. Whilst providing a signature might be seen as belonging in the adult domain, this task was re-interpreted by each co-researcher who made it their own. Of key importance to the researcher/therapist was not where on the form they signed their name, but that they were given opportunities to explore assent in both verbal and non-verbal ways using action and stillness. In this way the exploration was specifically developed for children to engage with by drawing upon child-oriented processes.

This fairly simple method involving a combination of questions, answers and potential action was developed by almost all the children invited into the study, who added words such as 'don't know', 'not sure' and 'ask me later' when asked questions which had an intended 'yes' or 'no' answer. In this way the voice of the child was present in the work from the outset, as the assent-gaining method was adapted and developed on an individual basis. Alongside verbally based evolutionary aspects to this method also came non-verbal developments, as some children answered 'yes' or 'no' by nodding or shaking their head. Some answered 'I don't know'/'I'm not sure' by shrugging their shoulders and raising their eyebrows. These observations reiterate points made earlier about the importance of acting upon the messages and communications made by children. This suggests that in order to engage children of their own volition in this complex process, the researcher/therapist must be significantly experienced in understanding the processes of listening, reflecting and engaging in actions derived from such communications.

The children were easily able to engage with imagination and creativity when engaging with Reggie, the research frog hand-puppet. Their ability to access playful processes was evident in their readiness to suspend their disbelief as Reggie, being a puppet, was a familiar symbol to the children from their play world vocabulary.

The responses of the children were engaged and focused throughout not only the sequence but also the entire assent-gaining session. Some children searched at times for information from the researcher/therapist's face. Others laughed at the questions from the various categories in a way which depicted a sense of uncertainty and, possibly, initially a little anxiety. In each case, however, whatever feelings had been evoked at the beginning soon passed, and in their place was a sense of ownership and confidence in the way that questions were answered and choices made.

The gaining of permission to engage with the start of the research study, whether seen in terms of 'consent' or 'assent', led to new discoveries being made by the children, witnessed by the researcher/therapist and felt by both as positive expressions of children's individual ways of relating to the material and to the associated tasks. Being asked to consider their own needs resulted in increases in confidence and engagement which had led to the children, now in the role of co-researcher, to finding out about their unique voices and having them heard.

Conclusion

Terms such as 'consent' and 'assent' may have, at root, generalized meanings. The tendency in the past has been to seek to avoid complexity by creating structures that argue for one position across all situations and contexts in relation to children's participation. It is as if by arguing that parental consent alone is the answer to gaining permission, other issues need not be acknowledged. The changing position, outlined at the start of this chapter, is one that seeks to redress this tendency to create a generalist answer by trying to define an effective way of engaging with diversity whilst answering important needs relating to protection and meaningful participation in complex areas such as capacity, the provision of information, informed choice and power dynamics in relation to research with children. The approach to research reflected in the vignettes emphasizes these children as active meaning-makers and decision-makers in relation to informed assent and consent. The practice attempts to meet the positioning of participation identified earlier in this chapter as involving areas such as children knowing the nature of their involvement, the freedom to be involved or to withdraw and communicating the choice. Consent from parents should not be taken to mean that permission has been granted to undertake research with children, but that it gives permission to seek assent from the children themselves in a way that is meaningful and accessible to them (Bray 2007). Such views of consent and assent challenge traditional, simplifying ideas and recognize that gaining informed consent or assent from young researchers is complex and requires imaginative and participative approaches.

The research also illustrates the necessity of developing ways of working, rooted for example in play, that prioritize how children communicate, assimilate and use information. The practice described demonstrates the importance of engaging with the complexity and individuality of this aspect of child assent, along with the importance of validating and giving due recognition to children's competency and decision-making. Questions must naturally arise from such work. Children are shown to engage in a valid manner with permission, and to have the capacity to make judgements about their own involvement in a meaningful way. It is natural to ask why such validity and capacity should not be given weight and value in the ways given to adult consent. The necessary complexity of this is no reason for a lack of recognition in the formal ways that consent-gaining is supported. The chapter has shown that the bringing together of consent and ethics, with the new attitudes towards children developing from fields such as sociology, results in challenges to traditional thinking and practice. To return to Field and Berman's assertion that opened this chapter: if the 'ethical principle of respect for persons' underlies the obligation of investigators to 'treat individuals as autonomous actors who must provide their informed and voluntary consent to participate in research' (2004: 147–8) then children – such as Lady Gaga, Stargirl and Rocksus – need to be recognized as worthy of ethical respect. The research's engagement with consent, assent and ethics indicates the value of change. It illustrates the need for these areas to acknowledge children as active meaning-makers, decision-makers and social agents, able to participate in research in ways that appropriately recognize and empower them and that ultimately enhance the quality of the data collected.

References

Bradbury, H. and Reason, P. (2008). 'Action Research: An Opportunity for Revitalizing Research Purpose and Practices', *Qualitative Social Work*, 2, 155.

Bray, L. (2007). 'Developing an Activity to Aid Informed Assent When Interviewing Children and Young People'. *Journal of Research in Nursing*, 12 (5), 447–57.

British Psychological Society (2009). *Code of Ethics and Conduct*, London: BPS.

British Sociological Association (2004). *Statement of Ethical Practice*. London: BSA.

Broome, M. and Richards, D. (1998). 'Involving Children in Research'. *Journal of Child and Family Nursing*, 1 (1), 3–7.

Bryman, A. (2004). *Social Research Methods*, Oxford: Oxford University Press.

Cuskelly, M. (2005). 'Ethical Inclusion of Children with Disabilities in Research'. In A. Farrell (ed.), *Ethical Research with Children*, pp. 97–111. Berkshire: Open University Press.

Fader, R.R., Beauchamp, T.L. and King, N.M.P. (1986). *A History and Theory of Informed Consent*. New York: Oxford University Press.

Fasoli, L. (2003). 'Reflections on doing research with young children'. *Australian Journal of Early Childhood*, 28 (1), 7–28.

Field, M.J. and Berman, R.E. (2004). *Ethical Conduct of Clinical Research Involving Children*. Washington, DC: National Academies Press.

Groundwater-Smith, S. (2007). 'Student Voice – Essential Testimony for Intelligent Schools'. In A. Campbell and S. Groundwater-Smith (eds), *An Ethical Approach to Practitioner Research*. Abingdon: Routledge.

Hill, M. (2006). 'Children's Voices on Ways of Having a Voice: Children's and young people's perspectives on methods used in research and consultation.' *Childhood*, 13 (1), 69–89.

Joffe, S., Cook, E.F., Cleary, P.D., Clark, J.W. and Weeks, J.C. (2001). Quality of Informed Consent: A New Measure of Understanding Among Research Subjects', *Journal of the National Cancer Institute*, 93 (2), 139–47.

Jones, P. and Welch, S. (2010). *Rethinking Children's Rights*. London: Continuum.

Kellett, M. (2005a). 'Children as Active Researchers: A New Research Paradigm for the 21st Century?'. Unpublished NCRM Methods Review Papers, NCRM/003. <http://www.eprints.ncrm.ac.uk/87> accessed 5 September 2009.

Kellett, M. (2005b). *How To Develop Children as Researchers*. London: Paul Chapman Publishing.

Kellett, M. (2010). *Rethinking Children and Research*. London: Continuum.

Langley, D. (2006). *An Introduction to Dramatherapy*. London: Sage.

Leeson, C. (2007). 'Going Round in Circles – Key Issues In The Development Of An Effective Ethical Protocol For Research Involving Young Children'. In A. Campbell and S. Groundwater-Smith (eds), *An Ethical Approach to Practitioner Research*. Abingdon: Routledge.

MedTran (2009). *Informed Consent and Assent*, Medical Translation Services: Medtran <http: //www.medtran.ru/eng/trials/protomechanics/ch3.htm> accessed 20 December 2009.

Morrow, V. and Richards, M. (1996). 'The Ethics of Social Research with Children: An Overview.' *Children & Society*, 10, 90–105.

Moss, P. (2005). 'Listening to children: beyond rights to ethics'. Thomas Coram Institute: <http://www.itscotland.org.uk/earlyyears> accessed 20 October 2009.

Ofsted (2009). <http://www.ofsted.gov.uk> accessed 28 September 2009.

Powell, M.A. and Smith, A.B. (2009). Children's Participation Rights in Research, *Childhood*, 16 (1), 124–42.

Prout, A., Simmons, R. and Birchall, J. (2006). 'Reconnecting and Extending the Research Agenda on Children's Participation: Mutual Incentives and the Participation Chain'. In E. Kay, M. Tisdall, J.D. Davis, A. Prout, and M. Hill (eds), *Children, Young People and Social Inclusion: Participation for What?* Bristol: The Policy Press.

Royal College of Nursing (2004). *Research Ethics: RCN Guidance for Nurses*. RCN: London.

Twycross, A. (2009). An Interprofessional Approach to the Ethics of Undertaking Research with Children, *Nurse Researcher*, 16 (3), 1–14.

11   Their life, their choice: Ethical challenges for supporting children and young people in the self-management of Type 1 diabetes

The 'Getting Sorted' programme: Its origins

The 'Getting Sorted' programme was established in 2006 by Liz Webster to support young people with Type 1 diabetes. Liz is an experienced children's nurse who has been working with children with chronic life-limiting conditions for over twenty years. One of her underpinning principles of practice has been to encourage the participation and engagement of young people in their own health-care provision, the ultimate aim being to facilitate knowledge and empowerment so that young people become better able to self-manage their conditions effectively and safely. The inherent challenge here is that the locus of control normally sits with adults – the parents/carers and medical staff – and any changes to these established practices would require these adults to trust the young people and believe in their ability to self-manage their conditions if they were supported in the right ways by the adults around them.

In this chapter, we describe how the self-help workshops (which the young people named 'Getting Sorted') and the related research that Liz and her colleagues have engaged in have helped in further developing their own understanding of how competent young people are at self-management. However, we also illustrate the substantial barriers to self-management that remain, as a result of established and unchallenged clinical practices and because of the uncertainties within families around the management of the condition. The chapter illustrates and discusses the problems that these contextual difficulties create for young people with Type 1 diabetes as told from their own experiences and in their own wways. In telling this story, the chapter also addresses the related ethical challenges that arose for Liz and her team as they sought to reveal young people's voices and ultimately to influence and perhaps change established medical practices.

Type 1 diabetes develops if the body is unable to produce insulin. It usually appears before the age of forty. It is the least common of the two main types of diabetes and accounts for between 5 and 15 per cent of all people with diabetes. Type 1 diabetes cannot be prevented. Children and young people in England have amongst the highest incidences and also one of the worst records of diabetic control in Western Europe. The recent national childhood diabetes audit (Lewis and Hawkins 2008) showed that less than 20 per cent of children with diabetes achieve the recommended level of control as measured by HbA1c (glycosylated haemoglobin). An HbA1c blood test measures blood glucose control and glucose control is a key feature of Type 1 diabetes management. Deaths from Type 1 diabetes in children and young people are higher in Yorkshire than elsewhere in Europe. In a recent analysis of data from the Yorkshire and the Humber region only 15 per cent of children achieved the National Institute of Clinical Excellence (NICE) guidelines, which provide recommended levels of control for HbA1c as being 7.5 per cent or below (Lewis and Hawkins 2007). Therefore the key to good diabetic control is matching insulin dosage with food intake, exercise level and other lifestyle factors so that blood glucose always stays within the recommended level as stated above.

As some of the young people involved in 'Getting Sorted' noted, getting the balance is a real challenge for them even though their condition can be life-threatening:

> To get my reading below 9 per cent means I have no life. The balance of school work and control is difficult. I am either an A class student and have poor control or the other way around. It's not easy to get the balance.

Poor diabetic control in childhood impacts on long term control and increases the risk of major diabetic complications such as kidney failure, risk of amputation and blindness in early adult life (Lewis and Hawkins 2008).

Developing the 'Getting Sorted' programme

> Workshops have helped with diabetes because I feel more in control, e.g. bloods used
> to be all over the place but over the course of the workshops they've been OK. I've
> learnt how to manage bloods better at GS.

The 'Getting Sorted' programme is located in the Carnegie Faculty of
Sport and Education at Leeds Metropolitan University. It provides a series
of workshops that were, over time, developed by young people for young
people. These workshops aim to develop knowledge, skills and confidence
to allow young people to take effective control over their lives and their
condition. Originally, Liz had been commissioned to investigate the appro-
priateness of an 'Expert Patient' programme based on a model developed
by Lorig (1999). This 'Expert Patient' model had been adopted by the
Department of Health and delivered in all Primary Care Trusts (PCTs)
in England between 2002–2007 based on key principles set out in Saving
Lives Our Healthier Nation stating that:

> People can make individual decisions about their and their families' health and
> Expert Patients Programmes can help people to manage their own illnesses. (DoH
> 1999)

The National Service Framework for children and young people (DoH
2004) had provided a ten-year blueprint and made a recommendation
that the Expert Patient programme should be accessible to young people
(Standard 6). When she had started the commissioned work around the
Expert Patient model, Liz had drawn on her own long-standing commitment to self-empowerment and self-efficacy, and had questioned whether
young people would want an Expert Patient programme developed from a
model for adults. A research project was subsequently undertaken involving young people with Type 1 diabetes (Webster 2007), which asked three
questions:

- What is it that young people want?
- What are their aspirations for managing their condition?
- What could health care providers create with young people to assist them in managing their condition?

Webster trained three young people (aged 18–22, all female, with Type 1 diabetes) to partner her in this initial period of research and data collection; the young women were also involved in analysing the data. Nine themes emerged and subsequently informed the basis for and the development of the 'Getting Sorted' programme. Those themes were:

- Diabetes, the condition itself
- The impact on life for young people
- Young people's perceived lack of control as adults around them took over the management of their condition
- Labelling by society and making and keeping relationships with others
- Acceptance by self and others of the condition
- Parents – being over-protective and not listening and parents' own development of coping strategies
- Information – receiving no information or the wrong information, needing more information to deal with the condition, gaining new knowledge to self-care
- Developing their own coping strategies for longer-term management rather than day-to-day management
- Role models – learning from other young people who have the condition and providing peer-support through friendships

These initial themes identified a key feature to emerge as the programme progressed – that young people need an holistic experience that addressed both their medical needs and their sense of self within the family and wider community. The title of the programme – 'Getting Sorted' – came from the many quotes from young people responding to the three research questions and from their individual and collective sense of whether or not they 'felt sorted' in relation to their condition. The majority did not 'feel sorted' at all and felt as if their lives and conditions were beyond their power to manage as the following quotes from this study revealed:

Of clinic staff:
[I go] Every 3 months – [they] keep telling you that you need to do better; [I was] left feeling shit with all the issues, wanted to cry, wanted something out of it. Wanted some solution, to be given help. What's the point?
The Doctor makes my mum cry – I don't like clinic so sometimes I miss it.

Of the clinics:
Clinic is dull, boring, smelly.
Magazines are for old people.
Toys are too young.
Toilets are horrible.
It smells of blood.

Of parents:
[They were] too involved when I was younger, now they don't want me to go to doctor on my own when I'm sixteen.
Parents don't let me stay out past 7.30pm.
Pushy parents.
Annoying parents.
Parents nag me to do my bloods.
If my bloods are high I don't tell my mum because she will get angry.
Mum asks all the questions in clinic.
Mum makes me go – have no choice.
Dad didn't cope, got angry with me – always questioning.

As these early findings emerged, Liz began experiencing some ethical dilemmas. She found herself wanting to defend the professional workforce as the young people became increasingly open in response to the questions and became critical of the care they felt they were receiving in clinic; she also experienced feelings of guilt that the research seemed to be encouraging the young people to be critical of their parents. She recognized herself defending and trying to justify the approaches that the young people were reporting, and realized that this made her potentially complicit in the silencing of their voices.

She also began to see more clearly how the relationships with parents and family as well as those with clinical staff were a vital part of successful management of the condition. She realized how strong the pull of her professional mantle was and sought for some understanding of this desire and of a way to suppress it or at least to re-direct it into a genuine hearing of the young people's voices.

She identified Kellett's work (Kellett 2005; Kellett et al. 2004) as helping her to come to terms with the need to allow the young people's voices to 'dim' the clamour of her own professional voice and long-standing views about 'who knew best'. This was a gradual development of understanding as she became more aware of ideas and concepts around children and young people as researchers. She realized she needed to shift from being an advocate for parents and professionals, and to move beyond more familiar traditions of working *on* young people rather than *with* them (France 2004). This would involve personal shifts in thinking, language and understanding. It would be necessary to think more explicitly about *power*, for example. Mayall (2000) talks of inviting children and young people to share their perspectives rather than pretending that we do not have power over them. Barker (2009) points out how different children's services use different terminology to reinforce and reflect different social constructions of the power relationships between those who deliver and those who receive services.

Articles 12 and 13 of the United Nations Convention on the Rights of the Child require that children and young people should be informed, involved and consulted with in relation to all decisions that affect their lives. This includes medical decisions relating to individual medical conditions. Recent policy initiatives have highlighted the importance of participation by children and young people in policy development and implementation – most notably, perhaps, Every Child Matters (DfES 2003; 2004a; 2004b; ECM 2008) and the Children's Plan (DCSF 2007). France (2004) identifies a growth of interest in listening to children and alongside this, May (2000) shows how understanding voice has become a fundamental objective within social science research within the wider construct of reflecting the meanings and significance of what people have to say (Silverman 2001). In seeking to more actively and meaningfully involve young people as researchers in the design of a development programme relating to the management of Type 1 diabetes, Liz therefore needed to confront her own pre-conceptions of young people's rights to be heard amidst the clamour of professional and parental voices.

Moving the work forward

The emancipatory road to joint research with young people was consolidated for Liz in a piece of research undertaken in 2007 for Asthma UK using similar workshops to those being developed for Type 1 diabetes (Webster and Newell 2008). This research was testing out the transferability of the 'Getting Sorted' model to a different condition. The lessons learned from the previous research in terms of involving young people in research design, data collection and analysis and dissemination assisted the forward movement of this later research project. Four objectives were identified by the young researchers (four females, aged 16–20, all with asthma), in their language:

- To increase self-confidence and to balance managing their condition against getting on with and enjoying their lives
- To increase confidence to take active control of their condition and apply problem-solving skills to meet new challenges
- To equip young people with knowledge and skills and to set personal goals and develop effective strategies for achieving them
- To explore and develop existing relationships with others and their condition to help them feel more in control

'Getting Sorted' was tested against these objectives and this influenced the developing programme. By October 2009, it had been developed with almost 150 young people across six primary care trusts and/or local health organizations. Discussions were ongoing for wider programme delivery and it was moving beyond the two UK counties of Yorkshire and Humberside. The following section back-tracks a little to look at some of the young people's reflections and to consider the ways in which the ethical challenges they presented began to be addressed within the developments in programme design and via its wider dissemination.

Within the 'Getting Sorted' programme, there are five workshops over a twenty week period. The evaluation is ongoing within these workshops and becomes an integral part of the workshop itself rather than a separate strand. The following workshop activities produced the research data:

- Focus groups are held; the young people renamed these 'talking groups' as a more relevant term for them. Some topics became substantial and remain under discussion for the duration of the workshops (one of these was the issue of transition from children's to adult services which is returned to a little later in the chapter).
- Oral presentations where young people can, in impromptu fashion and of their own volition, tell their own stories or the parts of their stories they wish to share. For example, one young person might have experienced an 'epiphany' prior to the session – a breakthrough perhaps in a parent's response to them – and may want to share this with the group. These would often generate further discussions as the group recognized the importance of the shared experience in coming to terms with their individual achievements or fears.
- Creative, reflective drama where, in the final workshop, each participant – working with actors from a local theatre company – rehearses and presents their story. This then leads towards the collective presentation of all stories by all members of the group, termed 'the grand performance'.
- One-to-one interview to which each young person brings their own story/script and a member of the 'Getting Sorted' team uses these storylines to frame questions to illustrate how the young person's experiences of self-empowerment and self-efficacy are developing and to identify what might be creating difficulties in forward movement. The interview becomes personal to the individual context rather than generalized thus replacing previous

methods where the researchers had pre-determined the questions but felt they were getting the answers that the young people might have thought they wanted, rather than an illustrative account of their own journeys towards self efficacy and empowerment and related challenges.

This latter example of working practice and data collection is illustrative of the wider ways in which the workshop activities have 'opened out' over time to be led by young people's interests rather than by the adult-leaders agendas. The workshops also have young people involved in facilitation and because they become increasingly confident in their roles, they are able to facilitate the 'turning up' of other, less confident, participant voices in the workshops. The commitment to hearing views and voices subsequently starts to have a cumulative effect in shaping the activities intended to enable young people to more effectively understand and manage their conditions and, over time, to allow them to use their voices more effectively in shaping the responses to them by medical staff and parents.

Re-framing ethical values and practice through listening to children and young people with Type 1 diabetes

These methods of data collection and engagement revealed trends and experiences that the young people began to articulate with increasing confidence as workshops progressed. As well as their voices gaining strength and momentum, Liz also found herself reflecting at deeper and deeper levels about her own role. She and the other members of the growing team recognized their responsibilities in relation to translating the voices of young people and carrying their views to the commissioners and providers of health care. They began to see the need for real change in how services were being provided but recognized that this would require a huge cultural shift within providing institutions. It would have to begin with small steps. Three aspects of particular concern for young people are illustrated below:

- Perspectives on clinical experiences
- Perspectives on transition from children's to adult diabetes services
- Perspectives on balance between the holistic needs of the individual and the need for treatment

Perspectives on clinical experiences

As some of the earlier comments have shown, many young people seldom enjoyed their experiences in clinic. Their comments and reflections showed high levels of stress, uncertainty, and concerns that they would be told off for not managing their conditions better:

> It feels like you're being told off if things go wrong.
> Too hot in clinic – I get headaches.
> The Doctor is too textbook, my HbA1c should be X but I can't achieve it.

In order to try and assist the young people in being pro-active in addressing these negative experiences in constructive ways, the reflective drama sessions were used to allow young people to work with actors to create their 'perfect clinical appointment'. In this drama, a 'consultant', a 'parent' and a young person acted out a worst-case scenario. The 'audience' are allowed to 'freeze' the action at any point and to comment upon what they are seeing in relation to their own experiences of clinical appointments. The ethical challenge here relates to the recognition that, on one hand, the young people are being encouraged to be critically evaluative of their medical experiences and – as previous reflections have shown – this can lead to a negative and downward spiral of reflection. To offset this, the groups are asked to reflect on how they can change this experience. Whilst they may not be able to change the medical practices, they can begin to develop strategies and solutions for how they behave and how they respond, and initiate conversations with doctors and other medical professionals. This also applies to their relationships with their parents during and in relation to clinical experiences.

As noted, the leaders have an ethical responsibility to support young people in moving on from initial criticisms of parents; it would be unfortunate and potentially very damaging if young people were to leave the workshops feeling this way about their parents and carers. To counter this, the actors are asked to offer a monologue as a 'parent' reflecting on how they feel about their child's condition and the ways in which they might want to manage it. This gives the young people a chance to reflect on how their parents/carers are feeling themselves and to distance themselves from their own feelings for a while and gain a new perspective on their condition. This helps the young person recognize the need to be sensitive to their parents' needs and to those of other family members, who are themselves seeking to understand and then help to manage the condition. It may take four of five sessions of reflection and discussion before the young people are willing to speak with the parent. There have been occasions when young people have decided they do not want a parent to come into the consultation with them and this has been successfully negotiated.

Perspectives on transition from children's to adult diabetes services

As the young people gave voice to their concerns about their treatment in their local diabetes unit, it became apparent how different this treatment was across units in different regions. This presented the team with a challenge in terms of how this information could be fed back. It seemed important not to hold on to this information as it directly affected the quality of care for young people. This information was subsequently fed back to each unit via a summary report. However, across the units, this began to reveal to the team huge disparities of practice and different levels of inclination in responding to young people's criticisms. One key area here related to the transition from young people's to adult's services for continued treatment which generally happens when they are sixteen years old. Comments from young people during the workshops included:

> There was no preparation time for a massive change.
> No one talked to me about transition, it was like a mobile thing, you get a card with five things on it roughly describing what it was, it didn't go into much detail.

> I hated my transition clinic so much I was in tears by the end of it because I had like twice as many doctors but they are all like pushing me to be on multiple injections and I really didn't want that because mine was well controlled and they were saying if you stay on this your control is going to be so bad with life complications it was every single doctor telling me that.

As a consequence of some of these experiences at transition time, some young people might deteriorate; this was becoming increasingly apparent as team members spoke with them in their talking groups or one-to-one interviews. Along with this realization of possibly serious deterioration comes a responsibility that clinics need to become aware that their preparatory work for transition could be improved with, potentially, very little effort on the part of clinical administrators. Sarah's story about her first appointment at the transition clinic provides a very illuminating and worrying case study around the challenges and dangers of transition:

> CONSULTANT: How are you doing?
> SARAH: Not very good, things get on top of me, can't cope, diabetes gets pushed to one side.
> CONSULTANT: I can't help with things at home, but you can control it yourself because you have been on the Daphne course. Bye, see you in 4 months.

As a result Sarah remarked that she

> Left feeling shit with all the issues, wanted to cry, wanted something out of it? Wanted some 'solution', to be given help. What's the point? Control getting worse if a doctor is not bothered.

Other young people also commented on their experiences of transition. These are grouped under the (often overlapping) themes below:

Inadequate 'handover' to adult clinic:

I didn't know I was in transition – no one told me at clinic.
You won't be seeing us anymore.
Not glad about going to see someone I didn't know.
No preparation. Sometimes see different nurses. Massive change in environment.
Can't do anything. I'm classed as an adult.
Negative, not good.

Lack of Information:

No letter, phone call, text message, email.
Too big a gap – it's 'too' different, not that I wouldn't cope, just need a clearer picture.
Didn't know the system or where to sit or go.
Am I just controlling it myself now? – DIY (DO IT YOURSELF) Diabetic Management.
Moved at 16, didn't know who I was going to see, who to ring, 'no-one' I knew.
Don't know who my doctor or nurse is.

Not given enough time:

Clinic wait 1 hour – not given chance to talk, two minutes tops.
An 'in betweener' – not as important as a real adult – an older woman in before me, in for ages.

Feeling 'alone':

Felt there was nobody.
Inadequate help when feeling upset and unable to cope.

Transition was a huge issue for these young people and was raised in many of the discussions across the programme; it was clearly something that needed to be addressed by the clinics.

Perspectives on balance between the holistic needs of the individual and the need for treatment

As the work progressed, Liz and the team began to understand that what was needed was a young person-centred model of diabetes care based on young people's views, experiences and knowledge but which also took account of the constraints of professional practice in hospital and clinical settings and the lives, needs and experiences of parents supporting a child or young person with diabetes.

They began to recognize the implications of the fact that Type 1 diabetes is managed by acute service provision and that this potentially inhibits the development of multi-professional approaches with other practitioners who might be better placed at bringing about an effective blend of the personal and the medical needs of young people in relation to diabetes management. Also, whilst the voices of young people were exciting and liberating as the workshops had progressed, the ethical challenge that the team needed to face was the right of medical staff and parents and family to be heard also. The biggest ethical challenge would be to strive for balance in order to bring about the necessary changes to facilitate institutional and cultural shifts in practice and provision. In the first instance the challenge was to hear the young peoples' voices and this created an important sense of solidarity for team members, but initially, this dimmed the voices of parents and professionals – this was no way forward if young people were to be well served. The key shift that was needed was towards treating the person and not the condition. The workshops provided an important venue for reflection and awareness-raising in young people and this young facilitator who had been involved in many workshops expertly articulated the need for an appropriate social context in the management of a medical condition:

> The discussions allowed all of the young people who took part in the programme to gain a sense of independence in an environment that was free of doctors and parents. This environment also allowed the young people to ask questions which they would otherwise be too embarrassed to ask, or felt uncomfortable with. The barrier between medical professionals and young people is broken in a more social situation like the 'Getting Sorted' programme.

Professionals do not have an opportunity to hear what young people are saying about their treatment; they do not hear these voices in clinic because here, the voices are dimmed largely because there is so little time during clinical appointments. However, as young people have also indicated they are, in their view, often disrespectfully treated in clinic; this does seem to vary from unit to unit as the written summaries that team members prepared for each unit began to reveal. On the one hand, doctors have a fundamental responsibility to draw a young person's attention to the dangers of the poor control of their condition; however for the young person, a small improvement in control of their HbA1c may require a huge shift in their life-style, feelings about themselves and attitudes to their condition. Their medical condition, for them, is not the only factor in their life; as teenagers, they are dealing with hormone shifts, puberty, body image, exams and much more (Gage et al. 2004). There are psycho-social conditions that surround their medical condition and their voices clamour for a greater acknowledgement of their wider lives and identity alongside their medical condition.

Conclusion

The workshop material reveals how young people want to keep autonomy, self-care and self-esteem at the heart of the treatment rather than sustaining a wholly medical model where experts make decisions with parents and, in so doing, exclude the young person's voice from the ongoing debates;

making changes here requires a shift in where the locus of power rests. The
'Getting Sorted' workshops have learned how to offer this power shift
over time by giving young people information about their condition and
its management whilst allowing dissent and creative solutions to be heard
and shared as the following quote powerfully illustrates:

> The new people I was able to meet as part of this programme, have enabled me to
> take control of my diabetes. Previously I did not check my blood sugar, and always
> guessed the amount of carbohydrate in the meal. Now, I take an active approach to
> my condition, asking the questions that I feel need to be answered by my Diabetes
> Nurse Specialist (DSN) and making myself knowledgeable about the different
> products available to me.

This young facilitator was diagnosed at thirteen and here she is at twenty-
one, only just recognizing – it seems – that she is able to control her diabetes; clinical attendance was not able to give her this realization, it was
becoming a facilitator on 'Getting Sorted' and listening to the discussions
and getting information in this context that pushed her towards 'taking
control'. This illustrates that 'taking control' is an incremental process; to
flourish, it needs a facilitative environment and an holistic acknowledgement of the complexity of young people's lives.

It is important to note that 'Getting Sorted' was never intended to
replace medical models of care but rather to give voice for the first time in
relation to Type 1 diabetes, to young people's perspectives on their care and
their own efficacy, or not, as the case might be, in the self-management of
their conditions. The aim of the programme became to let young people
drive changes in practice and the young people themselves have educated
the team because the team became increasingly able to hear what young
people were saying.

Future challenges that have more recently arisen for the 'Getting
Sorted' team as ethical forward-movement, include convincing medical
professionals that young people are worth listening to and that they can
effectively operate as partners in their own care and well-being – with the
right approaches. This construct of self-efficacy was at the heart of the
project but has also presented the greatest set of challenges because of
the well-established procedures in place in terms of offering diabetes

treatment to young people; invariably the approach is to treat them as 'patients' rather than as 'people' and the programme and its evaluation have shown that this needs to be changed to create better management of Type 1 diabetes in Yorkshire if HbA1c levels are to be improved and the likelihood of associated life-threatening conditions to be alleviated.

Maintaining the energy and impetus to keep the initiative moving forward; the team has grown from one person (Liz) to four members; there is a supportive infrastructure within a university faculty; there are now eleven facilitators working with young people in the workshops across the region, there is National Health Service Diabetes support with an evaluation project ongoing. Increasing numbers of health care professionals are listening to and acting on the clear messages that young people are sharing both within 'Getting Sorted' and in their increasing numbers of presentations at meetings, seminars and conferences. Consultants have nowhere to hide when a young person is standing before them and telling them: 'you're making me feel rubbish' or is suggesting to the consultants that they need to build their own confidence (as consultants) in building good relationships with young people. The work goes on.

References

Barker, R. (2009). 'Every Child Matters: Current Possibilities, Future Opportunities and Challenges'. In R. Barker (ed.), *Making Sense of Every Child Matters: Multi-Professional Practice Guidance*. Bristol: The Policy Press.

Department for Children, Schools and Families (DCSF) (2007). *The National Children's Plan – Building Brighter Futures*. London: DCSF.

Department for Education and Skills (DfES) (2003). *Every Child Matters: The Green Paper*. London: DfES.

——(2004a). *Every Child Matters: Change for Children*. London: DfES.

——(2004b). *Every Child Matters: Next Steps*. London: DfES.

Department of Health (DoH) (1999). *Saving Lives: Our Healthy Nation*. London: DoH.

—— (2001). *A New Approach to Chronic Disease Management in the 21st Century*. London. HSMO.

—— (2004). *National Service Framework for Children and Maternity Services. Core Standards*. London. HSMO.

Every Child Matters (ECM) (2008). 'The Children's Plan' <http://www.everychild-matters.gov.uk/strategy/childrensplan/>.

France, A. (2004). 'Young People'. In S. Fraser, V. Lewis, S. Ding, M. Kellett and C. Robinson (eds), *Doing Research with Children and Young People*. London: Sage.

Gage, H., Hampson, S., Skinner, T. (2004). 'Educational and Psychosocial Programmes for Adolescents with Diabetes: Approaches, Outcomes and Cost Effectiveness', *Patient Education and Counselling*, 53, 333–46.

Kellett, M. (2005). *How to Develop Children as Researchers*. London: Paul Chapman.

Kellett, M., Forrest, R., Dent, N. and Ward, S. (2004). 'Just Teach Us the Skills, We'll Do the Rest: Empowering Ten Year Olds as Active Researchers', *Children and Society*, published online 5 February 2004 DOI: 10. 1062/Chi.807. <http://onlinelibrary.wiley.com/doi/10.1111/chso.2004.18.issue-5/issuetoc> accessed 10 October 2009.

Lewis, I and Hawkins, J. (2008). *Final Report of the Yorkshire and the Humber Clinical Pathway Group for Children*. NHS Yorkshire and the Humber.

Lorig, K., Sobel, D. and Stewart, A. (1999). 'Evidence Suggesting That a Chronic Disease Self-Management Program Can Improve Health Status while Reducing Hospitalization: A Randomized Trial', *Medical Care*, 37, 5–14.

May, T. (2000). *Social Research: Issues, Methods and Process*. Buckingham: Open University Press.

Mayall, B. (2000). 'Conversations with Children: Working with Generational Issues'. In P.H. Christenson and A. James (eds), *Research with Children: Perspectives and Practices*. London: Routledge Falmer.

Silverman, D. (2001). *Interpreting Qualitative Data: Methods for Analysing Talk, Text and Interaction*. London: Sage.

Webster, E (2007). Development and *Evaluation of the Getting Sorted Self Care Workshops for Young People with Diabetes*. Yorkshire and the Humber Strategic Health Authority.

——and Newell, C. (2008). *Development and evaluation of the Getting Sorted self-care workshops for young people with asthma*. Asthma UK.

KAYE JOHNSON

12 Promoting ethical understandings in child co-researchers

For the past fifteen years ethical questions dominated my work as a primary school head teacher who wanted children to participate in school-based research. Conducting the research in my own schools posed a number of ethical dilemmas including my role:

- As 'an insider' with privileged knowledge that would not be available to external researchers
- As principal, which placed me in a position of power over the children with whom I wished to conduct the research,
- As principal with the likelihood of remaining in these settings after the conclusion of the research

These ethical considerations were further compounded because I wanted to include the children as investigators in school based research so I needed to teach them about, as well as enact the ethical principles of, informed consent, confidentiality and respectful treatment of all people associated with the research.

This chapter explores these considerations as I acknowledged children as competent contributors to improving their schools. It identifies some of the ways in which I addressed the ethical issues of consent and confidentiality when conducting research in my own school with thirty 8–10 year olds. In it I tell of the guidelines children devised for adults who wished to conduct research in their school and demonstrate how I used these to make explicit to the children the purposes and ethical conduct of our school based research.

Listening to children

> I begin by outlining my motivation for listening to children because identifying the reasons for asking children their perspectives is central to *what* children are asked, *which* children are asked, *how* they are asked and *what is done* with what they say. (Fielding 2001)

My commitment to enabling children to have a say in their everyday school lives – that is, to participate in decisions about curriculum, the daily operations and the governance of their schools – has been informed by those who have called for children's voices to be heard. These advocates for listening to children can be summarized as follows:

- Defenders of children's rights (Groundwater-Smith and Downes 1999; Alderson 2003)
- Proponents of school effectiveness (MacBeath 1999)
- Campaigners for distributed leadership (Gronn 1999)
- Supporters of civics and citizenship education (Pekrul and Levin 2005; Holdsworth and Thomson 2002)
- Those who maintain that schools' current practices are based on outdated constructions of childhood and who propose the New Sociology of childhood (Prout 2001; Rudduck and Flutter 2000)
- Promoters of critical literacies (Comber and Nixon 2004; Comber and Thomson with Wells 2001; Luke 2000)

These calls for the inclusion of children's perspectives are not mutually exclusive and their intersection influenced my thinking about inviting children to talk about their school. I had three main reasons for asking children their perspectives about their school. Firstly, I wanted to ensure that children played an integral role in determining their school experiences and provided feedback about their school and how it met their learning needs. Further, I wanted to work with children to co-create a democratic school environment in which they could develop expertise in having their voices heard in a variety of forums thus learning ways of operating as active citizens. Finally, I wanted to enable them to contribute to leading school change and to work collaboratively towards improvement for all children. I therefore decided to conduct research that would value children's knowledge about their lives and provide opportunities through visual research and action research for them to share their perspectives and take action.

Researching with children

Asking children

Children at my previous school had considerable experience in being asked about their perspectives and in participating in research (Johnson 2000). These children were confident in articulating their views because of their experience on school-wide reference groups and working parties. Rather than having a Student Representative Council where a small number of students operate as a decision-making executive, we had adopted a system of committees. This meant that more than one third of the children were involved simultaneously in the daily running and governing of their school. When issues arose that did not fit under the role description of any of the committees, additional working parties and reference groups were formed.

At a time when that school was overwhelmed with requests from external researchers, a reference group was initiated to explore the rights and needs of children being researched. That reference group was made up of eight children in years 4–7 each of whom had personal experience with research, that is, had been an active participant in research conducted by an external researcher. Each of the children was articulate about the rights of students of all ages to have a say in matters that affected them. Each of the children strongly believed that the child, as well as the sets of parents/caregivers, should be consulted about participating in external research. While our initial discussions focused on the areas of confidentiality, consent and safety, these concerns were quickly followed by children's emphasis on being treated well in the collection, interpretation and use of the information they provided. As an outcome of these discussions, the children devised a set of guidelines for adults wishing to conduct research with them. Known as *The Child Speaks to the Researcher*, the following guidelines form a child-centred ethical code of practice prepared by children (Prosser 1998):

1. Please treat me and my life with respect.

2. Tell me about this research
   - Why are you doing it?
   - Who will it help?
   - What is my role?
   - What will you do with what I say?

3. Ask me if I want to participate
   - Tell me how I was chosen
   - Tell me what I need to do
   - Give me a real choice to decide
   - Don't threaten me if I change my mind

4. Invite me to talk about things that are directly related to the research, don't trick me with smart questions or pry into the rest of my life.
   Show me that you are really listening.

5. Share my story in ways that don't
   - Put me down
   - Make it worse than it is
   - Make me unsafe

6. Please show me what you have done with my words.

These guidelines were then shared with any external researchers prior to allowing them access to that school as a research site. *The Child Speaks to the Researcher* also provided the basis for subsequent discussion with children in other schools about ethics in research.

Children as co-researchers

I wanted to engage children at my primary school in investigating issues they defined as central to their school lives. Rather than acting as sources of data or even becoming active respondents, children at my primary school were positioned as co-researchers (Fielding 2001). Co-researching with children was designed to

- Enable active involvement by children in research which privileged their perceptions rather than merely asked them to collect data
- Reduce passive or tokenistic forms of involvement by children
- Enable children to represent their worlds rather than have someone else portray their lives for them
- Enable children to contribute to the analysis of the materials they created, to determine which topics to pursue and decide which aspects of their school they wished to improve

Table 1 summarizes the children's roles as co-researchers in the research about their school.

Table 1

Project 1: Children representing their school places	Project 2: Children interpreting their school places	Project 3: Children changing their school places
Purposes: This project was informed by calls for children to have a say and the roles of children in research. It provided the context for conversations with the child co-researchers in Project 2.	Purposes: This project enabled children to interpret their own data created during Project 1. Children reflected on the places they like and places they want to change. Together with Project 1, Project 2 provided the data for the renaissance moment of action research in Project 3. This project informed reflections on researching with children.	Purposes: This project enabled the children, as co-researchers, to further analyse and act on their data from Projects 1 and 2. Reflections on the action research further informed learning about researching with children.
Research Questions: How do children represent their place(s) in the school? • Which places did children choose to represent? • What geographies do they convey? • What are the commonalities among the representations?	Research Questions: How do children understand their place(s) in the school? • Which of the school sites do children say they like? Why are these preferred places? • Which places do they want to talk about? • Who determines their access to and activity within these places? • How does access to and activity within places affect their connectedness with the school? • What do children see as their place(s) within the school?	Research Questions: How do children respond to the everyday spaces in the school? • What changes would children like to make to places in the school? • How could they enable this to occur? • Which research methods enable children to engage with the topic, pose questions they want to answer, collect and analyse data and share their stories?

Visual research methods:	Small group interviews:	Action research methodologies:
Children created visual compositions and photographs of places they liked or wanted to talk about. Adult researcher analysed children's representations using visual semiotics.	Children interpreted their photographs. Adult researcher analysed the interview transcripts to gain insight into children's perceptions of their places and concerns about them.	With the adult researcher, children analysed their data, responded to adult researcher's interpretations, determined which places to change and used the four moments of action research to implement and reflect on changes.

Ethical implications of listening to and researching with children

In this section I focus on three aspects of ethical research with children. Firstly, I consider the relationship between adults and children in school settings. Next, I reflect on the practice of informed consent and my responses to this dilemma. Finally, I address the difficulties of maintaining confidentiality.

Relationships between adults and children within the school

The commitment to co-researching with children and conducting the research in my own school posed a number of ethical dilemmas. While research always takes place within social relations and cultural contexts (Christensen and Prout 2005) seeking to conduct research in my own school further complicated ethical issues. Investigating aspects of one's own workplace, 'insider' research, has been cited as the single factor that impacts on all other ethical issues of research.

> The insider has responsibilities and relationships that are fundamentally different from those of an outsider doing research in schools ... (the insider) will struggle with issues of loyalty, confidentiality and trust ... They know that after this enquiry is complete and this report is written their own professional life will continue in the same setting. (Zeni 2001: xii)

In my case, these demands on the insider researcher were made more complex by having an adult co-researching with children. Two of the major challenges in researching with children have been identified as the characteristically hierarchical power relationships between adults and children and the intergenerational differences between the groups (Morrow and Richards 1996; Rudduck and Flutter 2000; Corsaro 2005). These challenges were intensified because of my role as the principal of the school. I therefore focused on redressing the power differences between the children, as students of the school of which I was principal, and me, as the adult researcher.

Combined with my position as principal, the discursive structures of schools prevented me from adopting approaches favoured by others who had researched with young children. I was well known to the children and their previous experiences interacting with me meant they had expectations of my role, my behaviour and me. I was therefore unable to assume 'atypical adult' behaviours used by Corsaro (2001), or to take on the 'least adult role' favoured by Epstein (1998) or to pretend that I could simply 'blend in' as Karlsson (2001) attempted. Instead, I sought to redress the power differences by adopting the role of a researcher rather that of a school principal. As a researcher, I made explicit both the purposes and processes of the research; I adopted image-based methods and enabled children to analyse the data they had collected; and sought to interact openly with them.

Informed consent

Informed consent is the process used by researchers to gain the permission of those who will be involved in the research. While there may be slight variations because of institutional protocols, professional practices and individual projects, the general elements of informed consent require the researcher(s) to:

- Provide potential participants with information about the nature, duration, purpose and risks of the research
- Seek an agreement, in writing, from the participants to be part of the project. This consent is to be sought without coercion and constraint and without using deception or fraud
- Promise that participant confidentiality will be maintained and that the participant can withdraw at any stage of the research without retribution

Informed consent aims to protect the individual from physical, psychological or social harm as well as ensuring that the research contributes to the development of a moral, rational society. The misuse of the trust of those being researched can have a cumulative and diminishing influence, not just on the individuals in the specific research instance, but also on society. Informed consent therefore requires researchers to be mindful of their roles in preserving the welfare of each participant and contributing to the store of trust about research. This was particularly relevant to research with children in my school because I had a duty of care to each of them, was bound to model the school's values, and would remain at the school at the conclusion of the research.

When inviting participants to consent to the research, there is an obligation for the researcher to alert them to the possibility that some research could impact on the lives of those involved and may generate emotional and interpersonal responses throughout the research. I found the guidelines in the *Child Speaks to the Researcher* useful for assessing the potential of humiliation or embarrassment during the data collection processes as well as the dissemination of findings. The children's caution in points 4 and 5 of the guidelines set out in *The Child Speaks to the Researcher* place the focus clearly on the well being of the participants and emphasize the relational aspect of ethical conduct in research. *The Child Speaks to the Researcher* was a standard to which I returned throughout the research projects.

Because of their ages, children in primary schools are not considered competent in making decisions about whether to participate in research and are therefore not legally able to give (or with-hold) consent to their own involvement. Institutional ethics practices do not require children to be provided with information about the research, or their roles in the research and they are not required to say whether they want to participate in research about them. Because of this, advocates for children argue that many ethics policies are essentially adult focused, legally oriented proto-cols which address the needs of adults, while ignoring and marginalizing the rights of children (Alderson 2003; Morrow and Richards 1996). They claim that parents make the decisions about their children's involvement while the children are silenced.

My thinking about gaining children's consent to participate in my research was informed by the practices of researchers who have attempted to include children in the decision to participate in research projects (Morrow and Richards 1996; Epstein 1998).

In developing a model to involve children in decision-making, I rejected approaches to determining children's participation in research based on both adults' and children's rights. Rather than adopting either of the polarized stances, I sought to balance the power between adults and children. I recognized children both as competent human beings who can articulate their needs and also as young people requiring the support of adults. I followed the technical requirements as well as the intent of insti-tutional ethical guidelines by asking parents to give permission for their child's involvement in the research before inviting the children to commit themselves to it. While this may indeed be asking children to 'assent' to their participation, I think that the term 'assent' relegates children to pas-sive roles. Because I provided the children with detailed information about the research, their roles and allowed them time to ask questions about it, I therefore apply the term 'informed consent' to describe the process of seeking children's active commitment to participation in my research and to positioning them as partners.

Although the children had been given permission by their parents to take part in this research and had themselves consented to join in the first project, they were again provided with formal and informal opportunities to withdraw prior to the analysis of their photographic images of the school in the second project. Even though they had initially consented to being part of the previous study, they had the right to withdraw from, without retribution, any of the subsequent research projects. Informed consent does not only occur at the initiation of the study but becomes a way of operating throughout the research, that is, 'informed consent is ongoing, continual negotiation' (Mathison et al. 1993: 3). I enabled participants to explicitly renegotiate their involvement at each successive stage of the research. I provide details about this and the children's responses to being invited to participate in the research within the 'Pedagogic approach' section below.

Maintaining confidentiality

Maintaining confidentiality is an integral aspect of reducing the identification and possible embarrassment of participants. In my co-researching with children, I considered three aspects of promoting confidentiality. The first was for the research not to identify any of the co-researchers. The second was to discourage the child co-researchers from disclosing specific details of their discussions with their peers. The third was to ensure that children who had not agreed to participate in the research were not photographed.

I made explicit the reasons for using pseudonyms as one way of maintaining confidentiality and invited children to disguise themselves appropriately. In an attempt to avoid the confusions outlined by Epstein (1998), I told the children of her research and some of the interesting observations she had made about encouraging children to select pseudonyms. When I invited children to choose a name that did not obscure their gender or cultural background and that did not indicate another class member, they entered the process of selecting an appropriate alias with great enthusiasm. While their renaming appeared to be part of the 'fun' of the research, children were thoughtful about their choices of name. Thus the first aspect of confidentiality, maintaining the anonymity of participants, was effective.

However, the second aspect of confidentiality that of not revealing details of the discussions remained a dilemma. Because the analysis of the photographs occurred in small groups, children had access to the visual representations created by others. Further, they heard the explanations about the reasons for the inclusion of each photograph by their peers and were therefore able to identify and make public the sources of specific ideas. Other researchers have noted that it is difficult to guarantee that children would not attribute comments to specific individuals (Prosser 1998). I addressed this by focusing in the workshops on children's understandings about confidentiality. I enabled them to generate principles that would guide their conduct throughout the research. Children suggested that essential ways of respectfully treating all those participating in the research would include 'being on the lookout for putdowns and embarrassment' and 'asking how would I feel if this was said about me'. These guides allowed the children to develop principles of conduct guiding research relationships rather simply applying a list of prescribed rules.

Similarly, the third aspect of maintaining confidentiality, that is, of precluding photographs of others who had not consented to be part of the research, posed some challenges for the child co-researchers. In the creation of their photographic compositions of the school places they liked and those they wanted to talk about, children often had difficulty in finding these places 'unpeopled'. Several of the research teams had to go back to their places a number of times before they found them absent of children at play or engaged in formal learning. During our research workshops these children debated whether photographs that included children who were not easily identifiable could be considered as not treating them respectfully. Another example of the children's consideration of ethical research behaviours as relational rather than technical was the deliberation about whether they could include visual images of themselves. One research team cleverly argued that photographs of themselves reflected in the glass entry doors fulfilled all principles of ethical treatment of people in the research, that is, those photographed understood the purposes of the research, their roles in it, had consented to participate and wanted to be photographed.

I now focus on the pedagogic approach I used to model and explicitly teach children about the ethical issue of informed consent.

Pedagogic approach

I took note of the cautions about research that assumes children are incompetent, that treats them as incompetent and which then produces findings which confirm that incompetence (Alderson 2000; Buckingham 2000). Even well-intentioned researchers may employ methods that construct children as passive, ignorant or incapable. They do this by oversimplifying the language and concepts used in their studies, by limiting the range and format of responses available to children or by involving children who are inexperienced in the areas being investigated. To avoid treating children as incompetent and to enable them to become co-researchers, I decided to implement a pedagogic approach to research as advocated by Thomson and Gunter (2005).

I constructed a highly specific and explicit program to teach children about research. This approach acknowledged children's competence, valued their unique perspectives and enabled them to develop the knowledge and skills to become co-researchers while simultaneously challenging the traditional positioning of children in research. I developed a series of workshops to provide information to the children in ways which would connect with their understandings about research; which would create spaces for them to talk about, reflect on, and to ask questions about research. These workshops challenged children to consider the ethical issues of informed consent, confidentiality and respectful treatment of all people involved in the research. Importantly, the workshops were designed to *model* respectful treatment of all as well as to raise ethical issues.

Informed consent

I produced a pamphlet (Figure 1) to explain to children my work as a researcher and their roles as co-researchers. The pamphlet addressed each of the points in the document *The Child Speaks to the Researcher*. In the initial workshop children who were contemplating their participation in my research discussed the prepared pamphlet in small groups and tested out the degree to which it addressed the criteria from *The Child Speaks to the Researcher*.

At the following workshop I posed the following questions to evaluate the children's understanding of the purposes of the research and their roles in:

- If you were going to tell another student what a researcher does, what would you say?
- If you were going to explain to someone what you were doing as part of this research, what would you say?

A further question ensured that children had the information they required to make an informed decision about their initial commitment to the research:

- If you were going to decide whether this was a safe and interesting activity to be involved in, what other things would you want to know?

These workshops were held prior to seeking children's agreement to participate. After a 'cooling off' time when children could discuss their involvement with each other, ask further questions of me or seek support from others, they were then invited to formalize their agreement to participate in the research by writing to me.

Figure 1: Pamphlet inviting children to participate in research

WHY AM I ASKING YOU TO HELP WITH THIS RESEARCH?
This research is about what children think about their schools. Although I will be asking you only about this school, I hope that together we will find out what can make many schools better places for children.

WHY IS THIS RESEARCH IMPORTANT?
I think that adults who work in schools can learn a lot from listening to the children who also work in schools.

Children are the 'experts' on their lives, so I am asking you, as the expert on your life and school, about your experiences and opinions. I will need to find out from the other experts (i.e., other students) about their experiences and ideas. As the main researcher, I will be leading a team of experts who will assist in this investigation.

I chose your class because
- we have shared our learning during the last year
- you have been practising asking challenging questions
- you have been looking for ways to extend your thinking
- you have the understandings to assist in this research.

WHAT DO YOU NEED TO DO?
1) You need to decide whether you would like to help with this research. *This is optional; you are not required to be part of this project.* There will be no consequences for not joining it or for changing your mind once it has started.
2) I will ask you to
   - work in small groups to talk about the photographs you took of our school;
   - talk with me about the photographs. We will videotape our conversations;
   - tell me about the individual pictures you created (painting, drawing, digital design) showing places in our school. We will audiotape our conversations.
3) Once the information has been collected and analysed, I plan to share it with children and adults from our school. I would also like to share it with other people who are interested in what children think about their schools. Before I do that, I will show you how I have put your ideas together. I will invite you to help decide on interesting ways of presenting the findings.

I hope that you will join with me in telling others what we discover.

Just as other young students had appreciated being consulted about their involvement in research projects (Danby and Farrell 2004), the children's letters demonstrated how much they had valued the right to determine their participation. Their written comments indicate how thoughtfully they had considered this invitation to become partners in the research:

> I'm sorry but it took me a long time to think it over. I'm glad I'm joining ... It's going to be lots of fun.

Several children emphasized their commitment to the process by expressing their willingness to contribute out-of-class time to the research project:

> I am prepared to take some of the work home to do.

Some had decided to participate because they were impressed by the research methods:

> I like how you are using technology ... I love digital cameras.

A few children had identified their current skills that would assist them to become co-researchers:

> I am good at taking photographs and I have a good attitude.
> I like doing art and I am good at writing.

One student identified the learning of new skills as a factor influencing her decision to join the project:

> I can always improve my skills and I would like to learn how people do their research,

Another student identified the topic as the motivating factor for her involvement in this research:

> I would enjoy sharing ideas with you about making schools better places for children.

I facilitated a similar workshop to explain project two to the original participants. I again made explicit the purposes of the research as well as outlined the organizational details, such as the days and time I planned to withdraw children from their class and the venue I had negotiated for the focus groups. At this workshop, I again provided children with a formal opportunity to consent to participate in Project 2. All the original participants agreed to continue with Project 2 so that they could analyse the data they had created in Project 1.

Because there had been a two year time lapse between the end of Project 2 and the commencement of Project 3, I explained to the original participants that when I had received written consent from their parents for their continued participation in the research, children would be invited to a half-day workshop. This workshop would focus on the purposes of the next research project, examine ethical issues that may arise and provide them with a forum in which to ask questions about the research and their roles within it, prior to making a decision about whether they would participate in the research.

As an extension of children's learning about research during the first two research projects, I invited the Research Degrees Coordinator for the Professional Doctorate at University of South Australia (UniSA) to talk with them about research. He illustrated institutional ethics requirements by telling the children about his own research and highlighted ethical issues that had arisen in other research involving children. At this forum, I provided children with information about the Researchers' Day that would initiate the action research phase of Project 3 and explained their roles as co-researchers. Children who wished to continue to participate in the research were asked to write to me telling me that they had considered their contribution and wanted to be involved.

Prior to consenting to participate in research Project 1, the prospective child participants had identified practices which would allow all research participants and their ideas to be treated ethically. These practices included 'maintaining open communication' and 'having lots of chances to keep talking about whether we want to continue in the project'. Since that time, children had participated in a whole school exploration of the school's agreed core values (Respect, Fairness, Mutual Trust and Social Cohesion) and had developed insights into others' definitions of respect. Revisiting these understandings of respect reinforced their previously stated commitment to principles of ethical treatment of all people participating in research, rather than to unquestioning adherence to a code of conduct. This enabled them to enlarge their definition of ethical treatment to include 'listening to and seriously thinking about the ideas of all others'.

Conclusion

My experiences in co-researching with children in my primary school have demonstrated children's competence and agency in reflecting on their daily lives, in identifying issues of concern, analysing possible solutions, making recommendations and implementing actions to change their everyday experiences.

Informed by other researchers about two problematic aspects of researching with children, namely consent and confidentiality, I crafted workshops with a specific focus on these ethical issues. A highly specific and explicit program to teach children about research is important because, while they have the lived experience, the intellectual capacity and the social competence to engage with research, children may have limited understanding of research. Pedagogic approaches acknowledge children's capabilities and value their unique perspectives. They further enable children to learn about research, to transfer existing abilities to becoming researchers as well as to acquire new skills and dispositions relevant to research. Pedagogic approaches allow the ethical issues to be made explicit and invite children to engage with them.

Although I had expected that children would willingly accept their ethical responsibilities as co-researchers, I had underestimated the degree of dedication with which they embraced these aspects of the research. Children's commitment to treating all people in the research with respect confirms for me the importance of adopting pedagogical approaches to research.

However, before pedagogical approaches can even be contemplated, it is essential that teachers undertaking research with children reflect on their motivations for listening to children's voices and including them in the research process. Such analysis may be within the context of a whole staff examination of the roles that children play in the daily life of their school. Or the review may occur on an individual basis where teachers identify their constructions of childhood and consider how these influence their interactions with children in the school setting.

Dispositions/convictions shared by teachers and school leaders who engage with children in their schools as co-researchers include their

- Acknowledgement that children experience the school differently from the adults who inhabit it
- Recognition that children's school experiences are not universal, that is, they are mediated by their class, gender, ethnicity, nationality, health and local contextual factors
- Acceptance that children are competent in commenting on their lives, generous in sharing their insights and able to work collaboratively for the good of all
- Genuine willingness to invite and listen to children's perspectives
- Readiness to reconcile the competing and conflicting opinions raised by diverse children with disparate voices
- Commitment to creating with children a democratic environment in which to conduct ethical research

These convictions are fundamental pre-requisites to promoting ethical understandings in child co-researchers.

References

Alderson, P. (2000). 'School Students' Views on School Councils and Daily Life at School', *Children and Society*, 14, 121–34.

——(2003). *Institutional Rights and Rites: A Century of Childhood*. London: Institute of Education, University of London.

Buckingham, D. (2000). *After the Death of Childhood*. Cambridge: Polity Press.

Christensen, P. and Prout, A. (2005). 'Anthropological and Sociological Perspectives on the Study of Children'. In S. Greene and D. Hogan (eds), *Researching Children's Experience*. London: Sage.

Comber, B. and Nixon, H. (2004). 'Children Re-Read and Re-Write Their Neighbourhoods: Critical Literacies and Identity Work'. In J. Evans (ed.), *Literacy Moves on: Popular Culture, New Technologies and Critical Literacy in the Elementary Classroom*. Portsmouth: Heinemann.

Comber, B. and Thomson, P. with Wells, M. (2001). 'Critical Literacy Finds a "Place": Writing and Social Action in a Neighbourhood School', *Elementary School Journal*, 101 (4), 451–64.

Corsaro, W.A. (2001). *We're Friends Right? Inside Kids' Culture*. Washington: Joseph Henry Press.

——(2005). *The Sociology of Childhood* (second edition) London: Pine Forge Press.

Danby, S. and Farrell, A. (2004). 'Accounting for Young Children's Competence in Educational Research: New Perspectives on Research Ethics', *The Australian Educational Researcher*, 31 (3), 35–49.

Epstein, D. (1998). 'Are You a Girl or Are You a Teacher?'. In D. Walford (ed.), *Doing Research about Education*. London: Falmer Press.

Fielding, M. (2001). 'Students as Radical Agents of Change', *Journal of Educational Change*, 2 (2), 123–41.

—— and Bragg, S. (2003). *Students as Researcher: Making a Difference*. Cambridge: Pearson Publishing.

Gronn, P. (1999). *Life in Teams: Collaborative Leadership and Learning in Autonomous Work Units*. Burwood: ACEA.

Groundwater-Smith, S. and Downes, T. (1999). 'Students: From Informants to Co-Researchers'. Paper presented at the Australian Association for Research in Education Annual Conference, Melbourne, 29 November–2 December 1999.

Holdsworth, R. and Thomson, P. (2002). 'Options within the Regulation and Containment of "Student Voice"'. Paper presented at the Annual Meeting of the American Educational Research Association, New Orleans, 1–5 April 2002.

Johnson, K. (2000). 'Research Ethics and Children', *Curriculum Perspectives*, 20, 6–7.

Karlsson, J. (2001). 'Doing Visual Research with School Learners in South Africa', *Visual Sociology*, 16 (2), 23–38.

Luke, A. (2000). Critical Literacy in Australia: A Matter of Context and Standpoint, *Journal of Adolescent and Adult Literacy*, 14 (2), 5–8.

MacBeath, J. (1999). *Schools Must Speak for Themselves: The Case for School Self-Evaluation*. London: Routledge.

Mathison, S., Ross, E. and Cornell, J. (eds) (1993). *Casebook for Teaching about Ethical Issues in Qualitative Research*. Washington: Qualitative Research SIG, American Educational Research Association.

Morrow, V. and Richards, M. (1996). 'The Ethics of Social Research with Children: An Overview', *Children and Society*, 10 (2), 90–100.

Pekrul, S. and Levin, B. (2005). 'Building Student Voice for School Improvement'. Paper presented at the Annual Meeting of the American Educational Research Association as part of a symposium on student voice, Montreal, 11–15 April 2005.

Prosser, J. (1998) (Ed). *Image Based Research: A Sourcebook for Qualitative Researchers*. London: Falmer Press.

Prout, A. (2001). 'The Future of Childhood'. First Annual Lecture of the Children's Research Centre, Trinity College, Dublin.

Rudduck, J. and Flutter, J. (2000). 'Pupil Participation and Pupil Perspective: "Carving" a New Order of Experience', *Cambridge Journal of Education*, 30 (1), 75–89.

Thomson, P. and Gunter, H. (2005). 'From "Consulting Pupils" To "Pupils as Researchers": A Situated Case Narrative'. Paper presented at the Annual Meeting of the American Educational Research Association as part of a symposium on student voice, Montreal, 11–15 April 2005.

Zeni, J. (1998). 'A Guide to Ethical Issues and Action Research', *Educational Action Research*, 6 (1), 9–19.

JO ARMISTEAD

13 Reflecting on ethical considerations around young children's engagement when researching children's perspectives

Introduction

This chapter critically reflects on the ethical considerations that arose during a doctoral study enquiring into the perspectives of English children on the quality of their nursery experiences (Armistead 2008). The focus will be on the research methodology and an exploration of the ethical challenges posed by the processes of empirical research with young children. In relation to these areas of focus the following themes have been identified from the literature, the relative power relations between children and adult researchers (Robinson and Kellett 2004; Lahman 2008); negotiating informed consent with children (Alderson 2004); and methodologies which demonstrate the competence of young children to participate in research (Christensen and James 2000, 2008; Lewis and Lindsay 2000; Fraser et al. 2004; Dockett, Einarsdottir and Perry 2009).

The chapter will examine how these themes were implicated in

- the research design;
- gaining informed consent and continuous consent as part of a longitudinal study;
- implementing a mixture of methods without coercion, involving children in the collection and interpretation of the data.

Each aspect of the empirical research involved the developing relationship between the researcher and the researched, aiming towards what Lahman refers to as 'intersubjective[ity] and an easy rapport with children' (2008: 293). The experiences of two of the core sample, Alan and Batman, will illustrate children's contribution to the research.

The context for the study was a dearth of young children's views within the wider literature around the quality of early years provision, encompassing education and childcare (Moss and Pence 1994; Dalhberg, Moss and Pence 1999; 2005). The wider policy context for the research was the substantial importance attributed to quality standards as an aspect of effective early years provision and the development of national, centrally imposed, quality frameworks in England (DES 1990; Abbott and Rodger 1994: QCA 2000; Sylva et al. 2004, DCSF 2008). This centralized approach is contested from a postmodern perspective which views quality as a socially constructed phenomenon, with multiple stakeholders defining quality early years provision at local levels (Farquhar et al. 1991; Dalhberg, Moss and Pence 1999; 2005). Adopting a postmodern position, the study aimed to develop a deeper understanding of what children as stakeholders valued within their own early years provisions, and also to highlight the continued absence of the recognition of children's views in government policy in the early years.

The research

The empirical research was a small-scale, qualitative study using an ethnographic approach. Research was conducted on a main site, where two phases of fieldwork took place over a fifteen month period. There was an additional phase, with a shorter data collection period, at a secondary site. Core and opportunistic samples of children aged three and four years were involved. In order to research *with* children, participative techniques were used to understand how children give meaning to their time in nursery

(James 2001; Christensen 2004). The children were viewed as active social agents (James, Jenks and Prout 1998) and a methodological objective was to give children voice to articulate their views, acknowledging their rights to be heard (Davis 1998; Landsdown 2004).

The research design sought a methodology which would make it possible for young children to convey their points of view through methods appropriate to their age within a natural and familiar context. According to James 'ethnography as a research method ... has enabled children to be recognised as people who can be studied in their own right 'permitting' children to become seen as research participants' (2001: 245). Children are subjects and participants rather than objects within the research. They are 'competent interpreters of the social world' (2001: 246) who can contribute to an understanding of their experiences. This 'represents a shift in perspective – research with rather than on children' (James, 2001: 246). Punch (2002) notes that an ethnographic approach offers 'prolonged ... periods ... in order to get to know [children] ... and gain a greater understanding' (2002: 322). However she cautions that as it relies on participant observation there is the inherent difficulty that adults 'are unable to be full participants in children's social worlds because they can never truly be children again' (2002: 322).

With children there is an 'additional responsibility' (James 2001: 252) placed on the researcher due to differential power relations. It was necessary to recognize and understand the inherent unequal power relationships between young children and adults when researching within a pre-school setting (Robinson and Kellett 2004; Dockett and Perry 2007). Children are able to distinguish the researcher from the practitioners who are responsible for them and may not see the researcher as occupying an 'adult position of power' (James 2001: 252). James argues that researchers should 'negotiate a new relationship with children – from children's point of view' and must acknowledge that they 'can only ever have a semi-participatory role in children's lives [in order for] ... the power differentials which separate children from adults begin to be effectively addressed – in this sense ethnography is powerfully placed to initiate this process. (James 2001: 252). Researchers must take 'seriously' the power differentials between children and themselves and seek to 'address these in the design, implementation and dissemination of their work' (Robinson and Kellett 2004: 93). In this study the researcher became a semi-participant observer who negotiated informed consent from children before employing a range of methods to elicit children's perspectives.

Before children were approached, information had been sent to parents to gain their consent. All parents of the core sample agreed to their child's inclusion in the research. Most other parents returned their consent forms, and three parents did not give consent. Alderson and Morrow (2004) advise that whilst children can give consent on their own behalf, parents should be asked to consent to their children's involvement; it is respectful and likely to engender trust. This was the position taken in this study and the research only involved children whose parents had given consent.

Participatory approaches to research: Gaining informed consent

The research design aimed to place children in control of their involvement. A pilot study had revealed that one barrier to children's participation had been their lack of prior knowledge of the research; children had not understood the purpose of the research or their role in it. After reflection, when designing the main study, it was decided to provide certain information to enable children to make an informed decision about their own participation. This is consistent with the professional code of practice for educational research when developing fieldwork procedures. The British Educational Research Association (BERA) Revised Ethical Guidelines (BERA 2004) require children to be informed and consulted if they are to be involved in any research. The guidelines advise that prior to the research children should have the opportunity to give fully informed consent, without duress. Participants should understand what will be expected of them and why their participation is necessary, how the research will be used and how it will be reported.

Gaining 'formal' consent, or assent, from children is an aspect of research practice that is emerging independently from different early years projects, though it is not well-established (Flewitt 2005; Harcourt and Conroy 2005; Dockett, Einarsdottir and Perry 2009). Some researchers have questioned the ethical implications of gaining 'informed consent' within educational settings due to the difficulty for children to 'opt out' of research where the power relations are likely to lead to children's acquiescence (David, Edwards and Alldred 2001). However, Masson (2004) argues that children can give consent when they can distinguish 'between research and other intervention ... and understand the impact on them of them participating' (2004: 50).

For this study, a booklet, called *Finding things out*, was devised which explained the research process to facilitate children's voluntary participation. It used pictures, photographs and simple sentences to introduce and explain the research activities, suggesting what the children would be asked to do and providing examples of other children's involvement in research. Significantly, from an ethical standpoint, it told children how they could avoid being part of the research. They were advised:

> Nobody has to talk to me if they don't want to. You can just walk away or say I don't want to talk to you now. You can shake your head, or you can use a thumb sign to say yes or no like this.

The outcomes of the research were also explained:

> [The researcher was]... going to think about the things we find out at nursery and write a book to tell other people what children think about nursery.

Following the first phase of field work the booklet was reviewed. It had been noted that children's interest focused on the images. One child, who showed impatience with the explanations, commented, 'Can we turn ... it's going to take all day. I don't like this page'. A revised version included more photographs to illustrate and make explicit children's involvement and reduced the words. Children were also introduced to the research tools. They were able to handle the note book, camera and an audiotape recorder, which possibly led to a belief that these were accessible and gave children a sense of ownership as will be reflected later in the chapter.

The children had met the researcher in their setting before being approached to give consent. She had visited the nursery and had been introduced informally to the children. During these visits the researcher made general observations and wrote field notes, recording the routines and the layout of the nursery. No approaches were made to the children, who took little notice, with only one child asking the researcher why she was there. The next stage in the research process aimed to provide information and start to gain the consent of the core sample. Singly or in pairs to give them confidence, children were shown and read the *Finding things out* booklet. They were asked to indicate their agreement using a consent form that provided two options, to join in or not to join in. Children were invited to write their name on the form, if they could, and to draw a circle round the face symbols on the form to indicate their consent or not – to join in or not to join in.

Each of the core children responded and other children, who showed interest in the research, becoming part of an opportunistic sample, were invited to give their formal consent. Joining in and taking part were not conditional on filling in a consent form. The formal process was used to signal the research process to the children, drawing attention to the activity and children's role in the research. Once the research was established it became less necessary to use the booklet as the activities and children's participation became evident in ways that were open to children to observe.

Alan was eager from the start to take part. He was the oldest child in the core sample. When offered the consent form, he attempted to write his name to give consent and he became a receptive and enthusiastic participant in the research. Of the core children he was the most consistently aware that he was contributing information, pointing out an aspect of nursery, or reflecting on his feelings. He took part in all the research activities offered but also volunteered additional material. He was aware of providing information and responded to the research tasks with competence and clarity. He chose the research name Alan Tracey that he wanted to be known by in the study.

Batman, one of the youngest in core sample, chose not to respond to the form when he was shown the booklet, neither consenting nor withdrawing. He decided to join in once he had observed other children take part and gave his verbal consent, becoming a competent and enthusiastic co-researcher. He demonstrated an understanding of the research process, as a provider of information, observing the practice of giving and withdrawing consent. Batman also chose his research name.

The initial consent was not viewed as a permanent permission. Continuing consent was requested and reiterated as the fieldwork progressed (Alderson 2004). Children were asked if they were 'OK' and ready to take part. They were able to withdraw consent to be observed or to have a conversation recorded. They were able to decline to take part in any research activity. The practice to reiterate consent at each stage of the research allowed children to withdraw consent, and at different times all the children in the core sample did, saying, 'No,' or in one case showing thumbs down. The aim was to protect children from coercive practices. A principle of research ethics is to minimize disruption, and the children's self-chosen activities were prioritized and respected. The ethnographic approach, researching over time, accommodated slow research procedures which responded to the children's pace (Lahman 2008).

Participative methods that recognize children as experts in their own lives

An ethical consideration was to include all children (core and opportunistic) who wished to take part in the research. Therefore methods were chosen which would maximize children's participation, taking into account their young age and their varying abilities to express themselves verbally. A basic premise, which influenced the choice of methods, had been that children are 'competent respondents, social actors' (James, Jenks and Prout 1998: 32), who are experts on the events, activities and encounters within the provision they attend (Langsted 1994). When enquiring into younger children's lives, Langsted advocates using a mixture of methods that are contextually appropriate, and ones which allow an 'open and listening approach' (1994: 41). Christensen and James (2000) remind researchers that 'children are not adults' and that when selecting methods they (researchers) need to 'adopt practices which resonate with children's own concerns and routines ... paying attention to the ways in which they communicate with us' (2000: 7).

Clark and Moss (2001; 2005) have developed a multi-method 'Mosaic' approach to involve children as research participants. It 'is a way of listening which acknowledges children and adults as co-constructors of meaning' (2001: 1). It uses visual methods, including children's photographs, combined with adult observations and talking to children 'to gain deeper understanding of children's lives' (2001: 3), and might involve children leading adults on tours of their setting. The Mosaic approach offers children a range of methods in which they can 'voice' their views verbally and non-verbally. It was designed as a model approach that could be replicated by other researchers, and was adopted in modified form for the study.

The combination of methods was believed to be meaningful to young children and aimed to elicit a range of responses. The 'mosaic' of methods in this study into quality comprised:

- Observations of core children's play and relationships, at different times over the period of the nursery day, sometimes elaborated through conversations with the children and illustrated by photographs taken by the children, and children's drawings.
- 'Child tours' of each setting, for children to show and tell what was important about their nursery. The researcher simultaneously noted children comments as she was led round, checking meanings when necessary. Children were offered a camera to record their tour if they wished.
- Photographs taken by and later discussed with children, in the context of observations and child tours, and if requested by the children or prompted by the researcher.

- Each respondent created their own nursery from small world play items, observed by and in interaction with the researcher. These were recorded on audio tape, supplemented by note taking in phase 1, and on videotape in phase 2.

Each method provided the opportunity for conversations (Cousins 1999) and communication between the children and the researcher. It was believed that the conversations or dialogues allowed children to elaborate on or clarify the meaning of their actions or comment on photographs and from these discourses would arise their perspectives on quality from within their own terms. Christensen identifies a 'dialogical research process' (2004: 166) where children can 'introduce their own themes ... on their own terms' (2004: 168). The researcher was open to responding to children's approaches to share information about nursery or other aspects of their lives. These encounters occurred naturally when the children knew and trusted the researcher, and a dialogical process became part of each of the methods. Exchanges were recorded in a field notebook as they happened, making clear to the children that what they said was important and demonstrating their participation. Through conversations children's 'construction of their world and the depth of their thinking' were 'exposed' (Cousins 1999: 9).

It was believed that using a range of methods allowed children to 'give voice' using a variety of media. Within ethnographic research James notes the use of:

> different kinds of research techniques designed to both engage children's inter-
> ests and to exploit their particular talents and abilities e.g. 'task-centred activities'
> adapted from those commonly used in development work for participatory rural
> appraisals ... techniques involve children in using media other than talk to reveal in
> visual and concrete form their thoughts and ideas about a particular research ques-
> tion (2001: 252–3).

Selecting a mixed-method approach provided methodological triangulation, offering reliability to the study. Each method contributed to an understanding of children's perspectives. The following section will illustrate how each research method enabled children to be full participants in the research process and focuses on the experiences of Alan and Batman.

Observing, listening to and talking with children

Observations form the basis of an ethnographic methodology and they should be 'prolonged and repeated' (Aubrey et al. 2000: 137). They provide 'thick descriptions' (Geertz 1993: 6) of human behaviour that offer a detailed account of an event or relationship, providing context and narrative. It appeared that dialogical observations, where meanings are checked with the children, produced rich data, from which clear themes emerged (Armistead 2008).

The following observation involved Alan working with a variety of small construction pieces. His interest in fantasy and media was reflected in his activity, and his spoken commentary that he shared with the researcher, elaborated only a small part of the story he was constructing in his head, and the strategies he was using to achieve the finished product. The observation demonstrates the depth of thinking and expertise of children in their play, interweaving skills and knowledge that are unique to the child. We see Alan withdrawing from other children initially, but once he has finished his invention he rejoins his friends outside.

> Alan was working on his own 'inventing' and asked 'everyone to go away in case ...' He made a 'mini-game console' from a set of interlocking pieces. Over the next fifteen minutes, working quickly, taking apart and reconstructing the pieces, he continued 'his secret invention', making 'a garage', then a 'ray gun' which became the 'Evil Emperor of Zugg invention', 'a missile' which he demonstrated against 'the baddies'. He continued to adapt the model, needing 'some more shorters and it will be done'. Realizing everyone was outside he decided to join them, taking his 'transformer' with him.

The next example tracks Alan's relationship with food. The extract aims to convey and understand his perspective of food in nursery. He used the research process to record *in words* his strong feelings for nursery food and record *in photographs* his distinct preference for food from home (and the supermarket). Influences on Alan from the media become apparent once again.

When Alan started to bring his own packed lunch he was observed to be much happier at lunch time. He asked to take a photograph of his lunch box and he listed each food item inside. It seems that his preference was for food sold in special packs designed for the lunch box market, such as cheese strings or dunking sticks. This is food that is media influenced. He brought crisps which coloured his tongue blue, and he proudly allowed another child to photograph the effect.

He later explained to the researcher that if his mother didn't pick him up by twelve on his 'short day' (i.e. the morning session) he would have to 'eat nursery food. I hate nursery food. I don't like it'.

The research study aimed to place participants in a position of control over data they were providing and the researcher sought methods that allowed children to influence what was recorded, and to reflect the children's control of the data when it was written up. Landsdown (2004: 7) refers to a level of children's participation as 'self-initiated processes ... where children themselves are empowered to take action'. Landsdown adds: 'Children's participation requires information-sharing and dialogue between children and adults based on mutual respect and power sharing' (2004: 8). Methods were chosen which directly involved children in data generation and collection; when recording observations, the researcher asked if it 'was OK' to write in the note book. Details were checked and some of what was written was read back to the children. The children were aware of what the researcher was doing. They asked what she was writing or if they could write or draw in the notebook, which they did. Some children were able to recognize words, for example, their name or numbers. They told the researcher to, 'Write this down'. In this way the book was perceived as common property, though the children referred to it as 'your book'. The book was also photographed by children. It appeared that children felt the notebook was accessible to them and this viewpoint was not discouraged.

The following vignette illustrates children's influence on the research process. Here Batman approached the researcher to record his sense of achievement in his play. He had a sense that his work would be appreciated by recording it in the field note book. Though he did not ask to take a photograph he took a total of four photographs when it was suggested to him.

> An 'anything you want it to be' area had been introduced to the nursery offering a diverse collection of natural materials including some feathers. Whilst observing other children, the researcher was approached by Batman, who told her 'I need you to come over; I've got something to show you'. He led her to the block area where he had created a display of carefully placed feathers, which he showed with pride and excitement and which he was prompted to photograph.

Photographs of and tours of the setting

In the use of the camera the methodology allowed children to choose what to photograph. Images were printed to make a series of albums, and presented back to the children, who were invited to add comments if they wished. Initially, due to the potential fragility of the camera the researcher controlled access to its use and supervised children who had not used a camera before. Children were asked to request consent from other children if they wished to photograph them. Batman was noted declining to be photographed, saying, 'My mummy said no', indicating his awareness of the consent process.

Some children were particularly interested and competent and took multiple photographs. Typically children made their own decision to stop photographing, either because there was nothing else they wanted to photograph or because they were distracted by another activity. Some children took only one or two photographs whilst others took up to twenty at any one time. As children became familiar with the camera they used it more selectively and with a growing sense of purpose. At the same time the researcher became more confident in the children's competency and the need for close supervision was reduced.

The child tours allowed children to record their experiences of nursery in photographs. Tours were followed by a discussion of the images, to provide further understanding of their significance for the children. In the example below, Batman explained his choice of photographs.

> *Batman said he had taken a picture of a rainbow canopy over a table:* 'Because it looked pretty because it's got all those colours on. It goes in the sky .. and you know what ... when it's raining and sunny you know what happens?'
>
> *He photographed some numbers:* 'It's because it looks nice'. *The researcher asked if he knew his numbers, and he counted to 20.*
>
> *He photographed himself in a mirror:* 'I took a picture of myself!'
>
> *Batman took photographs of several children and adults. He said this about one friend:* 'I have took a picture of Ria because she looks pretty'.
>
> *He photographed a world map and a globe:* 'I took a picture of the worlds. I love it cos it has nice pictures on ... the space rockets because I like them and went to blast up on the moon last night and I see one today, but not a real one.'

Alan would ask to use the camera, when he rarely restricted himself to one shot and the results were often illuminating. His photographs were from a child's perspective, for example, a sequence of photographs recording details that might have been ignored by an adult. Alan's comments on these photographs were:

> ALAN: I got the see-saw and the end of the five *(the number painted on the paving)*.
>
> RESEARCHER: Why are you taking these pictures? What are you choosing?
>
> ALAN: Stuff I like. I like the car and the slide and the house. The house is full of Halloween horrors that might get in your hair – the spider and the gruffalo. *(the house was covered by a section of camouflage netting)*

Alan and Batman both used the camera to illustrate their perspectives of nursery, capturing images of the resources that they valued, used and knew. These were personal and expert views of nursery from their own perspectives.

Play nurseries

The play nurseries method was devised by the researcher, based on personal experience of using small world play materials to encourage spoken language, and play therapy techniques to encourage children to discuss their feelings (Axline, 1990). Children were invited to 'make their own play nursery', using a collection of small world play items that reflected aspects of nursery. These 'toys' were particularly attractive to children and the use of the method within a busy nursery was challenging. It raised ethical dilemmas regarding the need to restrict the use of the items to one child at a time, to enable them to make their individual play nursery, by discouraging other children from interfering, for example by touching toys or taking them away to play with elsewhere. One tactic used was to wait until most children were playing outside and to then invite children singly to take part when the room was quiet. However, there was normally a small audience who over time learnt to interfere less on the understanding that would have their own turn with the materials at a later point.

As a novice the researcher was unsure and had less confidence in this method to generate useful data. However, the method revealed a distinct and more personal aspect of being in nursery that was more challenging than other methods. In the following two vignettes, both Alan and Batman revealed strong and possibly shocking feelings in their play:

Making his first nursery Alan carefully explored all the items in the bag. He found the computer and placed it on the computer table, explaining that the people were 'playing circus' on the computer. He placed the printer on top of some shelves 'for the big children'. He placed a baby on the table and said, 'The baby's got to go in the cot.' He was particularly interested in the 'hoover', and the telephone, saying 'somebody's ringing on the phone'. When he had finished playing, he was asked to talk about his nursery. Surveying the table he said, 'I really love playing with these and the telephone keeps ringing ... so ... I love it so much'. He added, 'I love the printer and the oven and I hate the babies ...'

Batman's searched through the play items, putting his head 'in this big bag', selecting one item at a time, naming it and deciding where to place it. When he was unsure he sought clarification, asking, 'What's that?' before placing an item on the table. With everything in place, he developed a play scenario around a baby in the cot. He had stacked a fridge on a table and was warned that it might fall and hurt the baby. Batman acted upon the idea that the baby was in danger and let the fridge fall on the cot. The baby was then subject to further hazards. Batman found a toilet in the bag and chose to place it 'here near the baby ... oh now the baby's going to get flushed down' pushing the baby into the toilet. Batman 'pulled him out' and decided to 'put a bandage on' since the baby had 'hurt himself. He's bleeding'. Placing the baby back in his 'pram', Batman found a watering can and 'poured water all on the baby ... I poured it everywhere on my nursery!'

It had not been anticipated that the research, via small world play, would elicit such strong and private feelings. Dockett, Einarsdottir and Perry (2009) discuss ethical tensions that can arise when children are invited to participate in research projects in relation to the interpretation and use of data they have generated. They present an argument for allowing children to censor the inclusion of such episodes from the research report. In the instances above it was felt that the data should be included as indicative of the need for a quality experience to allow the exploration of strong emotions. Alan's strong interest in technology and antipathy towards babies along with Batman's playful and exploratory approach, were felt to reflect the boys' relationship with the 'real' nursery and to reveal relevant perspectives relating to what a quality experience was for them.

Ethical considerations of children's involvement in the research

As has been made clear, the researcher aimed to make explicit the purpose of her presence in the settings. The children were aware of her interest and that she was writing about them in the notebooks. It was recognized that her presence and children's interest in the research would present some disruption but she aimed to minimize this as far as possible. It was also clear that not all children wished to approach or be approached by the researcher and their feelings were respected (Alderson 2004). Over the weeks of fieldwork, trust was established between the researcher and children from both the core and opportunistic samples (Lahman 2008). Children took part in the research activities, but they were just as likely to call upon her help, for example, to tie a shoe lace or find a name tag.

Reactivity or the influence of the researcher's presence was acknowledged and throughout the fieldwork period the researcher examined her own role and relationship vis-à-vis the children. She aimed to intervene as little as possible. However on occasions her position as responsible researcher was challenged and she was required to consider her practice. The core sample children were particularly sensitive to the presence of the researcher and aware of their participation, which perhaps allowed them some latitude in terms of their behaviour when involved in research activities. The possible effect of this is demonstrated in this sequence involving Batman and his brother Robin where they demonstrated some seemingly uncharacteristic behaviour.

> Batman and Robin were playing noisily in the construction area, observed by the researcher. They pulled the blocks off the shelves, covering the floor. Another younger boy approached, possibly wanting to join in. Instead of including him in their game they sided against him, cornering him against a wall, and threatened to push him. He was prepared to defend himself and did not back off. All the boys were standing on the blocks. The researcher realised both the physical hazard and the implications of the brothers' behaviour and felt it necessary to intervene to protect the younger child.

Keddie (2000) writes about the 'voyeuristic aspect … of collecting "good data" through observing conflicts and … risky or distressing situations' (2000: 74) when researching with children. She points out the 'paradoxical nature of research and the tension between raising awareness of these situations and the suppression of data through intervention' (2000: 74). It is important that researchers recognize their responsibility in such situations, both to protect children from harm but also to understand and minimize the effect their presence may have on participants.

It has already been acknowledged that adults can only be semi-participants in research with children. The semi-participant observer role adopted was not of 'least adult', attempting to experience the settings as a child (Warming, 2005). Whilst the researcher did not assert authority over the children she helped out in the nursery and responded to children's requests for help as noted above. However, when children commented on her role it was clear that they acknowledged a different adult status to that of the permanent practitioners'. One child identified the researcher as 'a student'; another asserted she was 'not a teacher'.

A further ethical consideration involves the nature of the research activities, which can be fun and offer attention to children (Christensen 2004; Cook and Hess 2007), and which may also be ethically problematic. Some of the research tools such as the camera or the small world play items, might be seen to offer enticement to young children, and so may be potentially coercive. In early years settings some children may be attracted to join in to gain adult attention. The researcher needed to be sensitive to ensure a respectful response to children's interest in the research, and that they understood the implications of participation (Lahman 2008). The research design aimed to achieve this by using an overt approach, which openly valued the children's contribution through simultaneous feedback and consultation.

Conclusions

The study used methods which enabled children to influence the outcome of the research by involving them in the research process and allowing them to control their levels of participation in the project. The intention was to redress the balance of power away from the researcher and towards the children, privileging the children's contribution and allowing them to take the initiative (Landsdown 2004). At times the results were challenging. However, methods were selected to enable children to project aspects of being in pre-school which would enable them to 'speak differently from adults in relation to the issue of the time' (Jenks 2000: 69).

The study aimed for an open and a consensual approach that acknowledged the children as co-constructors of learning and culture (Dockett and Perry 2007). The examples of the research in action illustrate the meaning given by Alan and Batman to their presence in their nursery that reflected experiences from home, from their wider lives, as well as the experiences provided in nursery. From these and from others, a wider understanding of the complexity of the experiences of preschool for children emerged, that were different from those in government documents. Children's expertise reflected a particular, personal and very local agenda in relation to the quality of their experiences, 'the stuff [they] like' to quote Alan that could only be understood by the use of a participative methodology.

The role of the researcher has been discussed, and it is clear that it is central to the ethics of research with children (Keddie 2000; Robinson and Kellett 2004; Dockett Einarsdottir and Perry 2009; Lahman 2008).

As a novice at the outset, this researcher carried a high level of responsibility to reflect truthfully the experiences of children, both as participant in the generation of data and as co-constructors of meanings around what constituted a quality experience in an early years setting. Each stage of the research required a reflective response; the research design; the process of gaining and reiterating informed consent; and through the implementation of a mixture of methods involving children in the collection and interpretation of the data. In addition to utilizing recent innovations in research with children (Clark and Moss 2001), some novel approaches were introduced which may influence future research methodologies. The study and this chapter have attempted to develop the rationale for involving young children in research and to consider some of the ethical dilemmas – both anticipated and unanticipated – that can arise.

References

Abbott, L., and Rodger, R. (eds) (1994). *Quality Education in the Early Years*. Buckingham: Open University Press.

Alderson, P. (2004). 'Ethics'. In S. Fraser, V. Lewis, S. Ding, M. Kellett, and C. Robinson (eds), *Doing Research with Children and Young People*, pp 97–112. London: Sage.

Alderson, P., and Morrow, V. (2004). *Ethics, Social Research and Consulting with Children and Young People*. Barkingside: Barnardo's.

Armistead, J.L. (2008). *A Study of Children's Perspectives on the Quality of Their Experiences in Early Years Provision* (University of Northumbria, unpublished thesis).

Aubrey, C., David, T., Godfrey, R., and Thompson, L. (eds) (2000). *Early Childhood Educational Research: Issues in Methodology and Ethics*. London: RoutledgeFalmer.

Axline, V.M. (1990). *Dibs in Search of Self: Personality Development in Play Therapy*. Harmondsworth: Penguin Books.

BERA (British Educational Research Association) (2004). *Revised Ethical Guidelines for Educational Research (2004)*. Southwell: BERA.

Christensen, P., and James, A. (2000). 'Researching children and childhood: cultures of communication'. In P. Christensen and A. James (eds), *Research with Children: Perspectives and Practices*, 2nd edn. London: Falmer Press.

Christensen, P., and James, A. (eds) (2008). *Research with Children: Perspectives and Practices*, 2nd edn. New York, Abingdon: Routledge.

Christensen, P.H. (2004). 'Children's Participation in Ethnographic Research: Issues of Power and Representation', *Children & Society*, 18, 165–76.

Clark, A., and Moss, P. (2001). *Listening to Young Children: The Mosaic Approach*. London: National Children's Bureau.

——(2005) *Spaces to Play; More Listening to Young Children Using the Mosaic Approach*. London: National Children's Bureau.

Cook, T., and Hess, E. (2007). 'What the Camera Sees and from Whose Perspective: Fun Methodologies for Engaging Children in Enlightening Adults', *Childhood*, 14, 29–45.

Cousins, J. (1999). *Listening to Four Year Olds: How They Can Help Us Plan Their Education and Care*. London: National Early Years Network.

Dahlberg, G., Moss, P., and Pence, A. (1999), *Beyond Quality in Early Childhood Education and Care*. London: Falmer Press.

——(2005). *Beyond Quality in Early Childhood Education and Care*, 2nd edn. London: Falmer Press.

David, M., Edwards, R., and Alldred, P. (2001). 'Children and School-Based Research: "Informed Consent" or "Educated Consent"?' *British Educational Research Journal*, 27(3), 347–65.

Davis, J.M. (1998). 'Understanding the Meanings of Children: A Reflexive Process', *Children & Society*, 12, 325–35.

DCSF (Department for Children Schools and Families) (2008). *The Early Years Foundation Stage: Setting the Standards for Learning, Development and Care for Children from Birth to Five*. London: DCFS.

DES (Department for Education and Science) (1990). *Starting with Quality: The Report of the Committee of Inquiry into the Quality of the Educational Experience Offered to 3- and 4-Year-Olds* (Rumbold Report). London: HMSO.

Dockett, S., Einarsdottir, J., and Perry, B. (2009). 'Researching with Children: Ethical Tensions', *Journal of Early Childhood Research* 7: 283–98. <http://ecr.sagepub.com/cgi/content/abstract/7/3/283> accessed 25 February 2010.

Dockett, S., and Perry, B. (2007), 'Trusting Children's Accounts in Research, *Journal of Early Childhood Research* 5: 47–63. <http://ecr.sagepub.com/cgi/content/abstract/5/1/47> accessed 25 February 2010.

Farquhar, S., et al. (1991). *Quality Is in the Eye of the Beholder: The Nature of Early Centre Quality*. Research Report No.2 to the Ministry of Education, New

Zealand. [Online]. <http://www.eric.ed.gov/ERICWebPortal/custom./portlets/recordDetails/detailmini.jsp?_nfpb=true&_&ERICExtSearch_SearchValue_0=ED341504&ERICExtSearch_SearchType_0=no&accno=ED341504> accessed 22 March 2006.

Flewitt, R. (2005). 'Conducting Research with Young Children: Some Ethical Considerations', *Early Child development and Care*, 175(6), 553–65.

Fraser, S., Lewis, V., Ding, S., Kellett, M., and Robinson, C. (eds) (2004). *Doing Research with Children and Young People*. London: Sage.

Geertz, C. (1993). *The Interpretation of Cultures*. London: Fontana.

Harcourt, D. and Conroy, H. (2005) 'Informed assent: ethics and processes when researching young children', *Early Child Development and Care*, 175 (6) 567–77.

James, A. (2001). 'Ethnography in the Study of Children', in P. Atkinson, A. Coffey, S. Delamont, J. Loftland, and L. Loftland (eds), *Handbook of Ethnography*, pp. 246–57. London: Sage.

James, A., Jenks, C., and Prout, A. (1998). *Theorising Childhood*. Cambridge: Polity Press.

Jenks, C. (2000). 'Zeitgeist in Research on Childhood'. In P. Christensen and A. James (eds), *Research with Children: Perspectives and Practices*, pp. 62–76. London: Falmer Press,.

Keddie, A. (2000). 'Research with Young Children: Some Ethical Considerations', *Journal of Educational Enquiry*, 1(2), 72–81.

Lahman, M.K.E. (2008). Always Othered: Ethical Research with Children, *Journal of Early Childhood Research*, 6, 281–99. <http://ecr.sagepub.com/cgi/content/abstract/6/3/281> accessed 25 February 2010.

Langsted, O. (1994). 'Looking at Quality from the Child's Perspective'. In P. Moss, and A. Pence (eds), *Valuing Quality in Early Childhood Services: New Approaches to Defining Quality*, pp. 28–42. London: Paul Chapman Publishing.

Landsdown, G. (2004). 'Participation and Young Children', *Early Childhood Matters*, 103, 4–14.

Lewis, A., and Lindsay, G. (eds) (2000). *Researching Children's Perspectives*. Buckingham: Open University Press.

Masson, J. (2004). 'The Legal Context'. In S. Fraser, V. Lewis, S. Ding, M. Kellett, and C. Robinson (eds). *Doing Research with Children and Young People*, pp. 43–58. London: Sage.

Moss, P., and Pence, A. (eds) (1994). *Valuing Quality in Early Childhood Services: New Approaches to Defining Quality*. London: Paul Chapman Publishing.

Punch, S. (2002). 'Research with Children: The Same or Different from Research with Adults?' *Childhood*, 9, 321–41. [Online]. <http://chd.sagepub.com/cgi/content/abstract/9/3/321> accessed 7 June 2006.

QCA (Qualification and Curriculum Authority) (2000). *Curriculum Guidance for the Foundation Stage*. London: QCA/DfES.

Robinson, C., and Kellett, M. (2004). 'Power'. In S. Fraser, V. Lewis, S. Ding, M. Kellett, and C. Robinson (eds), *Doing Research with Children and Young People*, pp. 81–96. London: Sage.

Sylva, K., Melhuish, E., Sammons, P., Siraj-Blatchford, I., and Taggart, B. (2004). *The Effective Provision of Pre-School Education (EPPE) Project: Technical Paper 12-The Final Report: Effective Pre-School Education*. London: DfES and Institute of Education, University of London.

Warming, H. (2005). 'Participant Observation: A Way to Learn about Children's Perspectives'. In A. Clark, A.T. Kjorholt, and P. Moss (eds), *Beyond Listening: Children's Perspectives on Early Childhood Services*, pp. 51–70. Bristol: The Policy Press.

14 Developing an ethic of care with children and young people: Opportunities and challenges

The potential of care

A six year old explains how she knows when a teacher really understands her, when it 'looks important, like they're really listening' (Cooper 2002: 64).

Quite young children are aware of people who take time to understand and interact with them. Every day, caring adults, in a range of educational, health and social services, value young people and make a difference in their lives, a difference which at times is significant. This creates hope and the realization that good relationships are possible, whatever disappointments or traumas have occurred in the past. Good experiences with significant adults can sustain young people emotionally when they encounter problems in the future. Harnessing such positive interaction and moreover multi-plying it, so that young people can flourish emotionally and subsequently replicate care and affection with others, seems to be central to creating a society which can nurture humanity and community, release individual potential, respect difference, remain tolerant and develop wisdom.

At every interaction between adults and young people, therefore, there is an opportunity – through the development of trust, however embryonic initially – to engender transformation, and in each moment of connection to sow the seeds for future relationships and development. Care can be revealed through thoughtful awareness of young people's pleasures, their personal interests and strengths. This allows relationships to be built on positive, already developing areas of understanding and experience (Gibbs

2006), augmenting self-esteem and fuelling motivation for further inter-action and learning. Taking pleasure in each other's company is vital for high quality relationships, as is a capacity for seriousness, sincerity and mutual respect.

Equally significant is the appreciation of problems. Care can be demonstrated by sensitive awareness of a child's immediate situation and related feelings, for example, recognizing unhappiness, appreciating the stressful nature of peer relationships in the playground, or under-standing the anxiety engendered for some children by the simple word 'maths'. Caring adults also recognize defensive behaviours which may conceal hidden but more damaging problems such as a critical or even brutal carer. Recognizing the experiences and feelings of another makes individuals feel valued as a unique person (Rogers 1975) and less afraid; some young people have much to fear – violence and abuse may have destroyed their trust in adults, whilst some institutions can be oppressive and uncaring (Chater 2006).

The quality of empathy is at the heart of developing an ethic of care and can have powerful and transformative effects on all age groups, as reviews of health care (Department of Health 2008) and the care of elderly people has also shown (Langer 1997). Profound empathy, and the moral bond it creates, drives one person to act on behalf of another with the aim of sup-porting their best interests and empowering them in their actions (Cooper 2002). However, empathy needs to permeate all levels of an organization and communication between organizations, if it is to be experienced by young people, especially the most vulnerable.

Caring adults need to understand the complex factors which both sup-port and hamper an ethic of care and to argue strongly for the conditions, which will enable future generations to thrive and develop each other's humanity. This chapter attempts to initiate an understanding of both the underpinning theory and processes involved.

The context and global challenges

This chapter was written in 2009, in the aftermath of a global banking crisis, in an era of disillusionment with the morals of capitalism and politics and after religious and ideological difference combined with economic, social and historical divisions had produced numerous horrific 'terrorist' and 'anti-terrorist' activities and – sadly – where incidents of students shooting their lecturers, teachers and fellow pupils in schools and universities were a too-often-repeated occurrence. The topic of global ethics was discussed avidly, since such events tend to cause moral panic. In the Reith Lectures of 2009, Professor Michael Sandel called for a new approach to citizenship, criticizing the intrusion of market values into the service spheres of education and health and advocating more communal and collaborative values.

The demise of capitalist values was predicted during the banking crisis, although in the aftermath governments struggled to curb the previous excesses of greed. The importance of a more ethical approach was frequently voiced but the means to achieve it remained more elusive. Although Appiah (2007) argues eruditely for a benign global cosmopolitanism in valuing people of all races, religions and ethnicities, he is less clear about the mechanisms needed to achieve it. Fielding (2007) and Ball (2000) question market philosophy, performativity and functionalism more boldly and advocate more humane systems which value human relationships.

While research revealed that more equal societies found their people happier and with a greater sense of well-being and respect for others, unequal societies seemed to reward excess, creating more unscrupulous behaviour and greater unhappiness (Bradshaw and Richardson 2007). Children in the United Kingdom and the USA for example, felt less happy than those in the Netherlands and Scandinavian countries. Extreme inequality is a major challenge in the pursuit of ethical development and needs to be addressed globally.

Inequality breeds resentment and lack of trust which can lead to increased regulation, centralized authority and control, whether in relationships, classrooms, institutions or societies. As people lose autonomy and become disempowered, they become alienated and learn not to care. When the values of competition dominate over collaboration, then inequality predominates, since competition is obliged to create more losers and greater inequality. Too often, the more extreme the competition, the greater is the greed for power and the more unscrupulous the tactics. To fight for others may be less motivating than fighting for oneself; nevertheless, altruism and exceptional moral courage do exist (Haste 1997), and for many feminist thinkers an ethic of care is central to their motivation (Noddings 1986).

Fragmentation, another global problem, also dehumanizes relationships by making connections between people less stable, increasingly tangential and fleeting. While this affects everyone to some degree, deprived sectors of global society suffer more because they need additional cohesion and community, to counteract the disadvantages which poor social and economic status can bring. Fragmentation affects many aspects of life and society, splintering individuals, families, schools, communities, social and health services and higher education. The hegemony of the Fordist business model ensures that every aspect of life is sectioned up and reduced to 'viable' units based on the principle of short-term mathematical or monetary worth as opposed to greater humanity or quality. When courses, curricula, services and communities are fragmented, so are the caring relationships between people.

When people-centred interactions in caring services are reduced to sets of objectives with targets for different aspects of mind or body function, then the human interaction becomes degraded, reduced to functional rather than personal exchanges. Assessments can become meaningless ticklists, without the glue of human dialogue to cohere them.

How do these challenges of global values and fragmented systems relate to the discourse on moral development and the micro interactions of human relationships which caring adults and children pursue on a daily basis? What can practitioners do to develop and sustain an ethic of care both as individuals and organizations?

Discourse on human interaction and moral development

Philosophy has always considered the complex nature of ethical interaction and how moral behaviour can be supported. Although empirical research on moral development is limited (Taylor 1994), there is considerable theoretical discussion. Whereas some theory emphasizes the nature of the moral individual, cognitive development and moral reasoning, others stress the role of affect, nurture and human interaction and others focus on the impact of the environment. Some philosophers emphasize the role of religion and others a humanistic perspective. Clearly psychology plays a significant role; however so, increasingly, do neuroscience and sociological research. This section offers a brief resume.

Despite the later dichotomy between the influences of emotion and reason on ethical behaviour, many classical philosophers considered both and the relationship between them. Aristotle valued the emotions, explaining that one should take pleasure in virtue and that it should lead to happiness and well-being (Benn 1998). Hume argued that sympathy was important in moral development and argued that we have a natural propensity: to sympathize with others and to receive by communication their inclinations and sentiments (1739: 316).

For Marx and Engels (1888), man cannot reach his human potential as an individual but only as a social being, in his relations with his fellow men and women. The denunciation of *naked self-interest* is central to their critique of capitalism and has particular significance in the aftermath of the banking crisis of 2008. For Marx, human relationships were not just functional but sensual and personal and made human beings complete (Fischer 1973). He believed that man acquires the world through his senses. Macmurray (1935), meanwhile, valued the senses for the sheer joy they give, rather than utilizing them for narrower intellectual or functional purposes. He considered the intellect subordinate to emotions and self-centred rather than other-centred. Macmurray perceives sensual sensitivity, and awareness towards other human beings, as the root of human communion and religion, whereas for Marx the ultimate human interaction was encapsulated in communism. The greater good is implicit in both concepts. Marx's concept of the 'species-being' is linked to the idea of spiritual awareness and both of these to heightened awareness and sensitivity by Hay (1997) who suggests that this awareness, which Noddings (1986) calls *receptivity* and Watson and Ashton (1995) call *openness*, is actually a physical state.

Kohlberg (1958) extended the concept of moral reasoning, envisaging several levels of moral development based around the response to moral dilemmas, but was challenged by the feminist critique of Gilligan (1982), whose emphasis was on the psychology of relationships. Hoffman (2000) emphasized the significance of empathy in relationships, in both the modelling and development of caring attitudes – as did Rogers (1975) and Aspy (1972). Others also argued that ethical development is modelled through human relationships. Murdoch (1970) calls this 'loving attention', whilst Noddings (1986) echoes the need for attention and emphasizes shared emotions.

The significance of affective issues was neglected in Western education at the end of the twentieth century (Best 1998) and also in countries which modelled their education systems on these more rational, technical models. Much of this neglect took place under the influence of monetarism and individualism, exemplified by the Thatcher era, when even care had primarily a monetary basis (Partington 1996). Best (2003) argued that more emphasis was needed on the role of relationship, love, mutual respect and spirituality, while critiques of the marketization of education and the public services appear in the work of Ball (1990; 2000) and also in Apple (1979; 2005) and Keat (1997).

Around the same time Koseki and Berghammer (1992) identified different types of empathy which had greater or lesser moral depth, including a phenomenon called 'adaptive' or 'moral' empathy, typified by leaders who took responsibility for others. This could be modelled by significant others to develop an ethic of care which is also related to 'love', a term which many adults struggle to discuss despite its centrality to their lives. For Halstead (2005) the concept of love is central to children's existence and needs to be discussed in school – whether initiated by spontaneous remarks, or through the sharing of drama, literature and poetry. Teachers demonstrating profound empathy (Cooper 2002) often used the word 'love' in relation to their pupils.

The revival of the affective

Developments in brain-imaging, have reinvigorated research into the role of emotions in human interaction, reinforcing and expanding previous psychological theories. Damasio (1999) explains how emotions have been derided by academics but that neuroscience places emotion at the heart of human consciousness and complex decision-making. He argues that the image of the self is recreated in the brain at every interaction and therefore intensive multi-sensory interaction builds the sense of self, increases engagement and speeds up mental processing, further reinforcing understanding. This powerful holistic process produces profound empathy (Cooper 2002), which enables the development of positive emotion, self-esteem and encourages the emulation of empathy.

Intensive interaction (Hewett, 1994) and augmented mothering (Ephraim 1986) are used in special needs education to support learning and development in students with profound and multiple needs. Empathy is also central to working with children from diverse cultures (Lang 2008) or who have to learn using an additional language (Bligh 2009). Appiah (2007) sees the empathic imagination as significant in his concept of cosmopolitanism and stresses the similarities between people as the source of understanding.

Cooper (2002), examining empathy in educational relationships, combined neuroscience with psychological and educational theory. An elaborated taxonomy of empathy was developed, showing the complex nature of empathic interactions in the learning process and their role in both modelling and developing morality. Narvaez (2007) similarly integrated research from neuroscience and psychology into moral development theory. Leal (2002) describes how the formation of identity in babies is bound up in socio-emotional interaction during intense non-verbal interaction and Winkley (1996) explained how babies' brains grow when they feel cared for. This notion renders the emotional and academic inseparable, a point emphasized by Vygotsky (1986). The nurturing of empathy through non-verbal and also later verbal interaction demonstrates care, which builds emotional capital (Cooper 2008) a term also used by Reay who describes it as, 'the stock of emotional resources built up over time within families and which children could draw upon' (2000: 572).

Rich interviews with teachers and student teachers – selected for their empathy – revealed the nature and powerful effects of profound empathy (Cooper 2002) that developed over time, and especially in one-to-one or small group relationships. It is akin to the empathy developed in counselling relationships (Rogers 1975).The most significant feature of profound empathy was the ability to develop positive emotions and interactions. Additionally the teachers possessed excellent self-knowledge, retained knowledge of other people and explained their own understandings to others. They appreciated the complex relationships children had with their peers, family and other adults aiming to know all of their students very well. Their engagement with others led them to care deeply for them, acting and taking responsibility for them.

These teachers created relationships which involved pleasure, happiness, fun and humour. They sought to find the good in all their students, masking negative feelings with disaffected students until they found a connection which could generate more positive feelings, often on topics beyond the classroom. They found time to talk to students and knew the importance of giving sole attention, of taking students seriously and responding to their feelings and understandings. This enabled them to assess more thoroughly, teach more precisely, engage interests more deeply, meet needs more fully and have higher expectations because trusting relationships enable constructive criticism. They created warm, more informal climates that were conducive to learning, where they became role models – enabling students to develop personally, morally and academically. Opportunities for significant personal interaction often occurred in the stolen informal moments, outside of the standard transactional interactions with large groups: corridor moments, chance encounters, the start and end of lessons and during extra-curricular activities.

Both experienced and trainee teachers in Cooper's study (2002) were very sensitive to students' emotional and academic needs:

I often think how I would feel. I put myself in that position. I've got a storming memory from my childhood of individual detail and I use a lot of my childhood experiences to analyse [the students]. ('Martin' 129)

I didn't want to sort of cry or anything like that but – when he was crying about [the reading scheme], I remember holding his hand – which is an instinctive response with me. But I understood how he felt, because I've felt like that even as an adult. ('Janet' 211)

Even young children in this study could identify characteristics of an under-standing teacher. The smile was a key feature but also such teachers listened to them, used their names, discussed topics they enjoyed, made them feel liked, offered praise and helped them. By contrast, grumpy teachers inhib-ited listening and motivation.

This and other research suggests that empathetic relationships sup-port both emotional and cognitive development (Cooper 2002; Black and Phillips 1982), supporting the evidence that schools with good relationships support and improve learning and behaviour (DES 1989; see Figure 2).

Figure 2: Profoundly empathic teaching occurs when teachers and students share large areas of understanding

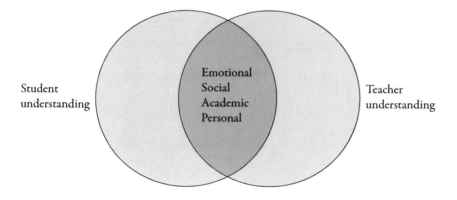

The effects of profoundly empathic relationships

Teachers in this study believed that empathy produced conversation, communication, personal exchange, emotional links, understanding and friendship. As empathy became profound over time, teachers came to understand children deeply and became aware of the significance of that knowledge in their teaching. Through a desire to understand and work with all individuals they supported inclusion and diversity. Over time the effects were transformative. Pupils developed greater self worth, a sense of security and trust, and an ability to emulate empathy. The creation of trust led to improved learning and risk taking and better behaviour. Teachers knew individuals deeply and learned more about their craft which tended to optimize learning by making assessment more accurate – taking into account the whole child – so that teaching could be pitched at precisely the right level. Empathy has a powerful effect on the climate and hidden curriculum, and sends a message of value, care and concern.

Not all empathy is profound however, for example one might only show empathy for some people producing prejudice, or use functional empathy, an adaptation for interacting with large groups which leads to stereotyping, or shallow or feigned empathy which can be short-lived or manipulative. Empathy nurtured in groups but restricted to members of those groups, can produce competition, even hatred leading to aggression, racism, and nationalism. Only profound empathy properly supports an ethic of care and generates caring in others (Cooper 2002).

Our biggest asset as caring human beings is our own emotional capital, created by our own experience of being cared for. An ethic of care does not emerge from codes or rules or lists of desirable qualities, but from the lived experience of being valued ourselves and of seeing others being valued. Every time an adult who is close to a young person takes a genuine interest in their motivations, interests and well-being, they model qualities which can be reciprocated. Everyone who comes into regular contact with a young person has the potential to model caring (or indeed not to model it) and can enrich self-esteem, enabling the building of networks of positive relationships which create community and social, emotional and moral support – promoting inclusion, social justice and greater equality.

Care through the curriculum or hidden curriculum?

Some educationalists argue that an ethic of care can be taught through the curriculum (Crick 1998), although this is disputed by Cooper and Clarke (2001). Others advocate strategies such as 'circle time' (Moseley 1997), whilst research in Italy has shown the effectiveness of supporting teachers to use such techniques (Francescato 1998). The British government now advocates such techniques in its national strategies (DfES 2003a; DfES 2003b). In some countries moral education is part of the mission of state education, in the UK for example it is enshrined in law. However, in the USA the concept of character education has been adopted separately by individual states for a diversity of purposes, and in China moral education now centres on schools – whereas the traditional Confucian teachings suggested a more holistic life-long learning approach (Fengyan 2004). In many faith schools, ethics can be central to the curriculum and a highly explicit aspect of daily life, whereas in secular schools the hidden curriculum is often where the ethos of institutions is revealed (Bottery 1990; Hargreaves 1982; Gibbs 2008).

The role of the arts, drama and literature has an important role in raising moral issues and supporting more complex understanding of people and situations. Allowing children to express themselves creatively and interact with others in real or imaginary scenarios can support a broadening and deepening of human understanding. Heathcote emphasized the role of empathy in drama in education (Hesten 1995) and, according to Brighouse (1991), drama can assist the understanding of differences in values. For Jones (1996) drama has the potential to enable emotional, political and spiritual change and narrative can develop empathy through engaging the emotions that are universal (Vandenplas-Holper 1998), and through that explain the moral (Winston 1998). Stories are all about human relationships (D'Arcy 1998) and enable children to develop perspective taking (Grainger 1997). The emphasis on basic skills, testing and exams at the expense of arts and drama in some curricula may lessen chances for children to develop compassion for of others.

The hidden curriculum conveys messages to children about they are valued. Both Dewey and Kohlberg recognized the power of the hidden curriculum (Hersch et al. 1980) as did Hargreaves (1982; 2000) and Gibbs (2008). Role models are central to children's behaviour (Bandura 1969; Blackham 1978; Kyriacou 1986). If adults are immersed in bureaucracy – racing through the curriculum or too busy to listen, talk and support while rushing to the next task, patient or student – young people receive the message, consciously or unconsciously, that they are not important. Care has to be enacted, not just imagined. The education system has often been criticized for creating negative responses in pupils and emphasizing power and control rather than learning, for alienating and subjugating rather than developing (Hargreaves 1967; Foucault 1977; Illich 1971; Freire 1970; Garratt 1996; Noguera 2007). These problems have not been reduced by the pressure of market policies, competition between schools and the increasingly prescriptive and fragmented curriculum adopted initially in the 1980s and 1990s in the UK for example (Ball 1990; 2000; Keat 1996). Staff and students feel both the concrete and hidden impact of such policies but the messages given to pupils are not universal. Young people are different and receive divergent messages about how they are valued in relation to others (Bernstein 1975). If the controlling, auditing and monitoring become so great that young people feel permanently compared, watched, supervised, and untrustworthy, what messages do we give and what are we preparing them for? Noguera (2007) argues that humanity and good relationships are absent from some schools in New York, which effectively prepare students for prison.

The bureaucratic, time-scarce regimes in which caring professionals work with huge case loads, militate against the relaxed one-to-one informal time needed to develop human relationships. When people become numbers, alienation is created and empathy reduced. Noddings (1986) argues that caring relationships require time to develop, not only through the curriculum but through normal conversations and interactions. Sometimes simple interactions can affirm students and their importance should not be underestimated, according to Watson and Ashton (1994). 'Off-task' interaction is more likely to enhance feelings of community than purely task-related engagement (Klein, cited in Clark 1996). Positive face-to-face interaction produces affirming sentiments between people and a sense of community can be destroyed by relationships which reduce other people to the status of objects (Clark 1996). Interaction should be frequent to maximize good relationships, and caring services need to build in time for this.

Practice in both faith and secular schools may belie doctrines and mission statements. A statement based on principles of equity, for example, may be mere rhetoric. Sometimes staff, or the system, or both, ensure children are labelled from the outset. The embedded immorality of inadequate resourcing in mass education, health and social services, and in housing, wages and work opportunities cannot only be addressed by empathic conversations as Appiah (2007) might have us believe. Power often rests in the hands of less benign, less dialogic individuals and organizations. Even religious organizations have found difficulty in matching doctrine with deeds and are sometimes riven by politics and power struggles, which detract from their stated mission. The abuse of children by religious institutions (Irish Government 2009) proves that intellectual indoctrination about morality does not ensure the emotional capacity to care (Blackham 1976; Aspy 1972). Even when intellectual discussions about care are facilitated across the curriculum and between staff, if that care is not modelled in institutions then people lack trust and messages are ignored (Bottery 1990). For example, do educators model care when they train teachers, nurses, doctors and social-workers – or are they too hurtling through a fragmented, overfilled curriculum in lecture theatres full of unknown students?

Facing the challenges

Needy young people

A primary challenge for developing an ethic of care is that large numbers of young people have only had abuse and neglect modelled in their early lives and have been unable to form the trusting relationships through which they can develop self-esteem and their own caring behaviour. They are in need of intensive demonstrations of care from alternative caring adults. This neglect often happens even before language develops and children struggle to find a voice for their feelings without intensive support (Docker-Drysdale 1990). Considering affective education in Germany, Fess (1998) called precisely for more consideration for such children and all agencies need to understand their needs and the actions needed to support them. An ethic of care needs to emerge from imagining the realities of these children's experiences. Given time and the opportunity, many adults would attempt to do this – so why is insufficient care demonstrated and how can we develop a more consistent ethic of care?

Improving individuals or contexts?

Training to enhance empathy is a possibility and has been debated in therapy, social work, teaching and nursing education. Considerable research has been conducted on the notion of empathy; in fact, recently the notion that nurses need more compassion and can be trained in it has hit the headlines again (Department of Health 2008). Early research into empathy did perceive it as a quality which could be improved (Rogers 1975; Aspy 1972). However, although training in education and health and social services can develop empathy test scores and empathy in groups (Walter and Finlay 2002) or support techniques to support moral development in schools (Francescato 1998), practice settings present a major problem where one to one time with individuals is scarce or an empathic culture is absent

(Reynolds et al. 2000; Cooper 2002) or where the emotional capacity of an individual is limited and also where care is associated with women and down valued (Tong 1997; Damasio 1999).

In statistical studies empathy is negatively correlated with an authoritarian approach (Black and Phillips 1982) which suggests that the tough-minded approach dominating the management of caring services could counteract a more empathic approach by those who work directly with clients. Black and Phillips concluded that although training can improve empathy scores, it does not for the more empathic student teachers, suggesting that selection may be more important than training. Cooper (2002) argues that for both empathic student teachers and experienced teachers, immediate working conditions are the key factor in supporting or constraining empathic relationships. Bassey (2003) also argues that working conditions have a powerful effect on behaviour. Nias (1996) argues that teachers are passionate about their relationships with children and display self-esteem when acting according to their values but display very negative emotions when the processes and management of schools run counter to their values. Valuing the human rather than the mechanistic seems to be central to nurturing an ethic of care, Nias was very pessimistic that this was happening in education at least and Chater (2006) similarly describes the embattled, war-like language of teachers steeling themselves against the authoritarian pressures of inspection.

Professionals in the caring services often become stressed and leave when obliged to act in ways which clash with their strong moral values, while others adapt or subvert the system in their own ways. Teachers in the UK enter the profession looking for good relationships with staff and pupils (Hobson et al. 2006) but the working conditions and oppressive nature of the system can distort relationships. Fifty per cent leave within the first five years, and social workers too are increasingly hard to recruit. Although governments stress training to develop and retain staff, workers are more concerned about the constraints of their working environment and the lack of quality time with their clients and colleagues. If profound empathy requires time and continuity to develop then this has to be embedded in systems. In schools, for example, many factors militate against the demonstration of profound empathy; these include poor teacher/student ratio, lack of time, unempathic management, a rigid, overfilled curriculum and competitive assessment and league tables – all within contexts in which resources are scarce and needs are great (Cooper 2002). Similar issues can apply across all caring services.

Modelling an ethic of care in institutions – Colleagues and leaders

For new staff, an ethic of care should be apparent in the way they are treated from day one in an organization, the way they are initiated into values and practices and made to feel welcome. Staff need to be valued and treated with respect in daily interactions. Only by both feeling valued and seeing people valuing others, can a strong ethic of care be nurtured. This means ensuring that good support, mentoring, collaboration, consultation and succession planning is built into workloads to provide stability and security for both carers and those cared for. Aspy (1972) argued that only staff who were treated humanely could reproduce a humane approach, which is the same argument that Hoffman (2000) makes for children.

Inevitably leaders and managers are very potent role models. They, above all, have to be seen to care and to respect everyone in their organization. Honesty, authenticity and respect permit people to have a voice and be heard. Friendship, commonality, sociality, are important attributes and leaders must be seen to both consult and take action when it is needed. Remaining aloof or working apart from staff, or expecting staff to come to them will model disinterest and produce alienation (Brighouse 1991). It is their responsibility to model genuine care through communication and interaction. Claire, an experienced teacher in the study of empathy, described an empathic head teacher: 'He understands people, he's got time for them and he's appreciative of what's done' (Cooper 2002: 183). Another, Charlotte, explained this could be achieved relatively simply:

> A head's just got to say, how's so and so doing? ... They are feeling people who acknowledge and take an interest in everyone. They are not self-absorbed, hurrying round, being important. They make people feel known, valued and appreciated. (Cooper 2002: 183)

Claire explained the alienating impact of an uncaring leader:

> If you're working with a head who's not empathic, she will just do things regardless of your own feelings and you'll feel well – 'why do I bother? What's the point of it all?' Your opinion's not sought and 'no feelings for me'. So I'll just do my job and go back home again. (Cooper 2002: 185)

Leaders at all levels are central to creating a culture of care. There has been considerable development in the understanding of emotional intelligence in leadership in recent years and a major shift from valuing heroic, charismatic leaders to more ethical leaders with a greater awareness of their staff, who have 'softer' skills but develop stronger organizations that appreciate and utilize the skills of their entire workforce (Alimo-Metcalfe 2009; Cooper 2002; Arnold 2005).

Inter-agency work

The multi-agency work essential for the most needy individuals also requires time and interaction for staff to understand and work with each other successfully. The life of a child can hang upon the weakest link in communication. What use the caring teacher informing social services of an urgent issue, if they are too overloaded to respond. It is not sufficient for the life of one child to be saved because another was not. The regular incidence of children who die at the hands of their families, demonstrates that caring adults can fail to meet the most basic need of protecting life. In large organizations, staff are under huge pressure of workloads and time constraints, with ever increasing demands made on their emotional and intellectual abilities. When faced with highly manipulative, emotionally disturbed adults, with all their own problems and addictions, the chance of finding time to discuss, assess effectively and act rapidly is scarce. Such scarcity of resources is morally unforgiveable. Part of an empathic approach means that the caring services have to be highly alert to cruelty and manipulation, highly communicative with colleagues and other services and fearless in taking action when signs warrant action. Systems need to be humanized and sufficient time and support embedded in them – if not society will continue to fail both the innocent children and the staff. Society, fuelled by media hyperbole, tends to blame individuals and seems happy to provide minimal support when only adequate time and support will begin to resolve the situation. Care is society's responsibility. If financiers alert to expense, or politicians alert to power and the populist vote, are allowed to dictate the rules without an ethic of care, the loss will be felt on a personal level by the most vulnerable and on a social level by everyone.

The future

Trusting, caring relationships are needed at every stage of life. Whether we concern ourselves with the well-being of tiny babies or elderly people in care homes, we need to embed profound empathy into the human relationships and systems which support them, especially for those with minimal familial support. This involves closely examining our practices – and if they do not provide sufficient time, sufficient care, sufficient sense of personhood in the human interactions and material provisions for people's well being, then it is our responsibility to argue for improvements, to identify need and request the necessary resources clearly, firmly and determinedly. Deferring to the motives of politicians and financiers is unlikely to support an ethic of care, as the events of 2008 have shown. The life chances of vulnerable children are ultimately at the mercy of financiers who – especially in recessions – reduce funding, increase workloads, destroy hard-fought conditions and pension rights, while bankers still head home to their multi-million pound homes.

Everyone involved in the caring services has an obligation to insist on high quality care at every level. It is insufficient to develop a personal ethic of care, if we do not expect that others do too. We have an obligation not to be cowed by cultures of deference; not to be alienated by indifference, but to develop a shared vision of what is good, what is right and pursue it with vigilance – asking others to be as demanding. From our financiers and managers we ask the same – to focus on people over budgets, to reward care not savings, value humanity over mechanisms and love over disinterest and dispassion.

Developing an ethic of care in all our services is essential for the positive future of individuals and society. Ultimately, all organizations would benefit from such an ethic – and even banks themselves are considering more open, fear free cultures which reward long-term quality for their clients (BBC 2009). Adopting longer-term values offers a better future for families, communities and the caring services, with happier, more effective staff, happier, better-supported young people and better learning and development. Fewer people will be deprived of stability and education and fewer people imprisoned – with all the attendant misery, expense and wasted lives for both victims and perpetrators. We can opt for a more positive building of human potential through personalized, humane caring, reducing the need for blame and punishment. Developing an ethic of care is dependent on each one of us, at whatever level, assessing personal needs, staff needs, system needs and both giving and requesting the necessary resources, in a joint venture to nurture everyone's life and to envisage and support everyone's potential.

References

Appiah, K.A. (2007). 'Cosmopolitanism'. Paper presented at the Association of Moral Education Annual Conference, New York University, November.

Apple, M.W. (1979). *Ideology and the Curriculum*. Boston and London: Routledge and Kegan Paul.

——(2005). 'Education, Markets, and an Audit Culture', *Critical Quarterly*, 47 (1–2), 11–29.

Arnold, R. (2005). *Empathic Intelligence: Teaching, Learning, Relating*. Sydney: University of New South Wales Press.

Aspy, D. (1972). *Toward a Technology for Humanizing Education*. Champaign, IL: Illinois Research Press.

Ball, S. (1990). *Markets, Morality And Equality in Education*. London: Tufnell Press.

Ball, S.J. (2000). 'Performativities and Fabrications in the Education Economy: Towards the Performative Society?', *Australian Educational Researcher*, 27 (2), 1–23.

Bandura, A. (1969). *Principles of Behavior Modification*. New York: Holt, Rinehart & Winston.

Bassey, M. (2003). Seminar at Leeds University.

BBC (2009). 'Rebooting RBS'. 26 August 2009, Radio 4.

Benn, P. (1998). *Ethics*. London: Routledge.

Best, R. (2003). 'Struggling with the Spiritual in Education'. Paper presented at the Tenth International Annual Conference on 'Education, Spirituality and the Whole Child', University of Surrey, Roehampton, London.

Black, H. and Phillips, S. (1982). 'An Intervention Program for the Development of Empathy in Student Teachers', *Journal of Psychology*, 112, 159–68.

Blackham, H. (ed.) (1976). *Moral and Religious Education in County Primary Schools*. Windsor: NFER Publishing.

Bottery, Mike (1990). *The Morality of the School*. London: Cassell.

Bradshaw, J., Hoelscher, P. and Richardson, D. (2007). 'An Index of Child Well-Being in the European Union 25', *Journal of Social Indicators Research*, 80, 133–77.

Brighouse, T. and Tomlinson. J. (1991). *Successful Schools*. London: Institute for Public Policy Research.

Broadfoot, P. (2000). *Culture, Learning and Comparison: BERA Stenhouse Lecture, 1999*. Southwell: BERA.

Chater, M. (2006). 'Just Another Brick in the Wall: Education as Violence to the Spirit', *International Journal of Children's Spirituality*, 11 (1), 47–56.

Clark, D. (1996). *Schools as Learning Communities: Transforming Education*. London: Cassell.

Cooper, B. (2002). *Teachers as Moral Models? The Role of Empathy Between Pupils and Their Teachers*. PhD thesis, Leeds Metropolitan University.

——(2008). 'Embedding the Person in Personalised Learning: Findings from a Studying Empathy in Learning Relationships'. Paper presented at BERA Annual Conference, Edinburgh, September.

—— and Clarke P. (2001). 'Moral Citizens – More Than Just a Curriculum Issue: Providing the Means to Moral Development through Empathic Relationships'. Paper presented at BERA Annual Conference, University of Leeds, September.

Crick, B. (1998). *Education for Citizenship and the Teaching of Democracy in Schools*, London: QCA.

Damasio, A. (1999). *The Feeling Of What Happens, Body, Emotion And The Making Of Consciousness.* London: Heinemann.

D'Arcy P. (1998). *The Whole Story*, Bath University, PhD thesis.

Department of Education and Science (1989). *Discipline in Schools: The Elton Report.* London: HMSO.

Department for Education and Skills (DfES) (2003a). *Every Child Matters: Green paper.* London: HMSO.

——(2003b). *Excellence and Enjoyment.* London: HMSO.

Department of Health (2008). *High Quality Care for All: NHS Next Stage Review, Final Report (Lord Darzi).* Norwich: TSO.

Docker-Drysdale, B. (1990). *The Provision of Primary Experience.* London: Free Association.

Ephraim, G. (1986). *A Brief Introduction to Augmented Mothering.* Hertfordshire: Report for Leavesden Hospital.

Fengyan, W. (2004). 'Confucian Thinking in Traditional Moral Education: Key Ideas and Fundamental Features', *Journal of Moral Education,* 33 (4).

Fess, R. (1998). 'Affective Education in Germany. Existing Structures and Opportunities: Are We Using Them Effectively?'. In P. Lang, Y. Katz and I. Menezes (eds), *Affective Education: A Comparative View.* London: Cassell.

Fielding, M. (2007). 'The Human Cost and Intellectual Poverty of High Performance Schooling: Radical Philosophy, John Macmurray and the Remaking of Person-Centred Education', *Journal of Educational Policy,* 22 (4), 383–409.

Fischer, E. (1973). *Marx in His Own Words.* Harmondsworth: Penguin.

Foucault, M. (1977). *Discipline and Punish: The Birth of the Prison*, trans. by Alan Sheridan. London: Allen Lane.

Freire, P. (1970). *Pedagogy of the Oppressed.* London: Continuum.

Francescato, D. (1998). 'Affective Education and Teacher Training in Italy'. In P. Lang, Y. Katz and I. Menezes (eds), *Affective Education: A Comparative View.* London: Cassell.

Gibbs, C. (2006). *To Be a Teacher: Journeys towards Authenticity.* New Zealand: Pearson Education.

Gilligan, C. (1982). *In a Different Voice: Psychological Theory and Women's Development.* London: Harvard University Press.

Government of Ireland (2009). *The Ryan Report of the Commission to Enquire into Child Abuse* <http://www.childabusecommission.com/rpt> accessed 20 September 2009.

Grainger, Teresa (1997). *Traditional Story-telling in the Classroom*. Scholastic: Leamington Spa.

Haste, H. (1997). *Moral Creativity*. Creativity Seminar, Open University, London.

Halstead, M. (2005). 'Teaching about Love', *British Journal of Educational Studies*, 53 (3), 290–305.

Hargreaves, D.H. (1967). *Social Relations in a Secondary School*. London: Routledge and Kegan Paul.

—— (1982). *The Challenge for the Comprehensive School: Culture, Curriculum and Community*. London: Routledge and Kegan Paul.

—— (2001). 'Nuttall Memorial/Carfax Lecture'. BERA Conference, Leeds University, September.

Hay, D. (1997). 'Spiritual Education and Values'. Paper presented at the Seventh International Annual Conference on 'Education, Spirituality and the Whole Child', University of Surrey, Roehampton Institute, London.

Hersch, R.H., Miller, J.P. and Fielding, M. (eds) (1980). *Models of Moral Education*. New York: Longman.

Hesten S. (1995) *The Construction of an Archive (on Dorothy Heathcote)*. PhD Thesis, Lancaster University.

Hewett, D. and Nind, M. (1994) *Access to Communication*. London: David Fulton.

Hobson, A.J., Malderez, A., Tracey, L., Giannakaki, M.S., Pell, R.G., Kerr, K., Chambers, G.N., Tomlinson, P.D. and Roper, T. (2006). *Becoming a Teacher: Student Teachers' Experiences of Initial Teacher Training in England*. University of Nottingham, University of Leeds and Ipsos MORI Social Research Institute Research Report RR744.

Hoffman, M.L. (2000). *Empathy and Moral Development: Implications for Caring and Justice*. New York: Cambridge University Press.

Hume, D. (1995). 'A Treatise of Human Nature (1739)'. In T. Honderich (ed.), *The Oxford Companion to Philosophy*. Oxford: Oxford University Press.

Illich, I. (1971). *Deschooling Society*. London: Penguin.

Jones, P. (1996). *Drama as Therapy: Theatre as Life*. London: Routledge.

Keat, R. (1997). 'Values and the Enterprise Culture'. In J. Conroy, D. McCreath and B. Davis (eds), *Changing Contexts for Values Education: Proceedings of the Gordon Cook Foundation Conference*. Stirling: Gordon Cook Foundation in partnership with St Andrew's College, Glasgow.

Kohlberg, L. (1958). *The Development of Modes of Thinking and Choices in Years 10 to 16*. PhD thesis, University of Chicago.

Kozeki, B. (1992). 'The Role of Empathy in the Motivational Structure of School Children', *Personality and Individual Differences*, 13 (2), 191–203.

Langer, E.J. (1997). *The Power of Mindful Learning*. Reading, MA: Addison-Wesley.

Leal, M.R.M. (2002). 'The caring relationship'. Paper presented at the Ninth International Annual Conference on 'Education, Spirituality and the Whole Child', University of Surrey, Roehampton Institute, London.

Lewis, M. and Haviland Jones, J.M. (eds) (2009). *Handbook of Emotions*. New York: Guildford Press.

Macmurray, J. (1935). *Reason and Emotion*. London: Faber and Faber.

Marx, K. and Engels, F. (1888). *Manifesto of the Communist Party*. Moscow: Progress.

Moseley, J. (1997). 'Circle Time: A Forum for Spiritual, Moral, Social and Cultural Development?'. Paper presented at the Fourth Annual Conference on 'Education, Spirituality and the Whole Child', June.

Murdoch, I. (1970). *The Sovereignty of Good*. London: Routledge and Kegan Paul.

Narvaez, D. (2007). 'Triune Ethics Theory: A Neurobiologically-Based Moral Psychology'. Paper presented at the Annual Conference of the Association of Moral Education, New York University, November.

Noddings, N. (1986). *Caring: A Feminine Approach to Ethics and Moral Education*. Berkeley: University of California Press.

Noguera, P. (2007). 'Safety and Caring in Schools: Addressing the Moral Basis of School Discipline Policies'. Paper presented at the Annual Conference of the Association of Moral Education, New York University, November.

Partington, A. (ed.) (1996). 'TV Interview with Margaret Thatcher 6th Jan. 1986, in the Times 12 Jan. 1986', in *Oxford Dictionary of Quotations*. *Oxford: 691* Oxford: Oxford University Press.

Reay, D. (2000). 'A Useful Extension of Bourdieu's Conceptual Framework? : Emotional Capital as a Way of Understanding Mothers' Involvement in Their Children's Education', *Sociological Review*, 48 (4), 568–86.

Rogers, C.R. (1975). 'Empathic: An Unappreciated Way of Being', *The Counseling Psychologist*, 5 (2), 2–10.

Sandel, M. (2009). *Reith Lecture: Markets and Morals*, 26 August 2009, BBC Radio 4.

Taylor, M. (ed.) (1994). *Values education in the UK*. Slough: NFER.

Tong, R. (1997) Feminist perspectives on empathy as an Epistemic Skill and Caring as a Moral Virtue, *Journal of Medical Humanities*, 18 (3) 1997.

Vygotsky, L.S. (1986). *Thought and Language*, trans. by Alex Kozulin. Cambridge, MA: MIT Press.

Walter, G.S. and Finlay, K. (2002). 'The Role Of Empathy in Improving Inter-Group Relations', *Journal of Social Issues*, 55 (4), 729–43.

Watson, B. and Ashton, E. (1995). *Education, Assumptions and Values*. London: David Fulton.

Winkley, D. (1996). 'Towards the Human School: Principles and Practice'. Paper presented at the Beyond Market Forces Conference: Creating the Human School, West Hill College, Birmingham.

Vandenplas-Holper, C. (1998). 'Affective Education in French-Speaking Parts of Belgium: A Brief Overview'. In P. Lang, Y. Katz and I. Menezes (eds). *Affective Education: A Comparative View*. London: Cassell.

15 New ethical horizons: Lessons learned for changing practices

This has been a fascinating book to edit and prepare, with each chapter bringing to the fore an opportunity for us as editors to think more broadly about the layered complexities of ethical issues in work and research with children and young people and for adults working with children, young people and families, many of whom live with personal difficulties on a day-to-day basis. Every chapter has contributed to our own learning and, cumulatively, the enterprise has forced us to re-think the sufficiency of our own ethical stances and knowledge. We hope these chapters work on our readers in this way, to further their own professional stances through professional learning. In this final chapter we aim to tease out some of these complexities in relation to two areas of focus:

- The challenges for ethical practices of care and education as integrated teams emerge and develop
- The challenges for adopting ethical research practices with children and young people

Our aim is to identify and articulate how new ethical horizons might look and feel, and indeed to move those horizons closer to home – enabling them to become accessible within all of our day-to-day practices. There is inevitably overlap across these two areas of focus, which of course also frame the overall structure for the presentation of chapters in this book. In order to move our thinking forward, this final chapter addresses the two areas by way of three themes which – we believe these chapters show – need to underpin professional learning. These themes are:

- Recognising and confronting challenges to ethical practice
- Deepening one's personal commitment to ethical practices
- Supporting life-changes through ethical practices

What is clear is the need for a substantial step-change in perspectives and practice for both professionals and researchers. From these might come the policy changes also needed to progress from the rhetoric of *hearing* the voices of the child, the young person and the marginalized adult – often a relatively superficial exercise – to enabling their voices to actively shape policy development and to subsequently and positively influence the quality of experiences within and beyond their own lives; a point that we made in the opening chapter, and which is a central tenet of this book and its purposes.

Recognising and confronting challenges to ethical practice

In seeking to draw from different disciplines and continents, the book is well-placed to address the global tensions between centralized systems of government and localized autonomy for action, and so to consider the implications for the development and framing of ethical practices internationally, nationally, regionally and locally. It would be hard to contest the view that the most ground-breaking work is undertaken at local levels, because it is here that human experience comes alive. However, if we fail to extrapolate from these local experiences in terms of expanding our funds of knowledge around ethical practices, then these local activities become nothing more or less than interesting stories set in a particular place, space and time.

We would argue that one of the potential threats to the expansion of the theoretical frames of ethical practice comes from centralized policy systems; in saying this, we do not seek to challenge the right of governments to frame policy but do contest the policy climate that demands rigid adherence rather than facilitating localized interpretations and applications.

English educational policy since 1988 has been critiqued as a contested political process where dominant groups replicate their own narrow visions of education, and inevitably of practice, as forms of social control (Ball 1991; 1993; Ozga 1999). However, these debates and concerns are international and we see for example, in the chapter by Pam Nason and Anne Hunt (Canada), a concern that early childhood services can become sites for producing subjects that are being expected to conform to the demands of globalized economies. In relation also to early years provision, Angela Anning (England) shows how the nomenclature of policy (with terms such as 'hard-to-reach' and 'deprived') can nurture discourses based on the premise of implicit assumptions about the value (or lack of) and worth (or relative worthlessness) of substantial sections of the population, who have become so marginalized by a prevailing policy ethos that they can seldom themselves contest these terms. Bruce Johnson's work (Australia) required a confrontation with Christian fundamentalist groups keen to maintain what they proposed were 'traditional values' in relation to sex education. When dominant discourses cling to central tenets based on the premise of the location of power, as in the power to determine policy and/or the power to mandate action on a significant scale, then local decision-making and autonomous and ethical actions become harder to achieve – but not, of course, as we have seen from the cases illustrated in this book, impossible.

Levinson et al. (2009: 767) talk about policy as a 'practice of power' and ask what would be needed to turn it into interdependent, socio-cultural practices, whereby interested communities might make policy meaningful within their own contexts through *appropriation*. As we can see in this publication, appropriation requires a principled stance but ethical position-taking even in the face of strong centralized tenets is by no means impossible. We can also see how such actions might of themselves influence policy-making at central levels, how the taking of a principled ethical stance or the unveiling of gaps in knowledge (Brock, Rankin and Swiniarski, Chapter 2; Groundwater-Smith, Chapter 8) might begin to shift the discourses and change the language of power and, most importantly for this text, begin to acknowledge the responsibilities of ethical engagements at all levels of policy-making, implementation and action. Anne Campbell and Doug Martin's chapter identifies the lack of prescription within the Every Child Matters agenda in the UK as a key feature of its potential for success in helping inter-professional teams to form in schools and begin the challenging processes of becoming ethically effective – even though this relatively non-prescriptive policy sits amidst the bureaucracy of a well-established and, some would say, punitive standards agenda.

Brock, Rankin and Swiniarski identify ethical practice as a central pillar of professional learning and practice, whilst Bridget Cooper argues persuasively in the final chapter for ethically informed relationships between adults and children; for relationships that are predicated on a lifelong commitment by the adult to developing an ethic of care that embraces the empathic and the affective as integral to educational experience and learning processes. Bridget Cooper points out, in this chapter and in chapter seven, that we must acknowledge the extent to which centralized bureaucracies militate against our engagement with such an ethical stance, and that as such – she argues – they threaten our very humanity. The Every Child Matters policy agenda in the UK, along with similar agendas established and emerging across the globe, encompass this principle of an ethic of care; however, as Bridget Cooper and others reveal to us, the principle needs a particular climate and levels of individual commitment in which to grow this ethic of care into the reality of informed practice. The climate also requires autonomy at local level to make mistakes that can be learned from, to take risks – as change requires risk-taking – and for individuals and teams to be willing to re-conceive of themselves in terms of new kinds of professional identities. For individuals to engage in the risk-taking of becoming ethical, the policy climate needs to focus less on centralization and marketization and more on confronting prejudice and discrimination. Cohen (2006) also argues that the goals of education need to be reframed to prioritize not only academic learning but also social, emotional and ethical competencies. The chapters in this book offer some powerful examples of such endeavours.

Deepening one's personal commitment to ethical practices

We have argued thus far that particular climates can more (or less) favourably support ethical ethos-raising and related practices. However, we have also seen that particular initiatives might work for 'climate change' with regard to both policy and the bureaucratic processes that maintain these policies and so potentially act to shift the scene from the use of shibboleths to that of counsel.

Many of the chapters have illustrated the extent to which empathic perspective-taking underpins ethical stances. Empathy is the ability to identify but, importantly, in these chapters we see that empathizing must lead to positive action rather than 'defeat in the face of'. As a consequence, Bruce Johnson and the colleagues he describes in Chapter 6 felt compelled to act in defence of what they saw as young people's rights to be recognized as sexual beings; their shared beliefs provided sufficient moral strength to resist strong collective antagonism from another powerful community and they needed to confront this over an extended period and in a range of ways. Dorothy Bottrell, in Chapter 9, draws attention to the social justice dimensions within positive action in relation to youth work, as she and colleagues sought to bridge the gap between young people's experiences and perspectives and those of the wider and older local community, with both groups seeking to share the same community spaces. Listening and questioning become stock strategies with each community, but also enabled Dorothy to reveal the young people's collective insights as theoretical frames of reference that might change a worldview for others who may be less disposed towards an ethic of care for these young people confronting personal challenges and difficulties.

Liz Webster and Pat Broadhead describe similar territory in Chapter 11 and, like Dorothy Bottrell, detail the unanticipated ethical challenges that gradually emerge for the initiating adults. In listening to marginalized young people, it is important not to lose sight of the rights of others. Webster and Broadhead speak of the temptation that Liz and her team experienced to marginalize parents and professionals in order to allow young people with Type 1 diabetes to find power in their own perspectives and insights. What they came to understand and act upon – based on joint reflection – was that care must be taken to maintain balance when listening to one group, so that other groups do not become marginalized or undermined. However, in their chapter, Webster and Broadhead argue that unless young people are heard their quality of life will not improve, so decisions must be taken relating to how those voices might be brought forward. This is powerfully illustrated in Susan Groundwater-Smith's chapter, which reveals the impact on young people of short-term alternative curricular experiences relating to accelerated literacy and how this impact sits alongside recurring dilemmas for school staff pertaining to the perennial debates regarding content versus process, truths versus problematising, individual learning versus social learning, holistic learning versus molecular, etc – the very debates that shift the educational ethos globally to and fro on a regular basis, and within which ethical stances must grow and flourish.

Resistance, it would seem, is a key feature of ethical action. In identifying the gaps in knowledge relating to ethical practices for teachers and librarians, Brock, Rankin and Swiniarski resist the notion that this status quo should be maintained and advocate a more explicit rendition of rights and responsibilities in relation to the experiences of young children. Like many chapter authors they broach the sensitive subject of confidentiality, which is of itself a form of resistance – a resistance to disclosure in recognition of the damage that inappropriate disclosures might bring. Liz Webster and team tussle with this throughout their work as young people disclose their neglect of their own medical conditions in favour of the more tantalizing and rewarding experiences available to them and to other young people who do not experience their condition – they want to be like the others and this broader context of aspiration and yearning must ultimately frame how the adults make choices relating to responsible action via disclosure. Angela Anning in Chapter 4 offers a possible counter-balance in her discussions around sensitivity, discussing how the immersion techniques of emancipatory practices can bring forward a capacity to become concerned for the welfare and dignity of others as expressed through our own actions; Webster and team found themselves able to move in such directions as their capacities to understand how this might be enacted were deepened. We see similar responses from school staff in the chapter by Anne Campbell and Doug Martin. Whilst school staff do not speak explicitly about resistance to their new responsibilities for inter-professional working under Every Child Matters, we see from their reflections how their responsibility taking has had to grow over time – and yet how they can now take a broader perspective on the special needs of some young people and their families and begin to relate this to that young person's wider entitlement to curriculum access and learning. These are significant and substantial ideological shifts; although perhaps experienced in small ways by select individuals, their collective resonance shows the possibilities of new ways of being for the powerful and the disenfranchised. Pam Nason and Anne Hunt's chapter reveals another dimension to resistance – the capacity of marginalized groups to resist supposed solutions. The new early years curriculum they developed in New Brunswick, Canada, was intended to be inclusive and sought to address the rights of marginalized First Nations in recognition of a colonial history of 'domination, silencing and assimilation'. However, their proposals were criticized by a First Nation woman as supporting the cultural genocide of Aboriginal people; this in turn led to more debate with new possibilities for solidarity and more empathic and ethical forward-movement in relation to curriculum development. Bridges (2009) discusses constructs of insider-outsider perspectives; urging a move away from this apparent dichotomy to a more collectivist view of human identity, he notes the need to acknowledge that individuals may have different 'understandings' at different points in time, shaped in turn by their own changing experiences and perspectives. Nason and Hunt's chapter, along with others in this volume, is illustrative of the need to recognize that one's own 'knowledge' – although potentially representing a significant shift in one's own position – remains only partial when set against the knowledge-stores of those in different positions.

Supporting life-changes though ethical practices

We began this last chapter with a focus on the bigger picture of policy, but must engage in this final section with the potential for ethical practice to impact on the individual. This includes the professional striving to be ethical in new worlds of multi-professionalism, changes in professional identity, the expanded demands of professional learning and the individual and group recipients of the emerging or established perceived-as-ethical practices. Here, perhaps, may reside a conundrum: is there such a state as 'ethical practice'? Or is there only the continuing search for an ethical state of being for individual enactors and for collective groups of enactors? Kaye Johnson in Chapter 12 gives us some insights into this in the opening words of her chapter, when she writes: 'For the past 15 years, ethical questions dominated my work as a primary school head teacher who wanted children to participate in school-based research'. For Kaye this seemed to have been more a search for a way of being than it was a state of arrival. Her concluding bullet points on the resulting dispositions and convictions necessary for deep and meaningful engagement with children and young people, alongside the testimony of the chapter itself, suggest that searching is more prevalent and more personally reconstructive than is arrival. Perhaps this is a fundamental tenet to be embraced; perhaps there are no 'truths' of ethical practice – the lists become rhetoric when the contexts from which they have emerged are omitted. However, it would seem that there are principles of ethical practice, and we hope the chapters in this book have signposted the way towards the adoption of such principles.

The search for ethical practice would seem to be, in every chapter of this book, a search for equity and morality. Angela Anning draws on Gilligan's work (1982; 2003) to suggest that men and women may do this differently. Men, says Gilligan, tend to espouse causes promoting social justice whereas women espouse in terms of their relationships with others and of their responsibilities within those relationships. This would suggest some welcome complementarities of practice, but we also know that some practices are ascribed higher status than are others.

One of the growth areas where we might further develop our principles of ethical practice relates to the emergence and development of work with children as co-researchers. By moving their voices into the policy spheres we change not only their perspectives of themselves as influential individuals but also the wider view of society that begins at last to engage with previously silenced voices. In Emma Ramsden and Phil Jones' chapter they consider at some length the complicated business of gaining the assent of children and young people for their participation and, along with Jo Armistead's chapter, they illustrate how the application of principles of practice require patience, persistence and the gradually developing capacity of the adult to become not only sensitive to but sometimes almost subservient to the child's actions and choices. Given the traditional relationships between adults and children in educational settings, this role reversal presents challenges to the normally 'powerful' adult, but it is only by confronting their inherent power base and seeking for new forms of action that adult-child co-researching can enter a new sphere of action and inter-action that moves beyond the traditionally conceived relationships of adults and young people in institutional settings.

Not only does the power base have to shift, but the adult – to conceive of this and enact it in an ethically principled way –must still work to protect the co-researchers interests in terms, for example, of their relationships with other adults on the scene and through acting out experiences that might not previously have found their way to public display. Giving 'voice' to the disenfranchised carries huge burdens of responsibility; we might envisage occasions when adults may fail to protect a child's or young person's interests because they encounter events beyond their own capacity for effective response. Being ethical, therefore, also means knowing one's limits; our aspirations for social justice and/or responsible relationships are laudable but potentially dangerous, as we bring to light what was previously hidden from wider public scrutiny and run the risk of leaving the previously invisible exposed – especially when this involves young children, young people and marginalized adults. Whilst ethical practices have the power to liberate all participants into new forms of knowing and being, the immersion in ethical processes is often a journey of discovery with unknown twists and turns for all participants. We can often find ourselves facing ethical dilemmas where we previously thought none existed (Mirvis and Seashore 1979) and then must seek within ourselves for resources to confront these dilemmas.

We hope this book has gone some way towards signposting this journey within our readers' personal and professional development experiences. Clearly, as every chapter has shown us, the ethical professional is a thinker – someone who recognises that they are acting politically because their work is about the location of power and the potential for shifts in power relationships. Developing and adopting ethical principles require a realization that it's easy to get it wrong and a continuing challenge to get it right.

References

Ball, S.J. (1991). *Politics and Policy Making in Education*. London: Routledge.
—— (1993). 'What is Policy? Texts, Trajectories and Toolboxes', *Discourse*, 13 (2), 10–17.
Bridges, D. (2009). 'Education and the Possibility of Outsider Understanding', *Ethics and Education*, 4 (2), 105–23.
Cohen, J. (2006). Social, Emotional, Ethical, and Academic Education: Creating a Climate for Learning, Participation in Democracy, and Well-Being. *Harvard Educational Review*. 76 (2), 201–37.
Gilligan, C. (1982). *In a Different Voice: Psychological Theory in Women's Development*. Cambridge, MA: Harvard University Press.
—— (2003). *The Birth of Pleasure: A New Map of Love*. New York: Vintage.
Levinson, B.A.U., Sutton, M. and Winstead, T. (2009). 'Education Policy as a Practice of Power', *Educational Policy*, 23 (6), 767–95.
Mirvis, P.H. and Seashore, S.E. (1979). 'Being ethical in organizational research', *American Psychologist*, 34 (9), 766–80.
Ozga, J. (1999). *Policy Research in Educational Settings: Contested Terrain*. Buckingham: Open University Press.

Notes on contributors

ANGELA ANNING is Emeritus Professor of Early Childhood Education at the University of Leeds and Visiting Professor at Leeds Metropolitan University. She taught in Nursery, Primary, Secondary, Further and Higher Education, including as head teacher of an inner-city First School. She is committed to working collaboratively with early years professionals. Substantial research contracts included DfES-funded evaluations of three Early Excellence Centres, ESRC-funded research into multi-agency team work in Children's Services and five years as investigator for the Impact module of the National Evaluation of Sure Start, based at Birkbeck College, in particular exploring variations between the effectiveness of Sure Start Local Programmes – including those transformed into Children's Centres.

JO ARMISTEAD is a part-time lecturer at Leeds Metropolitan University and York College. A qualified teacher, she has worked in a variety of social care and educational settings. In the period of the New Labour government she has moved from leading a pre-school SEN service, to become early years co-ordinator within a Local Authority early years service. She left that job to study for a full time doctorate, studying children's perspectives on quality, awarded in 2009. She has a curiosity regarding the impact of recent policy on practice, in particular its effect on the wellbeing of young children.

DOROTHY BOTTRELL is a Lecturer in the Faculty of Education and Social Work at the University of Sydney and Convenor of the University of Sydney Network for Childhood and Youth Research. Dorothy's background is in secondary teaching, juvenile justice, youth and community work and teaching in welfare studies. Her work aims to challenge categories of 'problem youth' and to situate young people's experience in relation to social and policy contexts. Resistance, resilience and identity work are central themes of her research, explored in relation to schooling and out-of-school learning, transitions, youth justice and community life.

PAT BROADHEAD is Professor of Playful Learning at Leeds Metropolitan University. Her main areas of research and publication relate to play and learning in early years educational settings. She has also researched and published in primary school development and aspects of teacher and curriculum development. She was an early years and primary teacher before entering higher education.

AVRIL BROCK is a principal lecturer in the Carnegie Faculty at Leeds Metropolitan University, leading Master's courses in Childhood Studies and Early Years. Before moving into higher education, she was a deputy-head, primary and early years teacher and has written books on bilingualism, early language development and play. Avril's longitudinal research resulted in a model of seven dimensions of professionalism for early years educators, which is now being explored across the professions in an interdisciplinary team. Throughout her work in Higher Education, Avril has participated in Socrates and Comenius European funded international projects and is involved in international, interdisciplinary partnerships with colleagues in West Yorkshire and the USA.

ANNE CAMPBELL is retired Professor of Professional Learning at Leeds Metropolitan University. Her research interests focus around professional learning through action research and inquiry. She has published widely in these areas and in partnership between schools and teacher education. Her edited book, with Susan Groundwater-Smith, *An Ethical Approach to Practitioner Research: Dealing with Issues and Dilemmas in Action Research*, established her interest in ethical issues across a range of contexts. She has directed and worked on various government research projects in professional practice. Before entering higher education in 1989, Anne worked as a primary school teacher, advisor and deputy head.

BRIDGET COOPER is currently Professor of Education at the University of Sunderland with a special interest in affective and moral issues in education and in how information and communication technologies can support learning. She has taught and researched in Higher Education for 15 years, first at the Open University, then the University Of Leeds and then Leeds Metropolitan University. Previously she worked in secondary, middle, primary and adult education and has particular experience in the teaching of History, Literacy, English as an additional language and in the raising of achievement for ethnic minority pupils.

SUSAN GROUNDWATER-SMITH is Honorary Professor of Education in the Faculty of Education and Social Work at the University of Sydney. In recent years much of her work has focussed on teacher professional learning and the conduct of practitioner research as a form of ethical practice. She works extensively with schools in Sydney that are facing challenging circumstances and has established The Coalition of Knowledge Building Schools, a hybrid community of action learning schools, crossing age, gender and sectoral boundaries. She has published widely in support of initial teacher education in the areas of primary, middle and secondary schooling. She also holds adjunct positions in the UK and the Netherlands.

ANNE HUNT is a member of the Early Childhood Research and Development Team at the Early Childhood Centre, University of New Brunswick. This team has developed the New Brunswick Curriculum for Early Learning and Childcare and continues to work with early childhood educators to develop curriculum support documents. Anne has had a long career as an entrance class teacher in the public schools and has also taught courses in Early Literacy, Play, Children's Literature and Curriculum at both the University of New Brunswick and St. Thomas University.

BRUCE JOHNSON is Professor of Education at the University of South Australia. His previous appointments were as Dean of Research Education in the Division of Education, Arts and Social Sciences, and Associate Director of the Centre for Research in Education, Equity and Work at

UniSA. He currently heads a large research project investigating Early Career Teacher Resilience, teaches research methods to undergraduates, and supervisors numerous doctoral students. He is the co-author (with Nerilee Flint) of *Towards Fairer University Assessment: Responding to Students' Concerns*, which will be published by Routledge in late 2010.

KAYE JOHNSON is an experienced primary school principal from Adelaide, South Australia. Her practitioner research has been published in both professional and academic journals on school change, student-negotiated curriculum, and student involvement in whole school decision making. In 2007 Kaye was awarded her Ed D from the University of South Australia for her research into children's perspectives on their place(s) in the primary school. In 2008 and 2009 Kaye was the National Co-ordinator of Australia's first national mental health initiative for primary schools. In 2010 she was appointed as Manager: Leadership Quality with the Department for Education and Children's Services in South Australia.

PHIL JONES is Reader in Childhood and Inclusion, Faculty of Education, Social Sciences and Law, Leeds University. Books he has authored include *Arts Therapies* (Routledge 2005), *Drama as Therapy* (Routledge 2007), *Rethinking Childhood* (Continuum 2009), *Rethinking Children's Rights* (with Welch, Continuum 2010) and *Childhood Rights: Perspectives from Practice* (with Walker, Sage 2010). He is editor of Continuum's 'New Childhoods' book series. His books have been translated and published in Chinese, Korean and Greek.

DOUG MARTIN is currently completing a PhD researching the implementation of Every Child Matters (ECM) in schools and communities. He led the development of ECM for a large Local Authority and contributed to ECM nationally through employment with the Department of Children, Schools and Families (DCSF). Doug is presently supporting family centred integrated work through teaching in higher education. He has most recently contributed to the development of integrated working nationally through guidance such as the Common Assessment Framework (CAF), Lead Professional and programmes to support leadership and management.

He is currently commissioned to work on Think Family to explore new ways of holistic working with vulnerable families.

PAM NASON was Professor of Early Literacies and Curriculum Theory at the University of New Brunswick. Her interest in maternal literacies, and the connections between home, community and schooled literacies has led to collaborative action research projects with parents and educators, and the publication of *Parenting for a Literate Community* and *Language, Literacy and Healthy Development: The Work of CAPC/CPNP Projects*. As co-lead on the New Brunswick Curriculum Framework for Early Learning and Childcare Project, before her death she worked with Dixie Mitchell and First Nations childcare educators to publish a curriculum support document that honours the ongoing work in Mi'kmaq and Maliseet communities.

EMMA RAMSDEN has a background as a dramatherapist and clinical supervisor in forensic psychiatry, education, homelessness and substance misuse. Emma has contributed to publications about her work in both forensic and educational settings. She is a doctoral research student at Leeds Metropolitan University for her study 'Children's Psychological Voices in Dramatherapy'.

CAROLYNN RANKIN is a Senior Lecturer in the School of Applied Global Ethics at Leeds Metropolitan University. She is a Member of the Chartered Institute of Library and Information Professionals (CILIP) and a Fellow of the Higher Education Academy. Carolynn lectures on the management of information and library services and the role of the information professional. Her research interests include information ethics, the provision of library services for young children and the development of information literacy in communities.

LOUISE BOYLE SWINIARSKI, a Professor at Salem State College in Massachusetts and a Visiting Professor at Leeds Metropolitan University, teaches and coordinates her college's Student Teaching Program in England and its Northeast Global Education Center. She earned her BS and PhD from Boston College and was a Visiting Practitioner Fellow at Harvard

University Graduate School of Education Principals' Center. Her research and writing interests include early education and international education. She received the Outstanding Educator Award and the Graduate School for Excellence Award from Salem State and the Fifty Faces of Boston College's Lynch School of Education Award.

LIZ WEBSTER is a Principal Lecturer and Director in the 'Getting Sorted' enterprise at Leeds Metropolitan University (<http:\\www.leedsmet.ac.uk/ health/sc4yp>). She gained a wide range of knowledge and expertise as an advanced practitioner and lecturer specialising in community child health. She established the Getting Sorted self care workshops through work with a group of young people with Asthma and Type 1 diabetes and supported them to undertake their own research about what impacts on their lives and what they wanted from a self care programme. To date, the programme has been delivered in nine Primary Care Trusts in Yorkshire and the Humber region.

Index

accelerated literacy 143, 149, 150
accelerated programme 152
action learning 149
action research 59, 68–70
affective domain 123, 131, 137, 265–6

Brock's seven dimensions *see* professionalism

capital *see* human capital development
children
    as co-researchers 184–7, 190–1, 202, 219–22
    participation of 224, 226–8, 238, 240
    perspectives 216–19, 226
    and play nurseries 250–2
    rights of 202–3
    as social agents 239
    taking photographs 248–50
Children's Workforce Development Council (CWDC) 19, 40
Christian fundamentalism 106–8
colonialism 87
    history of 95
    postcolonial critique 96
    transculturation 90
Common Assessment Framework (CAF) 41, 43, 47, 54
common language 92
compliance 93
confidentiality 31, 42, 46, 47, 52,
    and children 225–7
consent
    of children 179–83, 223–5, 240–3

informed consent 66–8
    of parents 240
    renewing consent 243
Council for Secular Humanism 105
'critical friend' role 150
culture
    differences 75, 96,
    issues 49
    texts 91
curriculum 143, 145
    framework 79, 89–90
    goals 86
    hidden 19, 29–30, 270
    materials 110
    pace 155
    statements 86
    texts 149

dilemmas
    curriculum 144–6
    ethical 15, 27–32, 159, 162–4, 170, 175, 201, 221
    moral 69
    research 66

early childhood *see* educators; librarians
early detection of needs 51
educators 15, 16, 18, 81
emotion 125, 127, 143
empathic relationships 268–9, 272–4
empathy 128, 132, 260, 264–6
ethics
    accountability 155
    of care 174, 223. 260, 268–9

challenges 45, 122, 284–6
codes of ethics 18–27, 24–5, 107
concerns 155
design 127
dialogical 84
dilemmas 15, 27–32, 159, 162–4, 170,
    175, 201, 221
ethical commitment 165, 168
as first practice 83–5
maxims 155
personal commitment to 287–9
in practice 16–17
in professionalism 16–18 , 28, 104
in research 65
resistance 288
responsibilities 207, 224
tightrope 39
virtue 103
Every Child Matters legislation (ECM)
    19, 38–43, 286
'Expert Patient' programme 199

'gate-keeping' 182–3
'Getting Sorted' programme 197
global challenges 261–2

human capital development 81

indigeneity
    Australia 147, 150; indigenous
        young people in Australia 154,
        168
    Canada 79, 96–8
    First Nations 86
inside reform 98–9
insider research 222
integration 100
inter-agency work 275–6
internet 123, 124
intervention 54

leadership 47, 51
learning
    inventory 153
    pedagogy 79
    power 153
    professional learning 79
    transmission mode 130
    with technology 122
librarians 31
life changes 290–2
literacy *see* accelerated literacy

Maryanne Lodge (respite care facility)
    147, 148, 149, 154
mosaic approach 244–5
moral panic 108, 109, 116, 119
moral purpose 117
    development 263–4
multi-agency work 61

New South Wales 149

observations 246–8
othering 166

policy
    background in the United Kingdom
        38–44
    borrowing 80
    neo-liberal 80
practitioner research 189
protection of participants 73
power 202, 212, 222
    relations 8
professionalism 94, 117
    Brock's seven dimensions of 16
    multi-professionalism 43
    professional identity 94
public spaces for discussion 87

quality 17, 238

realpolitik 120
relationships 16, 48, 52, 71
resilience 143, 153
rights 144, 182,
    of children 20, 28, 29
    of practitioners 19
rigour in research 60
risk 54

self-esteem 133
sex education
    programmes 105, 106
    defence of 117–18
social control 162–4
social justice 39, 62, 159, 161, 168
stereotypes 49, 75

technology
    differentiation 131
    ICT integrated classrooms 132–6
    unethical use 124
Training Development Agency (TDA) 19

transparency in research 62
trust 17, 70–2

values
    core 23
    human 124, 128
    personal 125
Virtual Learning Environment (VLE)
    124, 126, 129,
voices 59, 173–4, 182, 183, 201–2, 205, 216
    children's 245
    missing 95–7
    professional 15, 27
vulnerability 59, 63–4, 154, 161, 181–2
    shifting nature of 76
    vulnerable children 76

wellbeing 153, 154, 224

youth culture 166
    and community 165–7
    identity 171, 211
    self-empowerment 204–5
    stigma, feelings of 171, 172

New International Studies in Applied Ethics

SERIES EDITORS
Professor R. John Elford and Professor Simon Robinson,
Leeds Metropolitan University

New International Studies in Applied Ethics is a series based at Leeds Metropolitan University and associated with Virginia Theological Seminary. The series examines the ethical implications of selected areas of public life and concern. Subjects considered include, but are not limited to, medicine, peace studies, international sport and higher education.

The series aims to publish volumes which are clearly written with a general academic readership in mind. Individual volumes may also be useful to those confronted with the issues discussed in their daily lives. A consistent emphasis is on recent developments in the subjects discussed and this is achieved by publishing volumes by writers who are foremost in their fields, as well as those with emerging reputations. Both secular and religious ethical views may be discussed as appropriate. No point of view is considered off-limits and controversy is not avoided.

The series includes both edited volumes and single-authored monographs. Submissions are welcome from all scholars in the field and should be addressed to either the series editors or the publisher.

Vol. 1   R. John Elford and D. Gareth Jones (eds)
          A Tangled Web: Medicine and Theology in Dialogue
          288 pages. 2009.
          ISBN: 978-3-03911-541-9

Vol. 2   D. Gareth Jones and R. John Elford (eds)
          A Glass Darkly: Medicine and Theology in Further Dialogue
          254 pages. 2010.
          ISBN: 978-3-03911-936-3

Vol. 3   Simon Robinson (ed.)
          Leadership Responsibility: Ethical and Organizational
          Considerations
          Forthcoming
          ISBN: 978-3-03911-933-2

Vol. 4   Jeanne Kentel (ed.)
          Educating the Young: The Ethics of Care
          Forthcoming
          ISBN: 978-3-03911-984-4

Vol. 5   Anne Campbell and Pat Broadhead (eds)
          Working with Children and Young People: Ethical Debates
          and Practices Across Disciplines and Continents
          313 pages. 2011.
          ISBN: 978-3-0343-0121-3